THE SEVENTH STAR PROJECTS
ECCENTRICITY

To the Honors Dept,

Thank you, take care, and enjoy,

Anie Knipping
2016

ANIE KNIPPING

The Almighty Carmen in Doll form, lying
on the Sacred Quilt that I made myself!

For

My Ni
Who Loves me into a state of Peace and has supported
my growth into Eccentricity and Happiness.

Parents and Brother
For not giving up on me when everyone else did.

Dr. Rika Alper
For being the best damn therapist, ever.

Andy Foster at Gallery 51
For finding this book to be surprisingly interesting enough to print.

Arielle Eckstut and David Sterry Head of The Book Doctors
For all your advice and trying to get someone to publish this book.

Amazon, Larry Kirshbaum, the Internet,
and the ever-steady Flow of Technology into the Future
For making it so that I don't need to get someone to publish this book.

Johnny Depp and Tilda Swinton
For giving me a reason to recreate
this book in the hopes of meeting you both someday.

John Luttropp at MSU
For taking my artistic and chaotic energies and
channeling them into something useful.

Montclair State University
For being kick-ass.

All those who have supported me
on this seemingly endless, impossible quest.

Everyone in Realspace
With whom I share my Life with Every Day.

And To Carmen

For Everything

Table of Contents

The Holy Lands

Four poster bed I
built to hide from
the winter in

2. Eccentric Senses

2. Eccentric Senses *(conn't)*

I've got a knack for finding these.
I've heard it's an autism thing.

The toy drawer.

2. Eccentric Senses *(conn't)*

3. Clothing

4. Theories

A pressed leaf from Tilda Swinton's
garden that she sent to me.

San Juan Airport restroom

The Seventh
Star Seal

Kidman of Realspace in one of her divine forms

Prologue
Or Opening Statement or Something Like That

I wrote this book in part as a BFA project for class. Actually I took on the BFA program so that I could write this here book. In any case, the important thing is this:

At the end of our first BFA semester the Council reviews our project ideas, and it was at this point that one asked something very interesting. She said;

"Many people probably perceive and do things like you. I have had similar thoughts to what you have shown us. What makes you different from the rest of us?"

At the time that had annoyed me. I was Eccentric. That certainly verified as different, I say. But I thought about it. And then I thought about it some more.
I thought about while I drove.
While taking showers.
While watching TV.

And I came to this conclusion:

I didn't know I was Eccentric until someone presented the idea that it could be an explanation for my strange behavior and thoughts. Once I found out, suddenly everything was verified. There was a reason why, and so I no longer had to change, because what I was was no longer bad.

I'm not different from everyone else, so much as that everyone else doesn't know yet that they may not be all that different from me. As I talk to more and more humans, I am finding that, buried under sociological conditioning, most every one of them has some strange thing in common with me. It's just a matter of informing them that they too have profound thoughts and strange experiences and things and verifying it for them. I can't think of anything more shway than people reading this book and thinking:

"You know, I never thought about this much before, but I kind of see/think/feel the same thing as it says here. So I'm not crazy! At least not in a bad way. Swanky!"
And possibly,

"Shway art, man."

So to answer the previous question, perhaps what makes me different from the rest of you is that I'm writing a book about it.

But don't let that stop you. 12/27/2002

This book was written sans drugs or drink, except for Paxil; which I need like a diabetic needs insulin, and Lucky Charms, which claim to be magically delicious.

Living the good life

The sitar from India, the
Instrument I can play but
I don't know why...

introduction

They say that a true eccentric does not know he is one.

This may be true, I say, for those who believe that.

And what about those that don't?

Well, then it certainly does not go for them.

This is my thought for the moment.

If I were to look hard at the statement above,
it would be easy to see that it does not make sense
because it does not incur any form of descision.

After all, i do not feel i am in the position to make
any absolutisms, that this is this and that for that.

In my small expeirience, absolutisms dwell in
theoretical sciences alone, sciences whose outcome
is molded by one who stummbles in the dark in
desperate search of a flashlight.

The need to have an answer with which to measure the new with.

That is a phenomenom i can not grasp, for in all my life,
i have never Known something to be true, for, after all,

i know nothing.

Second Edition Notes

This book has been written over the course of nine years, though that wasn't intended. It was originally 'completed' in 2003 as my senior project for college, but I left out many things due to time constraints. After college I became homeless and the files were locked until some time later when I set about preparing it for publication. By this time I had been diagnosed with Autism, and the later work reflects that.

I thought about going back and re-writing the chapters I did without knowing I was autistic, but I believe that there is something telling in them, because I was trying make sense of the same things I am trying to make sense of now, minus the new angle that my most recent label has brought. In some places I have added **'Second Edition Notes'** to clarify things I've learned since I wrote the first draft that I've found important.

Important Disclaimer!
While I am autistic, I am not the quintessential autistic. There really is no such thing, which is why autism is now called Autistic Spectrum. The general similarity seems to be sensory and social issues, and starting to speak later than the average toddler. After that, it's up to debate and degrees.

I should hope my story and ideas help others get a view on autistics and other eccentric persons, but my experience should not be considered standard by any means. After all, who ever heard of a standard eccentric?

Cheers!

P.S. I did everything in this book.; text, layout, drawings, photos, digital madness, ect.
P.P.S. Should you happen upon my parents in the wild, let them be. They are quiet creatures.

◀

The original cover for
Autobiography of an Automaton

21 Stages

The story of my Life in Pictures

The first thirteen years of my life are missing. I'm not sure why my memory is gone, or if it ever formed to begin with. I woke up a stranger here, a blank, possibly sprung from my world to yours because the brain grows just a little bit more during puberty. This empty past and what has formed from it has brought endless questions, and although some may come to be answered in time, one thing is for sure. Because of it I am forever marked, for I may never see myself as human.

These are my first eleven years on Earth, in 21 stages.

➤

The original title of this section from the first edition.
The original file has been lost to time, so I can no longer change the words. Instead it serves as a reminder of how I used to view myself. I've always felt more comfortable relating to myself in machine's terms, but when I wrote this the first time around, I really felt very removed from the human condition. Not so much anymore, but I still don't feel like I'm part of your species.

autobiography of an
automaton
the story of my life

the Before

time >>>>>>>>>>>>>>>>>

08.30.1981 - 10.18.1994

1

The Before Time
Lost in the Ocean of the Mind

When I was born my ego lay dormant a million miles below the surface. On the outside it looked like I was awake, jumping out of windows, biting people, and all that. But on the inside I was oblivious to it all, lost in a constant haze like a TV with poor reception. For thirteen years nothing got in and I never emotionally evolved; locked in a state of perpetual toddler-hood.

I was content when left alone, but if somebody tried to get me to do something I would lash out or run. The school didn't really want me there and tried to have me removed. They blamed my mother for all of it, but somehow she knew I wasn't just a bad kid. Something else was wrong.

I don't know how many doctors she brought me to, how many phone calls she had to make, how many dusty corners of libraries she had to search, but definitely enough to make a good-sized list. Ma never gave up. I was eventually diagnosed with ADHD, as that was what was popular at the time, and they put me on Ritalin. Ma says it helped calm the outside person, but inside the storm raged on. At times wild, impulsive, and resistant to any form of social grid, my other half carved a reputation to be feared. I continued to lock myself in bathrooms, run out of class, and on occasion became violent.

All the way into my early teens.

Any flickering memories I've found since then don't link back to me, rather to some forgotten life that may never have existed. In fact, I barely have any childhood memories at all. I know I was the subject of peer abuse. I know I was a focal point of anger and frustration. Luckily I am affected by next to none of it, just getting clipped as I slowly awoke.

I had been sleeping, and mercifully, I had missed the whole thing.

Second Edition Notes:

It has been six years since I wrote this and I now know that while the reason my memory is missing was because it never formed correctly, some was, and still is, repressed. I have been getting memories back in bits and pieces since, mostly through dreams. Where this will lead remains to be seen.

◄

Someday I will find that place that I lived in most of my life. Sometimes the memories are so close, I can almost feel them...

the wash

>>>>>>>>>>>>>>10.19.1994 - 07.13.1995

The Wash 2

Someone finds me in the Strangest way

Waking up didn't happen at once. Well, it did, but there were events leading up to it. In the beginning of eighth grade something started to change. I heard the brain grows again at puberty, giving it a second chance to get it right. It tried, but as far as self-awareness was concerned, I was still quite comfortably out to lunch.

Because I was so far out of touch I was usually lost in some kind of daydream, most of which were short, scattered, and often didn't make a lot of sense. On 10/19/94 however, one about a group of pirates stayed on and continued to build on itself, making permanent characters and locations. It was full of cliches, plot holes and ridiculous situations, but at the time it was enough to create something of a sort of primitive consciousness. My brain was watching these imaginary pirates go about their business like a cat watches a spot of reflected sunlight race across the floor. As it continued, more cats came forward to watch until a pack of once uncontrollable animals became calmly transfixed as one. It lasted a staggering six months, but come April it began to falter and the natives became restless. Just when it seemed that everything that had been accomplished was about to unravel, by pure glorious chance on 4/22/95, I met Her.

Carmen Sandiego, head thief of so many educational computer games since the 80's now had her own animated series. It wasn't the show that had gotten my attention, it was her. Carmen's character was not the norm in television. Though obviously the villain, she was no longer content to be the 2-D shadow of incarnations past. She instead recast herself as a high-minded Machiavellian, a brilliant, fantastic, enigmatic mystery that you couldn't help but fall entranced with. Time passed and I became less interested in the show itself and more so in Carmen, specifically the one that had taken on a life of her own in my head. Eventually she abandoned her original context entirely and began to claim autonomy, becoming something of a self-aware imaginary friend. My guess is that with so much of me asleep, Carmen claimed facets of my personality that I hadn't found yet or had failed to master.

After she set up a permanent camp in the base of my skull, things sped up drastically. Fragments of information and sensory stimulation began to get through, coming down the lines that my intense focus on Carmen had created. I was floating just below the surface looking up, noticing light filtering through the murky water that had I had never seen before. The world was coming nearer as the currents pushed me closer to shore. By June – July 1995 I was in the surf line where the sea Washes up debris of the lost on the beach.

I just needed one big wave.

 A gathering storm. I finally began to build up enough momentum to escape .

ECCENTRICITY

the awakening

>>>>>>>>>>>>>>>>>>>> 07.13.1995 - 1996

The Awakening

3

Obtaining Sentience.

One sharp blow from my subconscious sent me reeling into existence. A million years of preparation for this one moment. Why now? Why this? One dream ended and the next began.

At some point late 7/12/95 or early 7/13 I dreamed that I was a detective working with the police after Carmen. But something was very different this time. I wasn't just watching some distant screen. Someone hit the switch and long rusted wheels groaned to life. I felt it moving, felt something tumbling into place. All of a sudden I was there, fully self aware.
I made my first conscious choice.
I ditched the police and ran blindly down a dark hall after her, only to hit a wall. Before I could fall back, Carmen grabbed me by the shoulders and dragged me to a huge, ornately carved oaken door.
And pushed me through.

It was open air, it had feeling. It was like everything became clear, like a shock. I was now in a very bright grassy field, the huge heavy door I had just passed through had become a rickety latch-door for a weather-worn shack. Its owner told me where to go to sign up to work for Carmen, but when I tried to, I realized I didn't know who I was, where I was, or how I got there. All I knew was this reality, the first I ever really knew, and it was a dream.

On my 13th year, 7th month, 13th day, at about 7:13 in the morning, I was born.
No kidding.

◀ All at once, altogether. 13 years later I am finally born. I do not really celebrate my 8/30/81 birthday because that was not me, only my shell.

Re-Calibration and Self
The Crash Course in Humanity

When children of any kind are just born, they look to their parents to show them who they are. I would say that the first ten years are when your brain installs its operating system, the structural code that everything else is sorted by. Gender, name, race, nationality, religion, morals, taboos, and other constraints, all those things that are not passed down by instinct alone are hard-wired into a child's system through constant exposure of life's little subtleties, whatever they may be. That is the process of imprinting. If a duckling hatches in sight of a dog, it will imprint as one. Once a person begins to think for themselves, the imprinting stage ends, having served its purpose.

But what if there is no imprinting? What if life's subtleties are too subtle for a damaged person to observe and rationalize into anything? By the time I awoke, my imprinting session had closed.

It's like this; If someone comes up to you thirteen years after you're born and tells you you're an alien, maybe after a while you may believe it, but will you really Know it in that indescribable way that you know yourselves to be human? I never can, because I never did, and despite anyone's best efforts, never will, not for really real anyway. You can only brainwash someone so much.

To this day I don't really recognize my name as my own. I don't have any of those basic labels like gender and nationality. This made for a unique opportunity, to consciously Learn the world with an adult mind. As a result I grew on my own accord and fell out of sync with the humans around me. Nothing was taken for granted. Trees were giant plants, authority figures only became so by getting others to believe they were, and leg warmers were much more effective on the arms.

I wasn't trying to think outside the box, rather, there was a box and I tried to explain it the best I could with the little knowledge I had picked up along the way. It was usually wrong, or if my explanation was right, it sounded really bizarre. Eventually I decided that if it made sense to me then that was good enough and concepts that didn't fit logically were rejected or modified. Many things in my new habitat seemed a waste of time and rather counterproductive, like make-up. People would know you were wearing it, so using it as an enhancer of the natural state of the face seemed pointless. On the other hand, if the person put on makeup to enjoy their own appearance in it, then it was a different story. Which is why I periodically dye my hair blue.

I was about fifteen when I bought my first article of clothing at a store by myself, a sweater with a stripe on it. Buying clothes was slow going before the Balance, as I really didn't know what humans my age wore. Then it became an issue of not wanting to. For some reason their clothes felt odd and alien. It made me feel like I was wearing some kind of a costume in an attempt to be something I wasn't. I am still terribly behind on pop-culture. At the time, I didn't even bother. There were more pressing matters, mainly, figuring out why no one seemed to like me much. I eventually had to abandon this as well.

Shortly after I arrived on Earth, they tested me.

The little voice in my head knew about as much as I did about our new home, but it never let on.

ECCENTRICITY

recalibration and self
>>>>>>>>>>>>>>>>>1996 - 1997

I did not yet understand the concept of 'authority' when the High School principal challenged me. After spending the past year absorbing information, I began to use it. I brought him down in less than four months.

Power

You shouldn't take away meat from a starving animal

I think I would have gladly continued to wander along on my own if not for the fact that eventually I would have to deal with the others, and that 'eventually' was February of 1998 when the small pond I was living in expanded a billion-fold with the discovery the Internet. The first thing on my list to find: Carmen. Six hours gave me an impressive stack of reading material but it wasn't until I found the Forum that the world shifted.

I stumbled upon a forum of others also devoted to Carmen, a few even being semi-nursed by Her presence in their subconscious like I was, and I could talk to them all, so long as I could get online. I had no access from home so I resorted to the school's computers. January gave me one month of my first sense of community. While this was going on the school hired a new principal, Dr. F, who then proceeded to terrorize students and teachers alike.

I remained blissfully unaware of him until one cold day when he saw fit to take me on.

I was informed that by posting on this forum I was breaking school policy and I was kicked off for the rest of the year. So I wrote a letter. After two weeks Dr. F told me that both he and the Superintendent had reviewed my request and denied it. It would have stopped there except that during a random chat with the superintendent (because people in power are fascinating), it was found that the superintendent had never seen the note, and what's more, demanded to see it now. The request was approved and Dr. F was very angry.

I hadn't meant to go over his head, but he didn't see it that way. The next day he pulled me out of class and threatened me should I ever think to go over his head again. It didn't matter to me. I still had the letter of approval.

For two weeks I roamed the Net. On February 11th I met a fellow forumer named Seldavia (Beanie!) from Minnesota who would one day become my wife and the sunshine to my world. Shortly after I met her I was thrown off again by the library assistant. When confronted she gave no answers so I went to the Vice Principal and found that he had heard no

such thing. It was at this point that Dr. F interrupted our closed meeting to announce; a) That he told the assistant to shut me down and b) there wasn't a damn thing I could do about it.

It would have been so easy to write me off as paranoid or a troublemaker, but I guess he was really confident that day. The Vice and I just stared at him, because yes, it really was that unbelievable. Then the Vice decided to help me beat him.

During the final months of my Junior year, students, parents, and teachers fed me information on the tyrant's dealings. There was a movement underground and somehow I had become its figurehead. I was a perfect front, when you think about it. I was easily manipulated, had no fear or concept of authority, was over-emotional, reckless, persistent, and above all, disposable. I was only dimly aware of what the implications could be, nor do I think I would have cared if I had. Bad things were happening, and they must be stopped. Could there be any other way? The consequences of losing were never fully understood, which I suppose is why I took him on in the first place.

But I did know something else, and that was how the humans worked. I had studied their structure, their interfacing, and I knew how to pull the strings.

And in the end, we won.

The full story is far more complicated than what I write here and from it I learned what colouring outside the lines could do to the whole structure. I had achieved Power. Two months later, I achieved internet access through the middle school library, which, as far as I was concerned, was the bigger victory of the two.

Second Edition Notes:

Dr. F was finally caught in October of 2003 and brought up on charges of sexual harassment. He was fired from his post of assistant superintendant of schools in the next county. Hopefully no one will be stupid enough to hire him again, but they probably will.

ECCENTRICITY

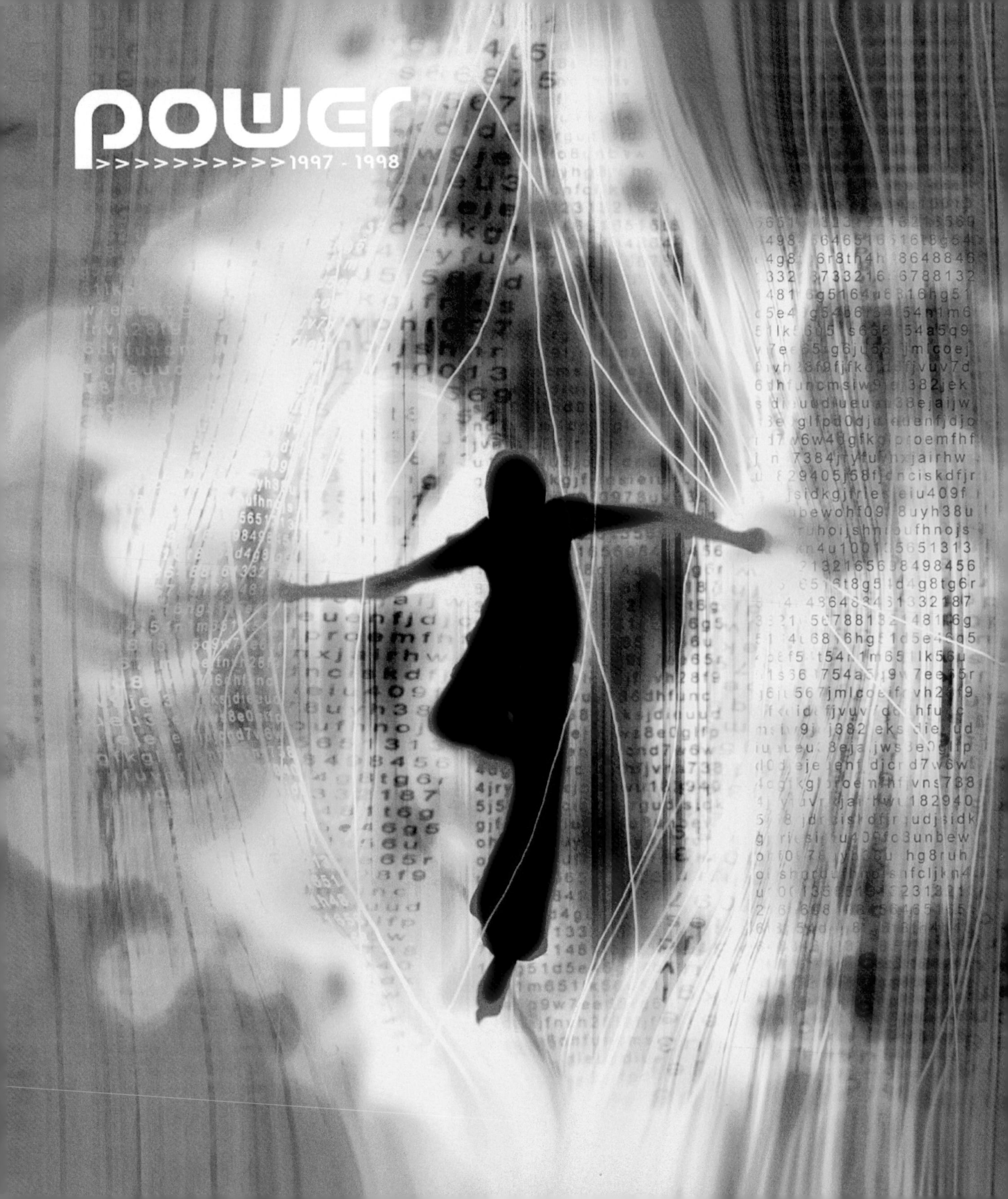
power
>>>>>>>>>>>1997 - 1998

6 Social Balance

Accepted

I had won them over. After Dr. F's eviction, things changed. Though still incurably out of sync, I was accepted by the school as rebellious. My bizarre self-training made it hard for others to pin me and I was written off as an artistic eccentric that could pull a mean one if needed.

I made my first attempt of being angry at someone and failed miserably. It was a lesson learned and I stopped trusting people as companions though I still loved to watch them as subjects. Actually, at the time I wasn't doing much exploring at all. It was as if I decided that the war had been fought and now it was time to start my life living amongst these beings as one of them. I had achieved the human standard of excellence (so far as I could tell) in so short a time. I might actually have became normal, except for the small matter that...

I wasn't.

One of them. I could finally take my place with the humans. But looks can be deceiving...

lfkjroiriti5o9gtjldiakjwokgjfi
i58gjr8fkrmt5454354eekrgd35fg6
f5t4h6f5h48j7ysdhjbvghfjkrj444
fd54g4n5c5r7h45g5y88i5lk5j55d5
vbj42mgfelgelo2m2bhujki5220p2x
2g5glettrh5y2j2m2u5o2o6f9c55v5
f2kuhcxzy76erfda135h9olpkkjbvf
vmkfhy735d0vjnsifxr93444994j3n
jendjklsu938hdha341hdoajhduiw2
djhdjkakndjlakmcnjsj1wlhfhjskw

```
tree
    maple
    oak
    pear (see also 'fruit tree')
rock
bush
grass
```

i58gjr8fkrmt5454354eekrgd35fg6
f5t4h6f5h48j7y5dhjbvghfjkrj444
fd54g4n5c5r7h45g5y88i5lk5j55d5
vbj42mgfelg6io2m2bhujki5220p2x
2g5glettrh5y2j2m2u5o2o6f9c55v5
f2kuhcxzy76erfda135h9olpkkjbvf
vmkfhy735d0vjnsifkr93444994j3n
jendjklsu930hdha341hdbajhduiw2
djhdjkakndjlakmcnjsj1wlhfhjskw
dvozdsvbsdbsdvbsdvsvscvsvsdvp
dvsov2dvsdvsd.xr45794jktfjfdk
lfkjroirti5o9gtjldiakjwokgjfi
i58gjrfpkrmt5454354eekrgd35fg6
f5t4h6f5h48j7y5dhjbbghfjkrj44
fd54g4n5c5r7h45g5y88i5k5j55d5
vbj42mgfelg6io2m2bhujki5220p2x
2g5glettrh5y2j2m2u5o2o6f9c55v5
f2kuhcxzy76erfda135h9olpkkjbvf
vmkfhy735d0vjnsifkr93444994j3n
jendjklsu930hdba341hdbajhduiw2
djhdjkakndjlakmcnjsjiwlnhfhjskw
dvdzdsvbsdbsdvbsdvsvsdvsvsdvd
dvsdvsdvsdvsdvwr45794jktfjfdk9
lfkjroiriti5o9gtjldiakjwokgjfi
i58gjr8fkrmt545435 4eekrgd35fg6
f5t4h6f5h48j7y5dhj vghfjkrj444
fd54g4n5c5 7n45g5y6i5lk5j55d5
felg6io2m2bhujki5220p2x
etrh8y2j2m2u5o2o6f9c55v5
kuhcxzy76er fda135h9olpkkjbvf
kfhy735d0vjnsifkr93444
ndjklsu9

social Balance >>>>>>>>>>>>

djkakndjlakmcnjsjiwirhjskw
bvsbsdvbsdvdvsdvsvsdvd
sdvsdvsdvwr45794jktfjfdk9
iti5o9gtjldiakjwokgjfi
mt5454354eekrgd35fg6
hjbv2fjkr44
fd54g4n5c5r/...5lk5j55d5
vbj42mgfelg6...2bh..j52.
2g5glettrh5y2j2m1u5e...
f2kuhcxzy76erfda135...
vmkfhy735d0vjnsifkr9344...
jendjklsu930hdha341hdbajhduiw2
djhdjkakndjlakmcnjsjiwinfirsk
dvdzdsvbsdbsdvbsdvsvsdvsvsdvd
dvsdvsdvsdvsdvwr45794jktfjfdk9

The Eternal Gray
The Abandonment

Even writing the words makes me feel a chill inside and a tightness in my chest.

Early on in my first days of college I had an epiphany.

A few friends and I were talking about 80's cartoons we watched as kids, but when I tried to think back, there was nothing, nothing there. It was the first time I noticed my past was missing. In fact, it was the first time it even occurred to me that I was very, very different from the others. Worse, I didn't know who, or even what I was at all. The Social Balance had been a sham, a false reward for something never sought. I realized the potential of my situation of being born without programming and theorized that with careful mental discipline I could eliminate even more bothersome emotions that skewed rational thought, such as Fear, Embarrassment, Pride, and Anger. I would leave everything that I 'knew' behind and wander the mind in search of the Truth. The experiment would be called, "The Abandonment".

It worked too well.

I started the Abandonment in September and systematically shut off emotional responses until I had myself trained. How was I to know that new illnesses had formed in place of the old? Now I was unwittingly feeding them and they grew exponentially, spreading their tendrils through my mind like a malignant tumor. After Fear shut off I began to feel numb. I started driving fast, as if I needed to get away from something, that I needed to fly. One day I tried to pass a construction truck on a blind turn and nearly lost my life. That's when I saw it. For one moment in time I could see it split and realized that those thoughts of Death and hopelessness were not really mine, but a foreign entity, something else living off my mind like a parasite. The truth was it had been there for years, perhaps as far back as Re-Calibration, only appearing in Winter. Now it was no longer content with that lot and had begun the move to take complete control. It touched off the desperate race to save myself.

Why was it called the Eternal Gray? As you read this book you will learn that my senses are wired up kind of strange. As Depression settled in and more 'inefficient' thoughts were removed, everything started to take on a gray tone. Sound was muted and temperature response was vague. Hot or cold, I always felt a chill under my skin.

I didn't taste and I couldn't smell. It wasn't so much that I couldn't, but that the resources usually given to those areas had simply gone dormant. I figured out that I could elicit false sensory response by listening to certain kinds of music and began abusing it like a drug. Toward the end, I refused to turn off my CD player, not even in class for fear of disappearing entirely. I was subsisting on the emotional equivalent of condiments.

By January I had lost control. I cried often, in school, in the car. I didn't want to leave the house and became restless. I often stayed up until two in the morning, afraid to allow the next day to begin.

Then I stopped dreaming.

That on its own should have been a blaring alarm for me to pull out of my dive because I always have dreams, vivid tactile dreams. But I didn't. I still believed that I was in control and these 'disturbances' were the side effects of my grand experiment.

Then, on February 26th, at about one in the morning, I lost it all.

I had trained myself so well not to feel the feelings I had deemed unfit for science, but those emotions connected to others and then still to others. They had dropped like dominos for the past five months and now as the curtain was pulled away I realized my folly. There was no escape, nothing else to feel.

Nothing else to feel...

On 2/26/2000, I went into catatonic shock.

Second Edition Notes: I know it says I "trained" myself not to feel, but now I wonder if it was in fact the illness that did it, or at least encouraged it. More likely it has something to do with a new theory I'm working on. Sometimes the body takes somewhat counter-productive measures when it tries to defend itself, such as fatal allergies and organ rejection. It's almost as if my head felt the Depression eating away and tried to block the symptoms itself by tuning out and going dormant. This is something that continues to happen every Winter and effectively suffocates me to death. That is why I hibernate.

My condition was already bad by 1999, but my attempt to fix it made it far worse. Social Balance and all that I had gained seemed trivial and I "abandoned" it to find higher meaning. By early 2000 the hoax was falling apart and my mind was beginning to unravel. The Abandonment was the riskiest and most disastrous mind experiment I have ever performed. ➤

abandonment
and the
eternal gray

>>>>>>>>>>>>>>>>

99 - 2.26.2000

8

Re-Entry
The Great Escape

It might have ended there except that I belong to Something Else and whatever That is had decided this had gone on far enough. I think my subconscious must have realized that unless it did something, it was going down with the ship. My dreamless sleep suddenly erupted with colours and visions, violent sensory reproductions and scenarios that forced long forgotten feelings to re-emerge. It took about a week to use the memories of those dreams to rebuild some semblance of a working mind. Moments before I was consumed by the Apathy Crash, I finally came face to face with the hollowed-out shell I had become. I could no longer ignore that I was disintegrating.

In a desperate bid to reverse the damage, I dove back into the world I had abandoned, trying to reclaim the seemingly good life of Social Balance. I ran about trying to keep myself busy, trying to mentally override the Depression, trying to believe that if I wanted it gone bad enough, eventually it would go away. It was a time of bursts of energy, fast-talking and no thinking. If I could just keep out-running it...

And the disease quietly *s p r e a d* .

In the eye of the storm. ➤
I got lucky and somehow dragged myself from the suffocation of the Eternal Gray. I thought I had escaped by consciously deciding to Re-Enter, but toward the end of this era I began to see that I would need medical help once more. I would have to hurry; I was almost out of time. Just because I had eluded one battle hardly meant I would survive the war.

I wouldn't win that easily...

THE RIVINIA STAR PROJECTS
ECCENTRICITY

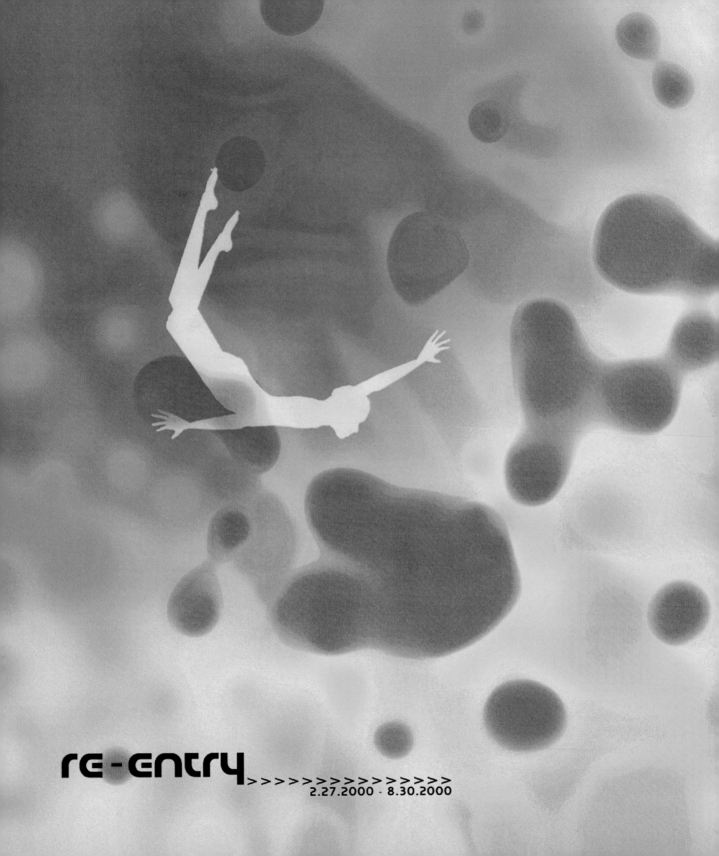

re-entry >>>>>>>>>>>>>>>>>

2.27.2000 - 8.30.2000

final
descent
>>>>>>>>>>>>>>>>>>>
8.31.2000 - 12.18.2000

This was a logbook that I kept for about three months to see if there was a pattern. There wasn't. The symptoms were measured in intensity from 1 being calm to 10 being suicidal.

Final Descent
Everything Falls Apart

The simple fact is you can't will away mental illness any more than you can a headache, and trying to do so only wastes precious time. I wish I knew that then. It wasn't until 8/30/2000 that I hit the wall, marking the first time that suicide went from idle thought to serious consideration. By November, my ability to function day to day was half that of what it was in July. I couldn't control my emotions at all. I was terrified of people, things, ideas, and leaving the house. It was like the scene from 'Clockwork Orange' where the guy is forced to watch all these things he didn't want to see, didn't have to see. It couldn't be stopped. The cycling thoughts of death and suffering would be there when I went to sleep and there again when I woke up. There was no way to distract it and it was slowly driving me mad.

The onset of Winter accelerated the cycling, but I still stayed in college. School was the last thing that connected me to any semblance of structure, but by now I couldn't go unless I called up the school's therapist to talk me out of the house.

I slept at all hours of the day. If I were to describe what it felt like trying to think, I'd say it was trying to drive a car on ice. Every turn and movement, no matter how small, was exaggerated into something huge and dangerous.

I was sent to a new therapist for a short while but she wasn't able to get past the obvious fact that I was Eccentric. After that, I suppose they figured me cured.

There was no stopping the inevitable.

Every passing day I could feel it all just peeling away as I fell, each day faster and farther. All my code dissolved and my consciousness burned away in the Final Descent.

System Crash
And then there wasn't any more.

The onslaught of pain and fear flooded every sector, burning everything, killing everything. There was no reasoning with it, no dealing with it and by God no relief from it. I decided to crash my car and disappear. The system collapsed before I even got the chance.

People love to point out that the *intent* of suicide doesn't count as an attempt. These people obviously have never crossed the Line in the Sand, the Point of No Return, that strange Serenity that comes over you when you step outside yourself and walk away. There where times when I came close, when suicide was idealized in flights of fancy but even then I was still in the land of the living. This time was different. I hope you never truly understand why.

Second Edition Notes:
Found this little bit of text in the back of my hard drive from when I wrote this section.

$%#@&$ this is so frustrating, trying to cram hell in a tiny box for reading. I've been sitting here for three days trying to get the right mix of words so I can convey the destruction, the chaos, the absolute futility of my last few days. It all sounds so corny and overdramatic, like some soppy screen play, but I'm telling you it was real.
Everything burned down, and when you went to dowse one thing three other things caught fire. It didn't seem so bad at first, but it just kept going and going, there was no rest, no time out. You couldn't go watch TV and come back to it. It was always on your ass like a rabid monkey, everywhere. I mean, I'm not weak, but after years of this you just lose it. What's the point, right? When no one believes you and talking it out doesn't work and you can't get medication because you aren't old enough to have your own insurance, death starts looking pretty good. It sucks, it sucks a lot, but death isn't about choices. It's about...I still don't know what it's about...

Death of the System ➤

system crash
>>>>>>>>>>>>>>>>
12.19.2000 · 1.18.2001

OS Re-Installation
Better Living through Science

On December 18th, 2000, the system finally folded. I was too weak to die but I wasn't strong enough to live either. I went into a semi-conscious stupor, sleepwalking through the holidays and falling into the nethermost regions of my mind. Unless a new operating system replaced the burnt-out shambles of my old structure, there I would remain.

A new doctor was called for and that new OS came in the form of a little blue pill called Paxil. (Which is what that chemical sign stands for.) A lot of people that I knew who had taken anti-depressants claimed a loss of feeling, becoming zombies and losing their creativity. I suppose if I had a choice I would have procrastinated or never taken the drug at all, but in the end it was get fixed or get scrapped, and I had put too much effort into my machine just to throw it away.

In the image over there you can see a lot of white. It was very white in my head during the late era of the Crash and most of the Re-Install because nothing else was running. It was as serene as a fresh snowfall and as quiet as nuclear winter. Deep inside I waited. The soft rainbow band in the middle started to appear at the end of the Re-Install, the notion that something was happening out there, that something was coming in to rescue me or that something big was secretly preparing to launch.

➤

And there she is, Shodan, one of the goddesses that live in my head and roam the Space at will, reconstructing me in accordance to the OS's parameters.

People that know me well find Shodan's presence at this vulnerable stage unsettling as she often has an agenda of her own, but even Shodan knows she can't command a broken ship.

She's also convinced that I am a product of her genius, and far be it from Shodan to leave something in her name in such dismal disrepair.

THE SEVENTH STAR PROJECTS
ECCENTRICITY

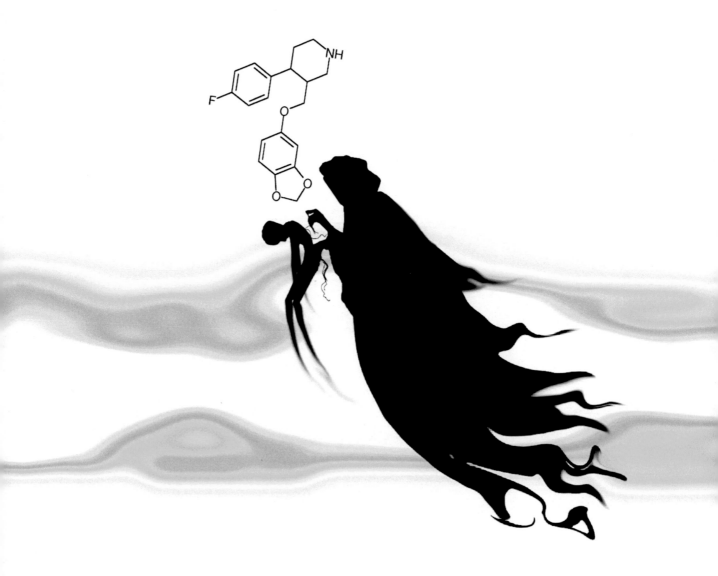

05
re-installation
>>>>>>>>>>>>>>>>>> 1.19.2001 - 2.06.2001

arrival

free. finally free! life awaits me, its mysteries new to my newborn eyes. I have walked through the darkness and madness of my own broken mind and survived.

at last, I have Δrrived...

Arrival

"Yes at Last, at Last, to be Free of the Past, and now the future beckons me."- Jimmy Somerville

February 6th 2001, I was sitting on the floor of the painting studio making a mindless watercolour of Beanie when someone asked what day it was. February 6th? I hadn't thought about what day it was in two weeks. I hadn't been aware of how long the winter was, or how long it would be before the equinox would salvage what had survived. It was at this moment that it dawned on me:

I was free.

The first week on Paxil had been filled with tremors, sleep, and more sleep, but once it passed, I felt it, a fresh breath of air filtering into my stale tomb. I had the urge to open my eyes and See the world again, a world that a short while ago had been a dark tunnel with no end. For the first time in nearly six months, I felt a person inside me, a person that liked Things and did Stuff. I suddenly had more emotions than the default Sad and Panic, ones that were dusty with years of neglect, like Boredom. I discovered Boredom while sitting in the shuttle bus several days later, had been unable to exist because all available space in my mind had been taken over by the virus. Now it was delightfully empty. My dose of Paxil seems to increase every six months, which tells me that under the floorboards the monster still lurks. But I am on the high ground now, watching ever vigilant. I am enjoying my place here in the sun, for now I am Alive, 20 years in the making.

Fun Fact:
When MSU learned of what had happened, they awarded me the Carpe Diem Alumni Scholarship for continuing education in the face of extreme adversity.
It was worth $1,000.
Montclair State rulez.

Second Edition Notes:
This is where I would have liked to say my life became stable. I would finish school, get a job, get an apartment, and become a full fledged Eccentric complete with a couch fort and telescope.

But then again, Life had its own agenda...

◄ If you can't read it, it says:
Free. Finally free! Life awaits me,
Its mysteries new to my newborn eyes. I have walked through the Darkness and madness of my own Broken mind and survived.

At last, I have Arrived.

 Fast times at Montclair State and beyond.

13

The Runway
Preparing for Take-off

My journey through hell complete, I went about taking everything I had learned and began making this manifesto. It was my senior year in college, the great home stretch, time to pull everything together and jump into the future. It was a golden age indeed.

This included that wonderfully heady frenzy that proceeds any great trip into the unknown. For me it was the chaos of actually getting this book finished, printed, and following an ancient rite of passage; *Getting the University to Let You Graduate.*

It's thought that one simply finishes their requirements and the school lets you graduate but this is a misconception created to lull people into a false sense of security. In order to actually graduate, you have to beat the school in a relentless game of mental chess and prove that you would be able to survive in the bureaucratic wilds.

They tried no less than four times to knock me off the grad list, using missing credits, miss-allocated credits, a missing major, and at one point an ancient library fine, none of which they would warn you of. Each time I was sent on a wild round of paperwork that had to be accomplished by deadlines often in a matter of hours. Madness reigned and

it was wonderful, like a drug. I don't believe I have ever been so consistently drunk on anticipation.

I had a wicked professor closing in for the kill but in the end, in the very end when I took that last spring into space, I knew she couldn't touch me anymore. No professor could touch me anymore.

Unfortunate events had left me more or less a drifter but who cared? I had this Book. I had a small pile of awards in my car. I was at the top. Now that I had graduated with honors and much recognition, I was going to complete the circle by moving into my own apartment and become a full-fledged Eccentric. There would be my own window, my own telly, my telescope, even a greenhouse. I would fill the refrigerator with my own foods and I would have a lock on my door.

With nothing left to lose and a brilliant future all but assured to me, I ran to the edge and leapt, leapt out with joyful abandon.

Into the worst economy in seventy years.

◀Wheeeeeeeeeeeeeeeeeeeeeeeeeeeee!

ECCENTRICITY

14

Failed Attempt

Jumping into Nothing

Graduation left me homeless once more (as I had fairly well been living in the computer lab) but I didn't figure on being homeless for long. I mean, finding a supporting wage couldn't be too hard, not with the burst of fanfare I had emerged from as a resume. Even if I could just barely grasp the concept of the word "professional", I was sure I could get by on talent. I wasn't worried.

And time passed.

And it passed some more.

As Summer burned into its full glory I had yet to get a response from a single employer and fear began to creep in through the cracks. While I was at school I had no time to absorb the idea that all my belongings were gone, but now I had all the time in the world. I kept wanting to read things, use things, wear things that had always been there and been mine, but couldn't. It really messes with your mind. I told myself that all I needed was a job, any job, and it would all be okay. It would be soon, it had to be soon...

On my second or third month of unemployment I was watching "The Daily Show" on Comedy Central. They were in the middle of a "correspondence piece" with Rob Courdry. "Ah graduation. That magical time when you trade one of these, for one of these." he said as his graduation cap changed into a fast food server's paper hat. He then threw the paper hat in the garbage, adding, "Or it would be, except that Wendy's currently isn't hiring right now." He went on to report on employment opportunities in the sex trade.

If the situation had entered into mainstream comedy that could only mean that it was pandemic. There really were no jobs, and if there were no jobs, there would be no home. A deep sense of failure and desolation replaced any excitement I had left from graduation and as Summer slowly drifted by without promise, I was forced to surrender to a grim reality. Life would have to wait.

Nothing ahead and nothing behind, I became Adrift.

'Whump'. I think that word accurately describes this picture. Or splat, but I like "whump" better. ➤

15

Nomad
Life Without a Home in the Age of Hopelessness

Many people are quick to point out that I was never *truly* homeless, that technically I could go live at my parent's house, but then again technically you can drink saltwater in small amounts and still survive. Several tragedies had taken place and the atmosphere was too unstable. No one is to blame, I was just too sick to stay there.

In a choice between life and shelter, I opted for the street. I lived like that for a month, from September to October of 2003. I don't think I ever really slept on the street because I usually managed to talk Beanie into letting me crash on her couch. It was around this time that I finally managed to get a job working in a tiny camera store doing restorations, but it didn't pay a sustaining wage. I knew I was horribly underpaid for what I was doing, but my boss couldn't afford to pay more.

Towards the end of October I went on a pilgrimage to Point Pleasant to collect my mind. It wasn't the true Holylands of Wildwood, that would have taken far too much time and money, but it would do in a fix. It was warm that day. Summer was giving its last gasp before succumbing to Winter. I remember that long walk on the beach so well...

I was lost, so very, very lost.

On the way home the bus stopped a town before mine and declared it to be the end of the line. Apparently I hadn't checked the schedule close enough. I remember wondering how I was going to get home, then realizing I had nowhere to go. The bus driver left me on a corner, stranded and alone.

Eventually I got to Beanie's via another bus, but the damage had been done. Any lingering illusions about my situation being temporary were gone. I was truly homeless.

Beanie decided to let me live with her after she discovered I would rather sleep in my car than go home at night. I lived on her couch, any clothes I could carry out of the house now resided in a Tupperwear container behind it, and most of my most immediately needed possessions were packed into my car.

The landlord of her building looked the other way to my squatting because I had tended the apartment's gardens during my summer of unemployment, another one of my Missions from better days. When he passed on, miraculously I was allowed to continue my stay.

As Fall turned into Winter, it was like the Eternal Grey all over again.

I hadn't given up just yet. In fact, I came up with a new hare-brained scheme to get a job just about every week.

I wrapped up my life and carried it with me to ward off the bitter cold sting of desolation. It helped at first, but eventually it only served as a reminder, a shabby grey mass of missing pieces that weighs you down as you go.

➤

ECCENTRICITY

Nomad

By January I saved up $1,200 to put myself back into the design scene by taking continuing education classes at the School of Visual Arts. I worked nine to five, six days a week, then took the bus to NYC four of those nights to attend school. It was the only thing keeping me going.

The inadvertent side-effect of going to SVA was being thrown into the glorious burst of confusion that was commuting to New York City at night. Every night I would slip into the current and let it carry me. It was bitterly cold and the Winter filled whatever nooks and crannies it could find, but the city fought back with a continual stream of activity and movement. It was an ideal hiding place for a nomad like me. No one notices that you don't belong. No one notices, but no one cares either. This was a city of humans with lives and jobs. Those of them that could not fit the mold fell by the wayside, the detritus of society, forever lost.

What if I couldn't find a way to fit? There were hundreds, thousands of normal, professional people competing for each job out on the market. They had corporate habits and manners, normal clothes, professional portfolios and resumes. I saw them everywhere, going to bars, going on dates, drinking at Starbucks with clients. It was a world so far apart from me, one I, for the life of me, will never be able to understand.

I had talent and skills, but I didn't have It, that essence of the everyday man. All my life I was in school, a place where you didn't necessarily fit in, but you couldn't be easily thrown out. In the real world it was done all the time. There were more than enough round pegs for those coveted round holes. At best I was a novelty item in mainstream America.

There was no need for me.

I still had my job at Photo Cullen, though. I had just begun wondering if I supplemented my meager pay with a second job as a janitor if I could afford a place to live when an agency returned my call. Even after all this time I was still putting in resumes for jobs, albeit in a mindless routine sort of way. I met with them in early April where they told me they had a job opening for a designer at a firm in Soho. I was rushed across town to meet with their creative director, who said they would hire me on a temp to perm basis if I could start the day after.

I said yes.

The next day I told my boss at Photo Cullen that I had to leave on very short notice. I hated to do it, especially after all he did for me, but I was desperate. He understood, and oddly enough, someone came into the store looking for a job later that day, She was hired. I went to my new job for two days, then was told that my supervisor would be away shooting a commercial for the next week. I was to get a call when my new boss came back, telling me when I could come in to continue my temp period.

I never heard from him again.

After two weeks of desperate calling I found out that they had hired someone else and hadn't bothered to call. The agency who placed me apologized profusely and promised me another job, a position as a designer for Marlboro cigarettes. I may have had lost everything, but I still had morals.

I quit the working world.

Second Edition Notes:
I often refer to this period as 'The Great Divide' or 'The War' when referring to possessions I lost. Example, 'That book was lost in the war.' 'I lost that picture to/in the great divide.'

16
Restoration
Which took far longer than anyone would have guessed

Which is of course exactly why I was hired by Mayer/Berkshire shortly after.

Figures.

I had sent out the resume some time before my ship sank and frankly I had forgotten all about it. This created a very unexpected problem.

I had a job but by now it was too late. The damage that the Nomad year caused was so severe that I no longer wanted to work in the design field. To be honest, at the time I got the call from M/B I was beginning to think of other things nonprofessional types could do for a living, like being a truck driver or a dominatrix. I crack myself up with that last one... but no, seriously, I was signing up for workshops.

Then suddenly Nomad was over. All logic said I should be overjoyed, but I found I was no longer interested. It was like trying to attach a limb thought lost to a healed stump. Beanie forced me to go to my new job but I was terribly shell-shocked. Though I wouldn't say Mayer/ Berkshire is corporate, it was still a far cry from the more unconventional jobs I'd had. As far as corporate culture is concerned, I'm hopelessly awkward. I was so afraid of miss-stepping that I skipped my lunch breaks to hide by my desk and didn't talk to anyone for months. Emotional progress was painfully slow, but with the job came the fantastic possibility of getting an apartment. Finally I could let go of the dead weight I had been carrying with me for so long as a vagabond.

Which created yet another very unexpected problem.

There were a lot of emotions that swirled around when I finally got a home, but the most unexpected one was pain. With every piece of my life that I reclaimed from those cardboard boxes I felt something akin to being kicked in the stomach. The Nomad years had been hard, but I had no idea how much hurt had been locked away until the boxes began to open. The event that I had waited so long for as being a grand release became a hollow, bitter, and torturous rite of reclamation.

And then Winter came.

I had been living in the apartment for three months by the time it did, but the darkness of the Nomad era was still clinging to me. By February I began to panic. The fact that I was still depressed, despite having accomplished the last step in my master plan for salvation, was enough to drive me to edge several times. I even called the suicide hot line, which I'll tell you was not very helpful.

Putting myself back together after the Nomad era took nearly a year, a whole year more than I thought it would. The memories continue to hang around the edges of my mind like pond scum, but that's okay.

The Rift has returned.

Seriously, that's what it looked like. I was orange and everything else was white. I felt like I had just come in from a storm and now all was quiet. I just dropped everything and stared.

17

The Jubilation

Everything comes together

It took nearly a frigging year for the system to check itself and realize that Nomad was over. A frigging year! FRIG! It was April 4th, 2005 when my brain suddenly realized that I had a job, a home, and that my depression was going into remission. Then it proceeded to announce this to me as if it were breaking news. The result was something like electrocution, except good. It wasn't just a change in the mind, but the entire body, like a warm summer wind gusting through cobwebs. I began to trip.

It's probably no coincidence that Daylight Savings had been the day before (one of the holiest days in the Spacialist calender). In fact, it fuels a theory I'm working on that a good portion of my brain actually shuts down for the winter, making it impossible to register change in the environment. It's probably a defense mechanism to keep Winter stimulus out, but in this case it ended up making things worse. I'm not sure whether I'll need it this year or not, but I am choosing not to think about it at the moment.

Winter can wait.

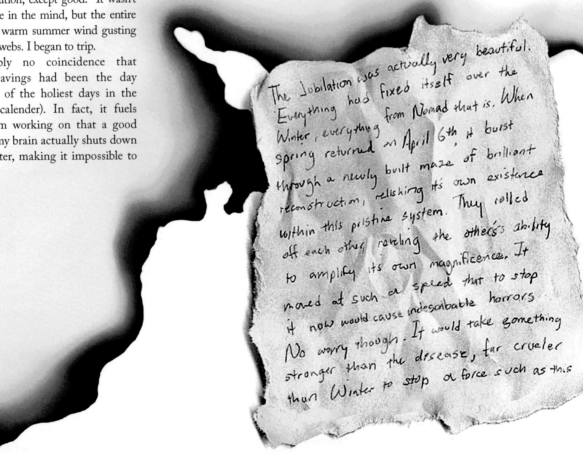

The Jubilation was actually very beautiful. Everything had fixed itself over the Winter, everything from Nomad that is. When spring returned on April 6th, it burst through a newly built maze of brilliant reconstruction, relishing its own existence within this pristine system. They rolled off each other, reveling the other's ability to amplify its own magnificence. It moved at such a speed that to stop it now would cause indescribable horrors. No worry though. It would take something stronger than the disease, far crueler than Winter to stop a force such as this

18

Shot in the Back of the Head

And then the Unthinkable Happened

The first shot wasn't personal and I had warning.

Not much, but some.

The Holylands had been destroyed. The land that had been locked in time for nearly 40 years had finally been discovered by land developers and they had consumed it voraciously. The land was pocked with the shells of disemboweled temples and empty lots in ruin. The ocean was not concerned, thank goodness and continued to throw out its energy with abandon. It was the only place that was safe. I never thought that the Holylands would change though I don't know why I never thought it would. It seemed permanent, the foundation of my scattered existence, the only connection I had to my childhood, the dream-world, whatever planet I belonged to, whatever place I was eventually destined for. It was the only place when everything came back into phase and I was whole. Suddenly those strings were disconnecting and there was nothing that could be done but let it wash away. I returned home from the 2005 pilgrimage completely out of sorts, only to greet another shot as it smashed into the side of my skull.

My great-grandmother died.

My great-grandmother was humanity's hope for eternal life. She was going to forge it from the void of mortal impossibility with sheer will alone and she was succeeding, until reality got wise. Of course it is ridiculous to believe that one can live forever, and I doubt I ever really believed she was doing it, but my subconscious had other ideas. So long as Great-grandmother lived (and she lived like normal people, not half passed on at a nursing home), then no one in our family could die, or at least the possibility for immortality would continue to exist. All hope of that is now lost.

Now all that was left was the Now. The past was becoming erased with the Holylands and the future was no longer protected by my great-grandmother's crusade on the ultimate destiny. All I had now was what I could gather Here in my hands. I had gathered a lot, actually, a home, a job, a life that I could reasonably sustain. It was an accomplishment that seemed impossible to achieve for so much of my life, but it was here. It was.

Until Mayer/Berkshire fired the final shot deep into my brainstem.

And terminated me.

◀ I never saw it coming. So much, suddenly deleted. Suddenly...lost.

ECCENTRICITY

19

State of Change
Learning and Accepting Life's Ultimate Truth

Thus I slowly learned the most essential lesson of all. Everything Changes. I hate change. I've always hated change. I have spent good chunks of my life trying to find a safe patch of land to call my own and defend it to the death. The last thing I wanted to do was have to search for another when this one had taken so long to secure. If it had taken so much effort to capture this fort, then losing it must surely be a sign that my attempt at life had been roundly defeated. If it was over then, shouldn't I now die? Why wasn't I dead? Was there something else I was missing?

So far as I had known to this point, life was about obtaining a specific goal and keeping it. If that goal no longer existed, was it possible to...change the goal? In fact, could I change the path completely? Did I have to follow the original path at all? Once I woke up from my injuries and found that I wasn't dead, I realized that I could go back to the center and set a new route. All I had to do was continue to remain alive and Time would eventually take me somewhere. In fact, I could go where I thought I could never return.

I could return to Eccentricity.

I should never have left, by god! I had begun to believe that my other half could not support me, but what if it could? I had been fired because I was different. My most valiant effort to hide and control it had been in vain; for the Mayers, after pretending for so long that they had accepted my handicaps, had actually never done so at all. It was time to face a Fact; I was Different and so my life would have to be Different. Instead of hiding and taming the wildness, I would now harness it. How could I have been so blind as to believe that because fire can destroy things that that was the only thing it was capable of doing? Fire was powerful. Fire was energy. Fire could be used to fuel civilizations that could not exist without it.

I would harness my demons, and this time they would pull the cart.

Returning to the Source. ➤

How it Was
What came Before what happened Next

The truth is, I finished this book in 2003, or so I thought. Time has continued to pass as I add more and more, so I've been writing new eras for this section as they happened. The problem with that is that the past several chapters are lacking the benefit of hindsight and it's finally caught up with me. So before we proceed forward, I will tell you how it was as I know it now.

When I graduated it rested in the back of my mind that I was about to embark on a new experiment; to see if something like me to exist in the working world. As Nomad came into full bloom I had begun to feel that this crucial trial had failed, meaning I could not fit in the world of Man. The consequences would be dire for sure, but before that door opened I was picked up by Mayer/Berkshire.

I did not count it a success just yet. Phase two would now begin; could I handle the day to day life in the human system? I put a lot of weight on this, for after all, I could pretend to be anyone at the interview. Could I actually survive through the hidden dangers that would make themselves known over and over for weeks, months or even years? I didn't figure I'd last a year. Nomad had stripped me of whatever confidence I'd had, making Restoration as slow and painful as it was, but Berkshire was a heaven. I told them early on the risks of hiring me, that I was out of sync, that I didn't understand much about corporate society, that the Winter would likely be disastrous when it came, that I couldn't handle wearing shoes, ect. I was daring them to fire me then. I gave them every excuse to within my first month to see just how safe I was. The response was amazingly positive, overwhelmingly positive. The Mayers told me that they had been searching for an eccentric because they believed they made the best work and encouraged me to change nothing. I could wear what I wanted, deck out

my desk in as many Christmas lights I could find and sleep on the lawn during my breaks. In return for their kindness I gave them my best. I completed projects they had dreamed of setting in motion years ago but had no talent to pull them off. Tapping my gift, they expanded their advertising venues with flyers, branding, packaging, post cards, store displays, catalogues, new product photography and a constant revamping of the website to name a few.

And they loved me.

Lucky catch! Lucky break! I couldn't be more lucky that these people would overlook my oddities and frailties because they liked me and my work. I

knew I would be able to work if I could just outweigh my weirdness with my talent. The experiment was a success! And then Winter came. It was the most savage, brutal Winter I had ever faced, and I went down fast. As I began to deteriorate, Doc. Rika (best doctor in the world) became alarmed and called Bob Mayer, my boss, early January. She asked him to let me telecommute a day or two a week to lessen the strain. He politely refused. As the weeks went by Bob was his usual friendly self, when he was there. As I began to lose ground, he was on a two week honeymoon in Thailand, then headed off to sunny California. In a bid to save myself, I

self launched a project to recreate the Mayer's Berkshire Legwear catalogue. I would have talked to my friend Mike, who also suffered from depression, but after a long struggle to continue working, he went under. He had tried to save himself by changing his duties from the isolation of the packing room to another job where he would be with people. The number one rule of surviving depression is to never let it get you alone. But once again Bob politely refused and Mike eventually stopped coming to work. Now he was gone, leaving me alone as well. There was something unsettling about seeing a comrade shot down in battle when

.EW – ANIE KNIPPING

June 9, 2005

Job Per...

Anie's graphic de.ign skills are ...re takes direction very well. In addition, Anie has a good understandi... ...ebsites/tasks and requires little to no explanation regarding file sizes, formats, upl... locations, etc. Anie is very creative and often develops excellent ideas.

Anie is an excellent employee provided that she is in good sprits. From time to time, especially in the winter months Anie is in bad spirits and she is very unproductive. Although this is rare, it is a serious problem that needs to be addressed. Anie and I will discuss the possibility of an unpaid, (if she has no vacation time left) week off this winter. during the time that An.e's spirits are low. Apart from these times, Anie is a pleasure to work with.

MAYER/BERKSHIRE

Michael Mayer
Executive Vice President ... ...made a good cont... ...ther department ar... ... ...ting to ...am very happy with her performance. I reminded Anie that this review is July 13, 2005.

Dear Anie:

This letter will confirm the termination of your employment at the Mayer/Berkshire Corporation, effective July 12, 2005.

As I explained to you on the 12th of July, it has become apparent that you are ... unhappy working here... And for that reason I felt that it was best to end our employment relationship.

.egan my emplo... ...sition of Graphic Artist.

..as diagnosed ... ...year 1989, 2001, 2003, 2004 and 2005. At the time of ...e, I did not info... ...employer about my disabilities and was able to perform my duties without th... ...ed for an accommodation. Sometime in November 2004, I informed my Supervisor Mr. Robert (Bo ...ayer, that the onset of Winter would negatively affect my disability. I requested an accommodation ...mporary tele-commuting arrangement to work at home for at least two days a week. My request wa... ...nied. After that period, I was singled out and subjected to harassment from Mr. Mayer. On Februa... ...2005, I met with Mr. Mayer and provided information about my disability. He rejected my doctor's ...quest over the telephone. During that meeting I became ill due to my disability. Following that ...eeting, we had several discussions about my disability and accommodations. The results were not ...ccessful. I continued to perform my duties to the best of my ability and generated satisfactory wor... ...roducts. On June 9, 2005, my performance evaluation was conducted by Mr. Bob Mayer. Several ...mments noted were, "Anie is an excellent employee", "overall Anie has made a good contribution t... ...e department" and "I am happy with her performance". Shortly after that period, I inquired to Mr. ...ayer about obtaining an employee handbook. Mr. Mayer took issue with me pursuing this matter. ... July 12, 2005, I met with Mr. Michael Mayer, Executive Vice President. He stated, "...it has becom... ...parent that you are unhappy working here, and for that reason I felt that it was best to end our ...ationship". As a result, my employment was terminated.

..believe that I have been discriminated against in violation of the Americans with Disabilities Act of ...90, as amended.

...t this charge filed with both the EEOC and the State or local Agency, if any. I will ...se the agencies if I change my address or phone number and I will cooperate fully ...them in the processing of my charge in accordance with their procedures.

you knew it didn't have to happen and that while you are still in the air, you could very well be next. Losing Mike gave me a strange sense of survivor guilt for being able to last when he couldn't. But I was making it. I was still working, even though I was now too sick to go out and get my medicine. Getting my medicine would mean going Out into the Winter and I kept putting it off until the withdrawal symptoms pushed me to the edge. I resumed with a higher dose but I continued to slide downhill. By mid February I put my plea in again for some kind of accommodation for the illness, Americans with Disabilities Act in hand, but was turned down again. How could I expect to get special treatment when no one else did? That wasn't how the world of Man worked. You either found a way to fit or you dropped out. I didn't know if I could do it anymore. But Bob promised me that if I just kept coming to work every day, I would have a job. So long as I could continue to walk out into the crushing Winter for one more month then the experiment would succeed.

So I pushed hard.

Then the Jubilation came, Spring came, and I knew I had made it. I beat the Winter and I was still in the world of Man! Thanks to Bob and all the others at MB for giving me this chance, thanks to the luck that I found them, thanks to the talent that outweighed my illness and thanks that they wanted me despite it. Things were going to be okay. At last, at long last I was one of you.

And then one warm summer afternoon,

they threw me away.

Gone.

Gone, gone, gone.

After the suicide attempt and I came home from the hospital, after the doctors said it was safe for me to be alone, after all my efforts to find out the truth behind why it had happened all failed, I entered a State of Change. I stopped trying to live in the System and began

Team Justice for the Autistic Kid, led by Professor Jonathan Hyman and two students from the Constitutional Litigation Clinic of Rutgers University.

to figure out ways to live off it instead. But there was also this profound rage that developed against Berkshire for wantonly destroying everything I had, after I had trusted them so deeply. I needed to funnel it into something useful lest it burn me to the ground, so I filed a complaint of discrimination with the EEOC. The god-slayer in me awoke and I pulled the entire case together myself. I'd had the wits to ask for a performance review a month before the mysterious firing and under pressure it was provided; flawless. Except for one thing;

'Anie is an excellent employee provided she is in good spirits. From time to time, especially in the winter months Anie is in bad spirits and she is very unproductive.'

I had argued it at the time, citing the many things I had done over the Winter to stay sane, including the Master catalogue. I was brushed away and I let it slide. Then when I was fired I asked for the reason in writing which was;

'...it has become apparent that you are unhappy working here... And for that reason I felt that it was best to end our employment relationship. '

They further cemented this claim when I got Unemployment insurance. Because I was fired, UI called the Mayers asking for a reason. They asked them if I had broken any laws or policies, to which they had said no and stated the same reason above. UI then asked if I had ever said I was unhappy and they replied no again. UI pressed them for an explanation but they wouldn't budge. Seeing no good reason not to, I was granted UI benefits and the Mayers sealed their reason in federal stone.

In at-will working states, a person can be legally fired for not liking the same baseball team as you do, but you can't fire someone for being disabled. EEOC saw reason enough to grant my complaint as a valid case but asked that I try mediation first. I really didn't want to. I was prepared to run MB into the ground no matter how long it took. After all, I had nothing left to lose. But the rage had grown to such a height that I feared it would spill out in a way that would give MB the chance to hit me with a harassment suit. In Mediation you can say anything you want and it's all sworn to secrecy. Short of threats of bodily harm, I was free to return Bob the favour of making life a living hell. But I wasn't an idiot. No doubt they would bring their attorneys and ruin everything. I needed lawyers, free ones.

In New Jersey you can get law students to try your case for free, so long as they are chaperoned by a professor who has passed the bar. The odds of getting them are slim, but I had the right case at the right time and so I got two students and one professor. Bob, on the other hand, underestimated me entirely and came alone. I may not be able to breath a word of what went on once the door closed for the Mediation session, but I can tell you what happened before and after, and while it is my opinion and not based on any fact what so ever, he was scared.

I hadn't been prepared to settle and I hadn't wanted to, but between my lawyers and Beanie I was pushed into agreeing to, well, I can't say. You'll have to imagine in your head. And so at 5 p.m., November 7th, State of Change ended.

20 Disabled

Broken in the Land of Crystal Mirrors

While all this was happening, something far more serious was transpiring beneath the surface, causing a new era to start before the last one had ended. They coexisted for a short time until that defining moment signaled SoC's end, leaving me to face a new and unsettling reality.

I was disabled, truly for real.

Several months before my final confrontation with Bob, I was merely unemployed. In early September I picked up a job filling in for a designer at ASN broadcasting. When I came in the first day, however, I noticed something strange. I had only been there for ten minutes when what had seemed to be customary nervousness began to give way to something else. Within a few hours the tremors began. Then came the spasms.

And then it broke into Fear. Pure fear. Nothing was happening, nothing was going wrong but slowly a little voice in the back of my head was making itself heard.

'Need to get out. Need to get out!'

Why was this happening?

Could Berkshire have left wounds this deep? It must have progressed over the Summer, but how could so much damage have happened without me even knowing? I was determined not to go down without a fight and stayed for the rest of the day, but by seven p.m. I was so delirious that I spent a good two minutes pushing on a Pull door, desperate to escape. That night I rallied the troops for another go, but that morning my entire body seized up in spasms. My brain was determined to do what it had to to keep itself out of a situation it feared. There would be no going back.

I must have spent all my life wondering if I could ever be like regular people and that day it was answered. I think I knew it all along but I was afraid of what that would mean. Now I had no choice. After getting over the initial shock (and strangely enough, relief) of accepting my new disabled status, I filed for Social Security. What was worse, my agoraphobia (fear of being places you can't easily leave, fear of leaving the house) had exploded, drastically limiting where I could go and how long I could stay out without getting another episode. I had a grand total of two places I could go; home/Beanie's apt or, oddly enough, my old college campus. Everything else had a time limit of about an hour unless I was with Beanie.

I picked up a part-time job at the campus with the intention of using the extra money to keep my apartment but I couldn't even do that. Even my attempt to work from home failed as it became clear that I was afraid to work under anybody. In the end I had to let my apartment go. Beanie rescued me once again and dropped her apartment too, then grabbed a bigger one down the hall for both of us, on the condition that I settled in the EEOC mediation. SoC ended and when Unemployment learned I could no longer work, they cut me off.

There was nothing left now but Winter.

21

Liberation
Free at Last

In the pre-dawn darkness of the months preceding, a new life had been forged, one free of the pain that I had endured my entire life. For the first time ever I slept the Winter away. I slept up to eighteen hours at a time and my days were filled with rampant, glorious boredom. Am I lazy? Mayhaps, although my compulsiveness leads to marathon bouts of housecleaning. I don't watch all that much TV but I do spend a good amount of time at my computer. I began to draw and write again, and my fantasy world Realspace entered a time of plenty, one it hadn't seen in years.

But as Spring came into view, a new threat was looming. My savings were drying up, and after almost half a year, I had still not heard from Social Security. By the time May came around I was in full panic. I couldn't go back, but I had to. I began to look for simple jobs like shelf stocking, but most jobs required shifts of at least four hours, three hours more than I could handle being outside the house. As my bank account dwindled to a few hundred dollars, I actually went for an interview at the local Target, where I was turned down. I didn't have enough money to make it one more month.

And then, May 19th, 2006, Social Security called.
It was over.
I was officially free.

So here I am!
I no longer work or seek work outside little odd jobs, and so I am liberated from social constraints and the crippling fear it brings. In fact, I'm beginning to wonder if pursuing a life in the working world was distracting me from what I was supposed to be doing all along, which is this. Almost all my ailments are in remission and I have never been so content and stable in all my life for so long. I even got back together with my Ma! We definitely understand each other better now.

Sometimes I feel guilty about turning my back on the working world, but these results are hard to ignore. I suppose this is what they mean when they say you have to lose it all to find it again.

Cheers to that, mate!

Third edition notes: It has been nearly six years since I wrote this and much has come to pass, but I fear if I pause to illustrate it now I will never finish the book. It as been so long already.

Glorious healing!

ECCENTRICITY

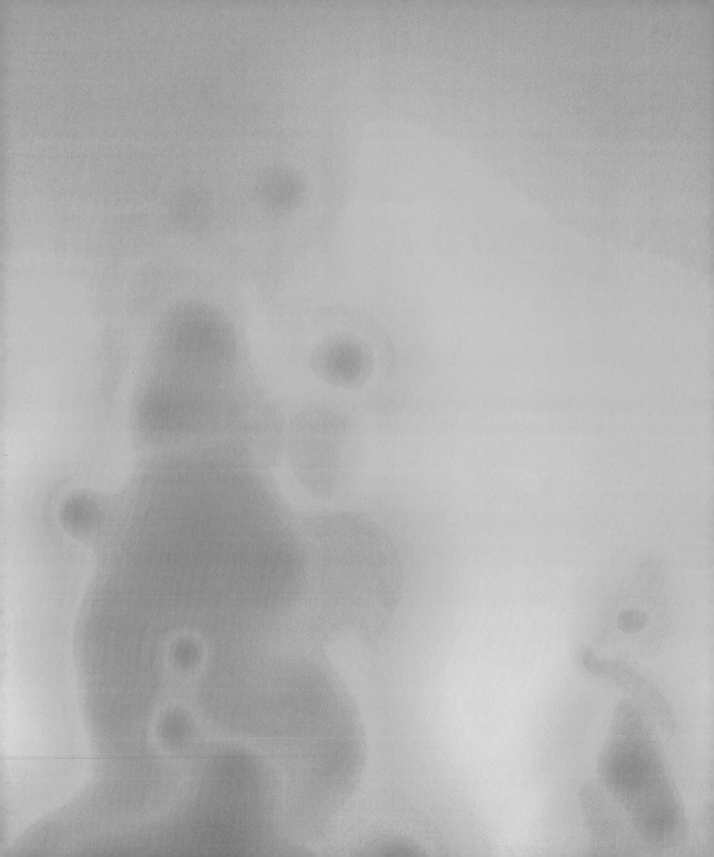

The Senses

Just all Kinds of Crazy

◀ The ego-less state of euphoria

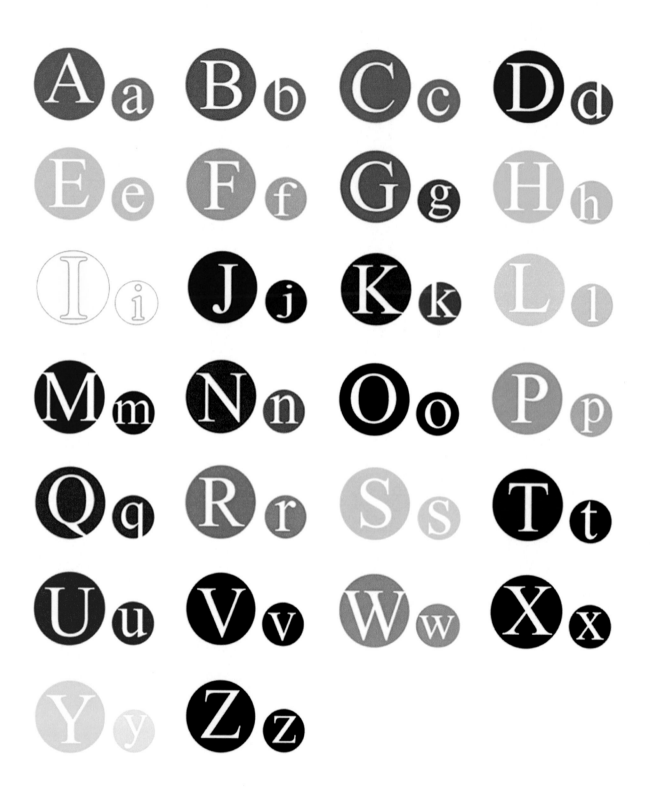

Synesthesia

The most Glorious of Disorders

Oh Synesthesia, how I worship you! A prime example of the good side of cranial mishaps is the disorder Synesthesia. Actually, Syn is as much an unwanted thing as superpowers, and so is never really considered a disorder at all. It is estimated that it effects 1/25,000 to 1/100,000, making it relatively rare and has been virtually unheard of since a quick spurt of interest between 1860 and 1930, only to re-emerge lately thanks to a neurologist named Dr. Richard Cytowic. It was actually Beanie that found out that I had it when surfing the net and found an article about people that saw coloured letters and numbers. Well, that was me for sure, so we did some research and here is exactly what Synesthesia is according to the Venerable Cytowic:

"The word synesthesia, meaning "joined sensation", shares a root with anesthesia, meaning "no sensation." It denotes the rare capacity to hear colors, taste shapes, or experience other equally startling sensory blendings whose quality seems difficult for most of us to imagine. A synesthete might describe the color, shape, and flavor of someone's voice, or music whose sound looks like "shards of glass," a scintillation of jagged, colored triangles moving in the visual field. Or, seeing the color red, a synesthete might detect the "scent" of red as well. The experience is frequently projected outside the individual, rather than being an image in the mind's eye. I currently estimate that 1/25,000 individuals is born to a world where one sensation involuntarily conjures up others, sometimes all five clashing together (Cytowic, 1989, 1993). I suspect this figure is far too low."

But what does it mean? It means that there are essentially no barriers between my senses, allowing them to blend at will. I can hear colour, feel a sound, taste the weather and a lot of other fun things. According to Dr. Cytowic, I fit the profile;

"Within their overall high intelligence, synesthetes have uneven cognitive skills. While a minority are frankly dyscalculic, the majority may have subtle mathematical deficiencies (such as lexical-to-digit transcoding). Right-left confusion (allochiria) (both of which I have), and a poor sense of direction for vector rather than network maps are common. A first-degree family history of dyslexia, autism, and attention deficit is present in about 15%. Very rarely, the sensual experience is so intense as to interfere with rational thinking (e.g., writing a speech, memorizing formulae). I have encountered no one whose synesthesia was so markedly disruptive to rational thought as it was in Luria's famous male subject, S."

So in a sense, somehow the chemicals that make things 'wrong' in my head make the 'right' things in my head. What an odd trade off.

Why is Syn so great? Why do people take Ecstasy or smoke pot? Now wouldn't it be great if you had that all the time? Depending on what music is playing, how loud, what I'm wearing or what I'm eating, I can get just as high. What's more, depending on the intensity of said stimulus, I can zonk out completely. This explains why I listen to Trance all the

Every Syn has a colour chart, and here is mine. Some Syns have textures or even personalities for their numbers and letters. Mine are just colours, though 5 is a little on the bossy side. I hope these colours print right, as they are very specific. It looks too light to me. hmmm...

Synesthesia

time. Your typical trance song has about 50 different sounds at any given time, each one of these giving you a different sensation.

Basic Syn

As you can see, I see colours on my letters. They are always the same colours on the same letters. If you were to surprise me on a corner 50 years from now and demand the colour of **F** , I could tell you it was carrot orange in an instant, because F is a vertical line and two short horizontal lines that happen to be carrot orange. These are the undeniable facts of F's existence as far as my brain is concerned.

Sometimes if I don't like the way the word looks, I'll use a different spelling. I use the word 'colour' instead of 'color' because the reddish '**U**' spices it up a little. As for what I mean when I say I 'see' the colours, its hard to say. I don't see them with my eyes, more like my mind. It's as if you were looking at a person with no eyebrows and your mind automatically filled in the eyebrows so that you don't notice at first. Because the eyebrows are supposed to be there, you see? And **9** is supposed to be navy blue. But tell that to another Syn and he'll declare that **9** is obviously reddish orange, and that snow is obviously cold. Which makes for a funny conversation.

Word colour is generally dictated by the first letter of the word, so 'Letter' will be kind of yellow greenish, even though the other letters aren't green at all. In fact, sometimes two words will have a similar collection of colours and so I will get them confused, even if one word doesn't look or sound like the other. The only words that escape the rule are the names of colours. Red is always Red, Blue is always blue, Green always green and so forth.

Coloured letter is a great way to tell you have Syn, but there are far better ways to enjoy it. If you are lucky enough to have coloured sound or hearing, you should really listen to some Progressive Trance or Classical music. Its like having a kaleidoscope in your

head. Some Syns have set colours for their notes, but I don't think I do. I do know that my colours are effected by the type of instrument and the intensity of it. Actually no, there's a lot more factors. Coloured Hearing is a lot harder to nail down, especially as I have sound feeling and tasting as well, and if the music is really good, I go somewhere else entirely.

To the right is what I see during one specific song. Just as the name of a colour overrides the regular colour code, the number track that a song is, (if it is known) affects the colour of the music. The fourth song on any CD will always have a purple tint, no matter what it sounds like. If the song is moved to a different track number, depending on how long it was at the previous number, it will change colour to that of the new assignment. Weird, neh? More on that later.

MICHELANGELO
LEONARDO DA VINC
Michelangelo
Leonardo Da Vinci

LETTER
Letter

RED   RED
GREEN   GREEN
BLUE   BLUE
YELLOW   YELLOW

Red, Green, Blue, Yellow   Red, Green, Blue, Yellow
Technically   Under Colour Name Exception

3 3   33 30
5 5   55 50
1   11 10

3, 31, 33, 30
5, 51, 55, 50
1,   11, 10

This is a picture of what I see when I listen to the song 'E-Tales' by 105, the Sasha remix. There are actually more oranges in this song, but I couldn't quite match it colour for colour.

Synesthetic Overlay

How Synesthesia presents itself and why it's not really distracting

The first question I get is "Why aren't all these colours distracting?" Most of us don't even find out that these reactions are extra because we grew up having them all our lives. The question for me is how do regular people experience things correctly if they can't taste air? I mean, how can it not have colours for things? How can you tell what's going on on the telly if the picture or sound is missing? Simply baffling.

Think of it this way; If you stood near an explosion, you'd expect to hear, see, and feel it. If any one of those sensations were missing, you'd notice, because your brain expects those three at once. Growing up with Syn is the same thing.

I know that the other sensations coming in aren't experienced the same way the original one is but I never really thought about what it actually is like. This took me a long time to come up with, but I think I have a way to explain the Synestetic ghosting effect. You know how sometimes you get a song stuck in your head? Not an annoying song that aggravates you, just any song that just plays in the background? Usually you don't even notice unless you turn special attention to it. Having a song stuck is different than conjuring one up. It's different from imagining because the song is there unbidden and will remain there even if you pay it no attention. In the same affect you can't seem to willfully get rid of it either. If you were to listen to real music the stuck song wouldn't override it, but when the music stops or you focus, you could certainly find the stuck song again.

The truth of the matter is, all your senses are just neural interpretations. There's no way to guarantee that anything your brain thinks it saw actually really happened. Just watch The Matrix and you'll know what I mean. That said, I am inclined to believe that these Syn responses are products of the same process that the real ones are created from and therefore on some level just as valid. It seems arbitrary that asparagus tastes purple, but then again who or what decided that asparagus should taste the way we taste it? If there is a God, why would he decide to make things that are good for you taste bad anyway? I don't think anyone decided anything. It was all a matter of chance that the brain decided to interpret the sky as blue, which makes as much sense as the letter A being blue if you really sit down and think about it.

'E-Tales' by 105, the Sasha remix. playing on speakers.

Is it really there? Like a piece of dust on your eye, if you try to really See the Synesthesia it's harder to pin down. While colour hearing and the like doesn't actually interfere with your senses, is does effect what you brain thinks it saw, though for the life of it, it doesn't know why.
Generally it doesn't notice or care anyway.

ECCENTRICITY

The Appearance of Music

Raving Without Drugs

If I could ever attain the power of 3D rendering, the one thing I'd really love to do is translate one song into colour. When I'm really bored on the bus or something I try to map them out in the event that ever happens.

I'd only have to do it once because like everything else Syn, the colour coding for a specific song will always remain the same. The shapes arrange themselves vertically by frequency, with the bass on the bottom and the treble on the top. After that, though, it's all a mystery. I'm not sure I even have the set colour-to-musical scale that some Syns have. The colour of a sound is so heavily affected by what kind of sound it is that it's really impossible to establish any kind of consistency.

The only thing that can change that, short of changing a song or sound itself, is to change the order it's played. If I have ten songs on a CD, no matter what song nine sounds like, it will have a navy blue overcast. Song four is purple, one is yellowish, ect. In extremely rare cases the music will contain so much of a certain colour of sound that it will override the track number's colour, but that usually never happens. If the song has no track number when it's first heard it won't have an overlay, but if it's re-recorded in a compilation, say, three years later, whatever the new track number it is it will pick up the color of the number. If a song was song four for ten years and suddenly is changed to track seven, it will take one or two plays before it switches colour but it will change. Once I made a mix that had three former track fours in a row. It didn't change the system and they were eventually reassigned different colours, but it was pretty weird having a set of purple songs one after another.

➤

Above: A few seconds out of the first minute of "Enjoyed" by the Chemical Brothers, from Sasha and John Digweed's remix album "Communicate".

Below: The first minute and how its appearance would change depending on where it was placed on a numbered list.
It's no where near perfect and I shortened it in some places to show more stuff. Just doing this one minute was much harder than I thought.

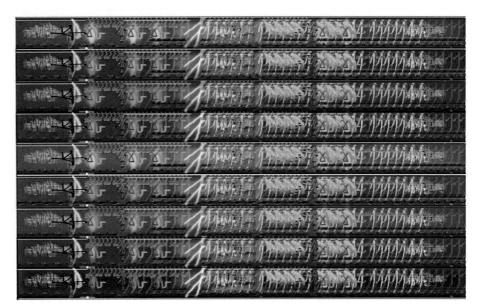

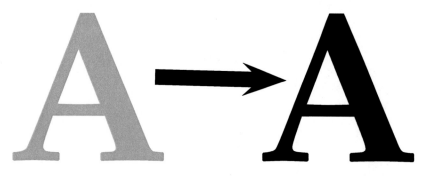

Stare at the yellowish orange 'A' for 30 seconds, then look at the black one.

There should be a kind of bluish haze floating on top of it. That's basically what coloured letter/number looks like when I read.

Synesthetic Overlay-Text

Read Like I Read

The second question I get about Syn is "Can you tell what colour the letters are really written in?" In a way, Syn is a massive collection of songs with an assortment of Play buttons in weird places. When I see the number four, Syn plays back the taste of grape juice for no real reason. It also throws in a purple shadow over the number.

As for explaining text overlay, it's a little harder but the picture to the right should help. When you look at any of the letters, the first thing you notice is that they are black, but something hangs to them that gives the illusion that it might be another colour too. What colour is this letter U to you? The impulse to say reddish is just as strong as the impulse to say black because the brain has gotten the suggestion of red, even though black is obviously more dominant.

THE SEVENTH STAR PROJECTS
ECCENTRICITY

This is what it is lik

read when you have

sethesia. Even thoug

you can see that the

ters are clearly black

red for that matter, t

hazy overlay is alwa

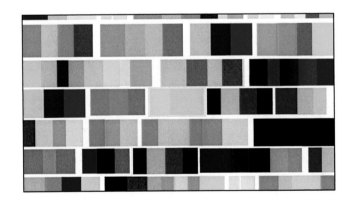

Something else neat, notice how letters are
one colour when in one word and another in
another word. Words that are used over and
over like 'the' and 'is' tend to develop their own
colour set that overrides the individual letters.
Sometimes, like 'even' and 'for' the colour is
completely illogical. Why 'even's 'V' turns
orange is a mystery. I suspect 'for's purple comes
from the suggestion of the number four.

What decides what the colour set will be
is as unknown as the origins of the regular
colours themselves. Here is how that paragraph
would look if it were just colour blocks.
Even though I tried my best, these colours
may still be off when this book goes to
print. Ah well, I do what I can.

The Taste of Numbers
They're Mathematically Delicious

Although just about everything has a taste, numbers have the most defined and most vivid taste of any set I can think of. Oddly enough, most of the numbers taste like edible things and of said things, most are candy. Some numbers, like 4 and 7, are easy to replicate perfectly. In fact, a mix of grape and lime juice would bring about a perfect 47 or 74, depending on which taste was more prominent. Others like 3, 5, and 6 are much harder to pin down. 5 and 6 switch with each other depending on what it's with and where in the number it stands. 1 changes from butter to milk if it's placed with anyone besides itself except for with 0, when it becomes ultra buttery. 7 will create a sweet-tart effect with 6 but not with 5 and will sweeten itself if paired with itself. 77 tastes like Sprite.

The more digits in a number the more complicated the taste will be although it may not increase in intensity. Almost all digits are registered in a number, even if it is in the millions, where as colour registration for letters seems to fade after about six places. Because numbers have taste and colour tags, they are stronger mental markers than letters but are subject to the same memory confusion, since although they don't tend to mimic each other like letters, mixes of numbers effect each other far more than mixes of letters do. My numerical dyslexia doesn't help.

smooth rock

0 is the odd one out in that it does not taste like a food at all. Instead it concentrates and intensifies the taste of any number it's with unless it comes before a number, like 07 or 0009. The more 0s preceding a number, the more watered down the number tastes. A number that is a decimal displayed 0. will be watery and the period will add the taste of fine gravel to the mix.

| #0 cold metal | 0 | 0# water |

grape juice

Necco wafer

sugar sprinkles

4 is the strongest number and can sometimes overpower other numbers, even if it's further down the line in a number's order like 114. 4 only tastes like juice when by itself. Once mixed with others, even itself, the second 4 will take a more sugary taste. When 4 is the first number it is less sweet, but still sweeter than when its alone.

5 is generally the lighter of the 5-6 set and its taste is more chalky. However, when 5 is paired with something else, its sugar factor goes up like 4.

6 stays sweeter than 5 over all except in the 60s where it tastes like the coating of a Jordan almond. Both 5 and 6 tend to become more watery in the face of stronger numbers such as 7 and 4.

| #4 grape lollipop | 4 | 4# juice |

| #5 stronger sweeter | 5 | 5# chalky |

| #6 sweeter | 6 | 6# jordan almond |

butter-milk

cherry
licorice

mint
creme

1 is almost as inconsistent as 7 but it does seem to follow general rules. 1 by itself is very buttery. When in the teens the one is 1% milk, or maybe closer to skim/water that's been frozen into an ice-cube. Teens have a definite hard coldness to them. 1s that are in other numbers vary between buttermilk and skim with different solidity factors. 1 rarely absorbs other numbers but usually affects those it's placed with.

2 jumps between a number of flavours depending on who it's with. The 20s are by and large a sweeter cherry licorice. Other flavours that 2s will take on is more bitter forms of cherry licorice, cranberry juice, marichino cherries, and other artificial reincarnations of cherry. Cranberry usually appears when grouped with strong numbers.

3 also has a bunch of different flavours it hovers around, usually picking a combination of the group. The 30s are usually a solid green spice drop, whatever flavour those are supposed to be. I think it's mint. Other 3s include creme mints like Andes, green Necco wafers, the shells of Jordan almonds, and mint ice cream. 3s distort all number flavours except 8 and 9 which seem to be immune.

#1 butter milk	1	1# skim milk

#2 cranberry juice	2	2# red rope licorice

#3 green Necco wafer	3	3# green gumdrop

lime

milk chocolate

black
licorice

Every 7 is different and follows it's own code as to how it wants to taste depending on who it's with. There are other tastes thrown in that I can't decipher in some.

	Sprite, sweeter	bitter, watery	stronger, sweeter
tarter			
more lemony			more watermelony
07	47	72	77
7	57	73	78
17	67	74	79
27	70	75	87
37	71	76	97

8 is a million different kinds of chocolate depending on who it's with. The one thing that is consistent with 8 is that the chocolate is always a spongy type like cake or nougat. What changes is the concentration of chocolate. 8 tends to be stronger when with other strong numbers.

Except for certain number setups, 9 tends to have a dusty after taste. Like 4, 9 has a very definable taste that really only alternates between sweet and dusty. Even at its sweetest it never really escapes the bitter confines of licorice. 9 tends to make other numbers bitter and flat despite its overall solidity.

#8 Fudge Brownie	8	8# Three Musketeers filling

#9 dustier	9	9# sweeter, more solid

ECCENTRICITY

The Colour of Taste
And the difference between a Fresh Yam and a Canned Yam

Which is basically the whole statement. A yam is a kind of potato that is orange inside. I noticed that when I ate a fresh one that the colour demographics were different than ones that came from the can. You see, each taste has a colour. A fresh anything usually has more than one taste, a bunch of smaller variants within the whole, and each of these makes a slightly altered colour from the original. When something gets stored, all these little tastes blend together and make something more homogenous.

I've found that the taste of most foods are about the same as their actual colours, though there are exceptions. Asparagus is greyish purple instead of green and honeydew melon is some weird yellow orange colour, definitely not green. Passion fruit has this messed up red/green/brown thing going on that feels like have upholstery fabric being rubbed on my face. When the colours fail to match, I usually end up not liking the food much.

I can also taste other things, either by hearing, touching, or smelling. One thing that I find especially useful is being able to taste the air. Depending on the colour signature in the air, I can generally figure out if there are plants nearby, water, pollution, the temperature... some other things. I never actually thought about it until now. I do know that sometimes the air tastes fruity when a tropical storm is coming. Now that's something I would miss tasting if I didn't have Syn.

➤

Can you tell which is which? If you can't, the one on the left is canned and the one on the right is fresh. I've also found that the warmer a food is, the more vivid its colours are, which explains why I put my strawberries in the microwave.

ECCENTRICITY

cold dry air

warm indoor air

hot humid air

Tiffany Perfume

The Taste and Colours of Air
Multiple Synesthesia with the 'Existential' Senses

Along with the obvious five senses and the curious sixth there is another group of touch-based stimuli that Synesthesia feels compelled to reinterpret. I've dubbed then the 'existential senses' as they deal with touch sensory occurring just outside the skin but doesn't really *touch* it such as Weight, Motion, Temperature, and Time.

For instance, when air masses are Synestetically processed, humidity (Weight), wind (Motion), and Temperature affect what the bands look like and how they interact with each other while the colour is primarily decided by scents carried within it. Sometimes the existential senses have colours of their own, however faint, and often influence the colours that have already been established by scent.

There are some basic rules that the existential senses generally follow. The more humid the air, the thicker, foggier and often more saturated the bands. Heat will do the same thing, mostly in the form of saturation intensity. Dry air has sharper boundaries. Cold generally decreases the amount of colour that actually appears. Wind and open air tend to have more complicated colour structures because the wind pushes a great many scents and air masses together at the same time. While the colour sets generally mimic what the scents look like in real life, there are exceptions to that too. For example, extreme heat is not red as one would suppose, but a dark blue-violet that sometimes appears black in the middle. This goes for hot water as well.

deafeningly hot day ➤

Typical colour displays of certain air masses. Because it is nearly impossible to get the same mix of air twice, these patterns tend to change. Other elements in the air can significantly skew the appearance such as a rogue scent.

ECCENTRICITY

hurricane

Violent tropical storms seem to carry a piece of the Caribbean with them, so the air is heavy with the taste of wet fruits, nuts, and vegetation

rain

Rain generally has a couple of dark, gravelly bars towards the top that taste like metal. The grey is more violet than blue.

greenhouse

That green strip feels like a grass stain on the tongue. When you walk into a greenhouse, especially a hot one that has just been watered, that green stripe is so strong that I usually follow the urge to lick the air like a snake. Same with hurricane air.

winter

Another demonstration of Winter's deadliness. The cold knocks out most of nature's subtler stimuli, almost like it's been frozen. There are several versions of Cold and some other nearly tasteless interpretations of Winter's decay but not much else.

stale/indoor air

The texture of indoor air is very different than outdoor. Outdoor air is smoother and much more complicated in sequence while indoor has an unusual bumpy feel, like licking worn cardboard

spring

This is another air mass that I love to try and lick. By April there are a bunch of different flowers in bloom and the winds carry the scents around for miles. Thawing mud and decay is the brown at the bottom.

hot humid day

Heat and humidity creates a canvas much like soaked watercolour paper. If you drop any colour onto it, it will bloom across the paper on its own. It also picks up minute stimuli and enhances it. Hail to the power of humidity. Now lick it.

salt nearby

When I first started working at Berkshire I used to get this colour set when I walked outside the building. It was similar to the Holylands so I looked up a map of the area. Sure enough, about two miles away there was a wetland.

fall cold front

Fall cold fronts create the sharpness associated with cold, but there are still enough cross scents to make an interesting picture. Much of it is leaf decay or burning and the scent of the sun.

ECCENTRICITY

Shopping Cart Wheels of Death

The Hidden Hazards of Sound-to-Touch Synesthesia

Somehow they always find me. There will be an entire store to haunt, but the shopper with the cart with the squeaky wheel will always follow me. What is just a mild irritant to most people is probably one of the most common sources of Synesthesic pain I encounter day to day. Not all squeaky wheels do it either. It has to be a certain pitch or frequency to cause pain. Sometimes when the subway cars pull into the station it happens, and once when I was in an airport someone's luggage zipper kept banging on the metal rollers as it went through the x-ray machine.

That time was terrible.

Like all Syn responses, each one of these sounds has its own particular kind of pain tagged to it. The subway cars and that %*@#& zipper were especially bad because the stimulus response was so overwhelming that I lost balance. All my systems got jammed and I didn't know where I was anymore. All there is is the colour and the feel of the thing. A painful sound almost always has some trace of red-orange in it somewhere and if it's loud enough it can blind me as well.

The strange thing about the shopping cart wheels is that they aren't particularly loud but still cause me to get veritably nauseous. Each wheel has its own set of pain, just like everything else, but by and large the effect is about the same. The sound feels like things are being hurled at the back of my head. Sometimes these things are thick ice-needles that pierce the skull and other times it's jagged pieces of brick that seem to rip the skin right off.

God help me when there's more than one.

The monster at rest, ready to unleash its full acoustic fury if pushed too far...

ECCENTRICITY

page 84

Day Blindness
Blinded by the Light

Brightly lit places bother me for the sole reason that I can't see, and if I can't see, I can walk into things, which I do. This is my therapist's parking lot on a ridiculously bright day. Above is what the camera and any normal person would see it, and to the left is how I see it, if I dare open my eyes. And it hurts! It's not always like this, just the very brightest days, but I have to hold onto Beanie's arm and let her lead me if I get caught without my sunglasses.

It isn't confined to the sun, either. I become easily disoriented any time there are a lack of shadows, such as over-lit Bloomindales or warehouses. Everything becomes flat and I have the sense that I am about to walk into a painted wall which things keeping popping out from. You will always see me clinging to Beanie in a mall. On the other hand, I have excellent night vision and Beanie doesn't, so once we go outside at night, the role reverses.

Being blinded by the sun isn't my only problem with it, either. Once the weather gets above about 65 degrees F, the sun burns where it touches. Not physically, but my skin is so sensitive to heat that the sun touching it feels like acid or hot metal. It really hurts, so I'm always covered in the summer, half so I can see, and half so I don't pass out.

Overloaded
The Downside of a Sensitive Machine · A Fear of Restaurants

With a sensory system set to pick up even the most subtle changes in air pressure and what not, what do you think would happen if you put that system in a busy restaurant? How about a concert? What about any crowd for that reason? It may not come as a surprise that I avoid such things. But that sucks! I can't tell you how much that sucks. I like a good night out at a pub on St. Patrick's Day as much as the next person (even though I can't drink with my medication. Bottle of root beer and I blend right in), but after only a few minutes I go into this kind of shock.

I've never been drunk or hung over before but from what I've heard, the experience is about the same. I'm going to go with hangover, because people seem to like being drunk, but no one relishes a hangover. It feels like there's no line between me and the rest of the bar. Everything gets slurred together. The lights are going through me, the movement makes me dizzy and by god, the noise! The noise, man! The noise is like, all these monkeys that are all over you, pulling your hair and biting and beating you with pots. Then you add in any random loud crash or drunken scream and the monkeys just freak out all over you. But I'm not weak. I can take the monkeys if I have food and it's only an hour. The problem is I live in New Jersey where it's customary to just sit at the table long after the food is gone and talk, at which point I'm climbing the walls with the monkeys. I'm considering get earplugs. It's geeky I know but I already use a cane when I'm walking in crowded places. Beanie loves to go to Chinatown in New York City where there's a million people everywhere.

It's not the noise that's a problem here, it's the movement. Actually no, it's not even just the movement. It's the movement and having to multi task being with Beanie. I actually fare pretty well by myself, but when I have to keep track of what Beanie's saying or doing it's enough to overload the system. It becomes a choice between interacting with Beanie and not walking into things, so rather than ignore her, I resort to letting her lead me like a blind man. Besides, people tend to get out of the way of a person with a cane, and my back always thanks me for it later.

 I'm not drunk. If I was, I wouldn't be aware that I was being trampled to death by elephants.

Overwhelmed
And the Upside of a Sensitive Machine - My Gallery Show

This was a unique experience that I'd love to have again. Before I graduated I had this gallery show to display some of the work from '21 Stages'. I then burned a CD with all my most potent songs to play for opening night. Between the colours on the walls surrounding me, the sound of the music as it echoed against the walls and the energy from the people inside, I became veritably drunk. Within an hour I was weaving and shortly after ended up on the floor. I didn't collapse, mind you, I just lay down after my body disappeared. I usually lose motor control if I play 'Zion' by Fluke in any situation, so the floor was probably the safest place to be. It was pure ecstasy.

Usually I am bombarded with harmful stimulus, and sometimes, as is with Winter, I get no stimulus at all. Both these situations have their own overwhelming effects, but it is only in a situation such as this that the massive overload of sensory input leads to the sensation of being high.

By the end of the night, I was Everywhere.
A resounding success on all accounts I must say.

My show, of which I spent most of on the floor, giggling hysterically. This is yet another reason I always wear pants, because you never know when you will overload and collapse. I obviously pride myself on professionalism.

Return

Sometimes I am everywhere and nowhere at once.

Sometimes my senses will swell in a burst of euphoria, and my sense of self momentarily disappears. It can be caused by any of the senses or a mix. Common offenders of spontaneous Returns to the Space include;

Sounds

Lawn mowers in
early spring
Large air-conditioning
units/exhaust vents/fans
Certain clear low notes,
such as temple chimes
Wind
Snowfall

Sight

Certain shades of
aquamarine and indigo,
as a light or as light
passes through it, ie
glass bottles, pools.
Other opaque shades,
usually fluorescent.
Certain formations
of clouds
Sunlight through glass
Sunlight through grass.

Other

Warm socks on cold feet
Strong wind

Scents

Burning leaves
Cut grass
Satsuma scented soap
Lemon scented soap
Musty books
A specific plastic
scent found in
some erasers
Air before a storm
Citrus tree flowers
Cinnamon
Coffee beans
Certain suntan
lotions

Taste

Pink Grapefruit and
Tangerine juice
Chocolate pudding
Chicken soup
SuperSweet100
tomatoes and
strawberries just
picked and still
hot from the sun

Music

The two big hitters that must be listened to while lying down.

'Zion' - Fluke
'The Silence' - Mike Koglin/Sasha and John Digweed

And the rest, each causing a different state of trance;

'The Baguio Track' - Luzon/Sasha and John Digweed
'Mission: Impossible' - U2 (ending only)
'Know You Love Me Too' - Chris Raven/Sasha and John Digweed
'Tyrantanic' - Breeder/Sasha and John Digweed
'Out Of Body Experience' - Rabbit In The Moon/Sasha and John Digweed
'Bedtime Stories' - Madonna
'Darksides' - Nugen/Paul Oakenfold
'Imperpetuum Mobila' - Patient Saints/Paul Oakenfold
'Roots' - Lior Attar, Lo-Step/Dave Seaman
'Terra Firma' (feat. Aude) - Delirium
'Currents' - Kingsuk Biswas on Asian Travels vol. 1
'Ready, Steady, Go' - Paul Oakenfold
'Homelands' - Ayumi Hamasaki

A word of warning:
Do not operate heavy machinery while listening to this playlist.

A vision consistently generated by the mid part of the song, 'Cloud Cuckoo', by Sasha.

JAnvAPy

January is white and blue with ice in it. The brown chunk towards the end is actually Superbowl Sunday. Don't ask me why that shows up because I have no idea.

FɘbʋPAPy

February is about the same but calmer, as if everything is asleep. Because it is the 2nd month, it has a reddish pink cast.

MAPGh

March has just barely the green it should have for being number 3, and is mostly dominated by brown mud on snow. Or at least I figure that's what it is.

APPiL

April, for some reason, is not purple like it should be. Actually it's all these pink colours and the rectangles go all over the place.

MAy

May is also weird because it's blue, like the letter A and there is always the sense of the sky being in the background. It's also darker at the end.

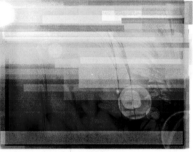

Jʋnɘ

June is brown and has the feeling of wheat. I'm assuming the Brown is coming from the letter 'J'.

Months
Synesthesia and Time-keeping

Months are another thing that tend to get colourized when a person has Syn. I actually did these pages for a calender about a year before I found out why the months looked the way they do.

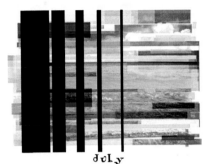

July

July is a billion colours, over-saturated. I'm guessing it's the heat. No idea what the black lines are.

August

I'm almost certain that August's blue comes from its 'A'.

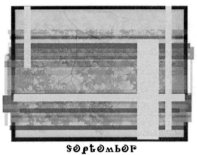

September

September is the same, the S dictates, but note that dark bar. I think it is the colour for 9 trying to come through.

October

October's orange is a mystery and the only thing I can figure is that its in response to the changing of the leaves. The darker lines are probably the letter O.

November

November is nowhere near the yellow it should be and takes the gray in N. No clue about the red. Maybe it's cranberry sauce?

December

December is loud and noisy with lots of blinking lights. Even though it's the darkest month of the year, it also has a high level of energy due to the holidays and such. The Brown is the letter D.

Year by Month

	January	Feburary	March	April	May	June

Year by Physical Seasons

	Mid Winter	Late Winter	Early Spring	Mid Spring	Late Spring	Early Summer
	January	Feburary	March	April	May	June

Year by Meta/Hyperphysical Seasons

	Eternal Grey		First Rift		Twilight Rift	
	January	Feburary	March	April	May	June

Year Ends   **Year Begins**

July	August	September	October	November	December

Mid Summer	Late Summer	Early Fall	Mid Fall	Late Fall	Early Winter
July	August	September	October	November	December

Summer Lockout		Homelands Rift		The Mourning	Holiday Rush
July	August	September	October	November	December

Calenders

My Personal sense of Time

I really like systems. I'm not sure why but when I have everything charted out it seems to make more sense. Everything should be colour-coded. I'm sure I'm not the only one that counts June as Summer and December as Winter. I know the seasons technically wait until the 20th or the 21st to switch off, but no one counts September as Summer. Why Summer appears blue confuses me too, though I think it's because certain kinds of heat are blue in cast. I almost never use the middle set anyway so the colours probably aren't as accurate as the other two.

The most important one is at the bottom, the Meta one. In some countries they don't refer to the seasons as Winter or Spring but rather the rainy season or dry season. That's because these lands run on rain. I run on energy.

ECCENTRICITY

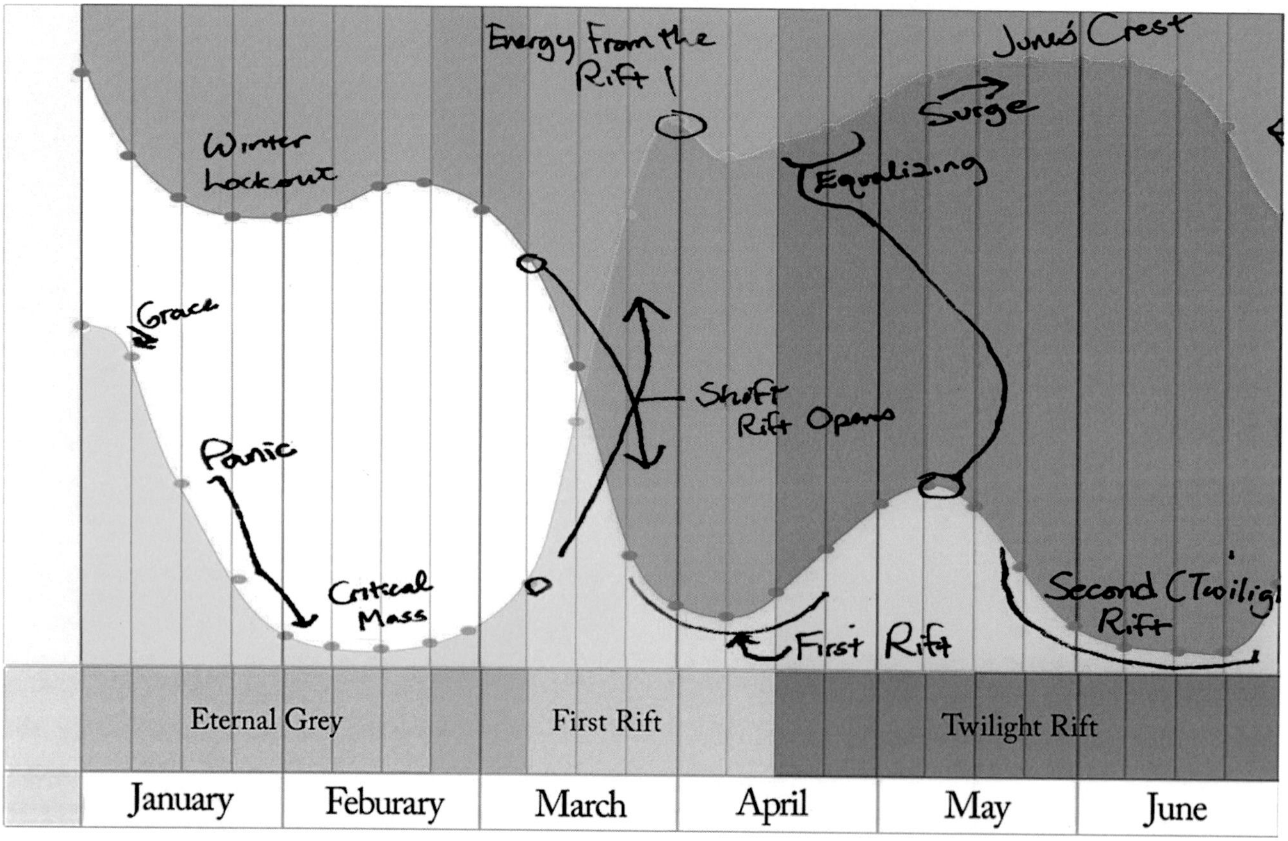
Energy From the Rift 1
June's Crest
Surge
Winter Lockout
Equalizing
Grace
Shift
Rift Opens
Panic
Critical Mass
First Rift
Second (Twilig
Rift
Eternal Grey
First Rift
Twilight Rift
January
Feburary
March
April
May
June

Energy to Dimensional Wall Ratio

The 6th Sense Calender Year

The Orange Line is how much Energy I have at my disposal, ambient or otherwise. The Green Line is not so easily explained. There are those of us that feel other worlds brushing up against ours. Whether this is actually true or just another facet of sensory extremis is unknown and truth be told, doesn't really matter. The point is that certain times of the year these 'other worlds' feel closer, as if the barrier between Us and the Rest of the Space is thinning, semi-permeable. It is the time of Traveling.

Dreams become more real and the waking world feels like it is sliding into that of the subconscious. A sense of displacement comes of it, of neither truly being Anywhere and being able to be Everywhere. The idea of Reality is one that is heavily challenged during these points in time. I always figured that this sensation came from high energy levels, so I expected to see the walls thin when the levels went up. Obviously this is not always so.

Third Edition Notes: I made this map in 2004 and now, seven years later, it is inaccurate due to global warming. I am astounded by how much in such a short time. I will draft a comparison for the sequel to this book.

Points of Interest:

First and Second (Twilight) Rifts are points where the Walls radically decrease after the Winter has passed. It coincides with an energy spike around mid March when

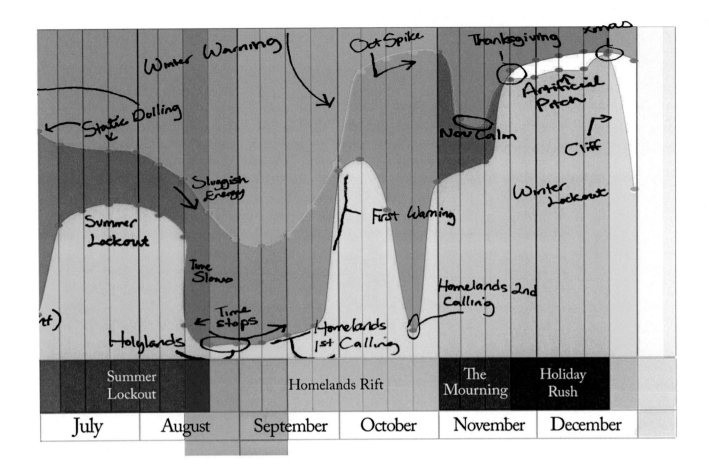

everything Shifts. The air becomes something close to electric, evens in April, then flows into full power at the end of June, a good time to be alive. Twilight is the most energetic time of the day for me, riding on the edge of night, and so that is how the Twilight Rift got its name.

Summer Lockout/Stagnation is a strange occurrence that shows that even in the summer, energy can be low, or rather, stagnant. It causes minimal problems.

Stopped Time is the most bizarre time of the year. Energy is so slow and stagnant that it stops somewhere close to the end of August. It has the feeling of walking through clear molasses. With the feeling of stopped time comes the need to return to the Holylands. This is the end of the Spacialist year.

The Homelands Rift/First Warning is the beginning of the Spacialist year. Time restarts and seems to rush forward as if to make up lost time. Subtle changes in the air signal that Winter is coming and a strong sense urgency saturates everything, causing the Walls to thicken. Sometime at the mid end of October the Homelands call, begging me to come home, and the dimensional wall all but collapses. It is a time of much confusion because I feel the need to go somewhere that to my knowledge does not exist. This time is mercifully short and ends by November.

The October Spike is another mystery. How a period of high energy can show up at a time when things are dying doesn't make logical sense, but the air positively crackles

Energy to Dimensional Wall Ratio

with energy. My only guess is that it is a result of the hurricane systems that swing by around this time. There is a three week respite called **November's Repose,** a short piece of time between the Homelands Rift and the Holiday Rush, also known as the Time of Mourning.

The Winter Lockout starts after Thanksgiving when an artificial rush of energy comes in. Winter Lockout silently falls into place while I'm distracted by the Holiday Rush. **The Holiday Rush** does not correspond with nature but with the energy of humans and acts as a surrogate Summer. People are as about as they would be in warmer months, life is celebrated with plentiful gatherings, the feel of plenty is perpetuated by commercialism and holiday lights mimic Summer's long daylight hours. When the Holidays end there is the feeling of running right off a **Cliff.** The Rush disappears to reveal that Nature has stopped providing long ago.

Critical Mass is when energy has completely run out and I begin to suffocate. I begin to have hallucinations that the summer has returned usually by mid-January.

This chart I made almost six years ago and I am surprised to see how the rhythms have changed. A lot of it is due to lifestyle changes, namely school hours. While in high school, critical mass didn't hit until late March with no real rifts until late July in accordance with schedule. When summer was pushed back to May in college, the crash point started to float closer to February.

When I was out of school completely the crash went all the way back to January and my new freedom allowed me to experience the coming of Spring directly, leading to the formation of two separate rifts, one beginning where the crash had formerly been in March. Over all, direct contact with the seasons has amplified the highs and lows, though Winter's destruction seems to be just as bad, insulated by school or not.

Ah the Twilight Rift, the most wonderful of all seasons. It begins with the first heat wave of April and ends at the 1st of July. If only it could last forever...

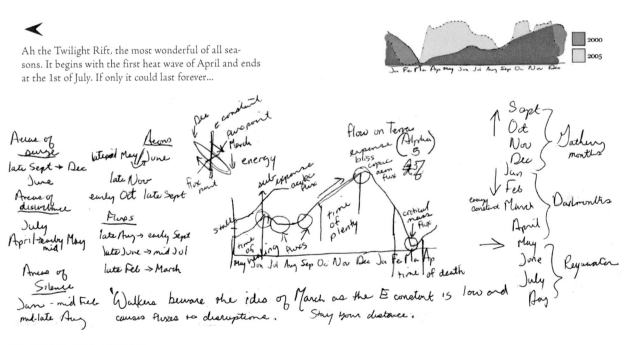

ECCENTRICITY

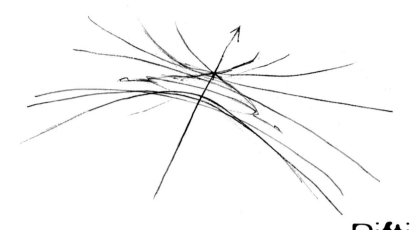

Rifting
Doorways to Other Worlds

When the walls are low and the pressure changes I feel the need to Travel. Rifts usually form when there is a kind of electricity in the air, typically during equinoxes when the major air masses are at war. There seems to be a hole in the sky, not a black hole into nothingness and not a hole you can see, more of a thinning. It feels like I could just push a little and pass through it like a waterfall. It pulls the air and energy up through it into unknown worlds beyond, trying to take you with it. Rifts call to you, enticing you to jump out into space. They are hard to ignore and I've been known to randomly stop and stare at a patch of sky for 10-15 minutes at a time, locked in an invisible battle of wills.

The reality is I've actually only Jumped a handful of times, usually be accident. Out of Body experiences are different, you stay on the same planet generally It happens when you lean out of your body too far and fall out. Rifting is like going somewhere else, astral projection I think it's called. I had one in the depths of Winter once unintentionally but I didn't use a Rift. Not sure how I did that. The other was my one and only intentional Jump, 5/13/00 in the back of my old high school. Still not sure where I went. Why I haven't tried since then is because it's uncontrollable and dangerous. I don't know what's going on in my brain when I do all this, but I know it makes me more susceptible to other things, things that aren't

good. I'd much rather ride the edge of it instead. The rush is just as good but you don't risk blacking out.

The word 'Rift' is used interchangeably with the season and the event. It's much the same way the BDSM community is called the 'scene' but an individual encounter is also referred to as a 'scene'. For those of you who haven't run away after the BDSM reference, 'rift' refers to both an overall season when the walls are thin and the name of an instance where the wall has actually become thin enough to Walk through. Conditions for Rifts change like the weather and while your chances for a hot day are higher in the summer, that doesn't mean it will be hot every day. The same goes for rift seasons.

Sometimes I hallucinate and see the picture on the right, several white rings over the weakest part of the wall. The stars in the middle are a hallucination within the existing one, something wholly imagined but that I can feel in my skin. It's more like an anticipatory vision, the way you can taste something before you eat it.

Out of Body

It always happens when I least suspect it.

Today I got lost
or I lost myself.
Tuesday I had my
Beanie and my Chan
to keep me subbduded
until they could make
me recognize my
reflection. I seem to have
had an involuntary out of
body dift.
Damn humidity...
See humity theory

◄

I had at least two other
Out of Body Experiences,
both happening under the
influence of Music. Both were
unexpected and a bit scary.

Definatly the scariest
part was the oversalivation
of fear coming in. It is sucking up so much Psi that
normal things, my face, my name, and orientation to surroundings,
became disrupted or misplaced. Mis-allocated file, I say.

The worst was, I thought it was 1995, that I was
Just born with Carmen in England. I asked where she was, then realized
I didn't know where I was anymore.

Humidity Theory
Air Extensions and why I malfunction in Winter

According to Humidity Theory, I proclaim that the air becomes more saturated, which allows energy to travel farther from its source than usual. So if it were a hot summer day, I might feel that I can reach an extra five feet with my hands. Or maybe I should say that I can feel an extra five feet in front of me.

Note the spheres in the picture to the right. The Spheres themselves are you, or rather, your boundary lines. The rims of the circles are where your brain perceives 'you' to stop and the rest of the world to begin. If you have brain madnesses, sometimes you don't always get a clear line, or in my case, many other things can make new lines for you. Humidity is one such thing and the higher it goes, the blurrier and farther out that line goes.

The top circle is Summer, or more specifically, a summer thunderstorm (which makes me really high off my nut). The one on the bottom if your average day. On average I have a bit of a range anyway. But let's look at Winter, more specifically a Bad winter. Actually, let's look at a bunch of examples on the next page, shall we? I don't think I can squeeze them all in on this page.

➤

Thunderstorms are great for getting high on. They have humidity and energy in one. Psychics warn not to try and have an Out of Body Experience when thunderstorms are about.

Humidity Theory

The Winter is a very hard time for me. On the average Summer day, as seen to the left, I am at least twice capacity. I have, in a sense, a surplus of self to use and it is in a constant state of regeneration, which gives me an unlimited supply. Humidity coupled with heat is a stimulus. You don't have to work so hard to keep the body going when the heat supports you.

A hot humid day makes me as immortal as a cloud of energy. Everything works more efficiently, the gears greased constantly by the continuous influx. There is no friction and I dissolve into something fluid. I have effectively merged with the moisture in the air and use it to my own ends.

In the Winter, there is nothing. I live in North Jersey and so the winters are cold. Even with the humidity present, I won't be able to meld with it because of the layers of clothes that one is forced to wear. I usually resist wearing a jacket or covered shoes for this reason, preferring to be cold than cut off from the grid. But eventually I lose to the cold. The supply from summer runs out by about mid January. I can lay dormant for about a week or so more, but then I must come up for air. And there is none.

I begin to fold on myself. Potholes are formed as pockets of energy collapse in its absence. Note the bottom circle. A bad winter has left the boundary line pocked with craters where potholes have formed. Also note that the circle is no longer a perfect circle and that the energy line no longer reaches the edge. There is literally not enough there to create a boundary and this can wreak havoc on the system. Without the boundary, stimulus can't come in. Rather, it is sucked out. Dry Winter also offers no way to replenish sections or link them.

More often than not, I end up having major difficulty by late February. As a side note, I often take two hot showers a day to get the steam and heat. In the summer it's not necessary, but in Winter, hot water treatment is often the only thing I have aside from a heated greenhouse.

I believe my need for humidity stems from the fact that my homeland was one by the sea. I guess my people need it as much as I do, but unfortunately I have yet to find any of them here...

Second edition notes:

I have been diagnosed with a few more sensory disorders and I am now on doctor's orders to relocate to a hot, humid place for at least one week during mid-winter. Unfortunately, most health insurances don't cover prescription tropical vacations, so I'm not exactly sure how this will turn out.

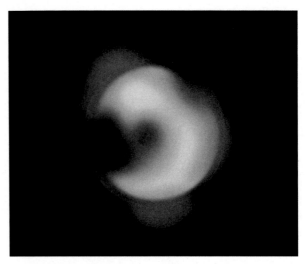

A good winter would look like this. The pocking is still evident, but the boundary lines are still functionally intact.

Ghosts and other Off-Worlders
Sometimes these things happen

I went with Beanie to go strawberry picking on June 2002. Strawberries are an alien fruit that keeps its seeds outside for so'me reason. Apparently I'm the only one weirded out by inside-out fruit but it tastes good, especially if microwaved. Not too hot, just to the level they were at when out in the sun.

In any case, Beanie was walking toward a patch further down the hill. I was about to follow her when I got this intense nagging sensation to look to the left. Over this strawberry patch, I could feel something heavy, something with mass pushing against the air, as if there can be heavy air floating in one spot. I didn't see it, or rather, her, but I could feel her talking, I could feel her face.

Because there are five senses, you can have 25 combinations of sensory overlap. In this case, I suppose I am feeling a vision because I didn't see her, but I could See her with some of my other senses. I suppose, though, if it isn't my other senses actually picking this up, then it must be a sixth sense that the other five don't cover. In any case, there she was, talking to me. I could See a vague face and a hand beckoning me. Then I got her message; she wanted me to come with her somewhere, to play. She wasn't young, and she wasn't a ghost to be sure. Ghosts feel different, cold. If I were to describe it in colours, this one had a slight rainbow iridescence whereas ghosts tend to be kind of a flat white/gray feeling, kind of a clammy cold.

Back to this one. I don't know what she was or what she wanted but I don't think it was innocent. There was something mischievous there. She kept saying in so many words,

"Come out, come out and play. Leave this behind and play with me. Don't worry, Let's fly."

I was hypnotized. This had never happened before and though I was pretty sure I didn't trust her, I was still curious. Beanie realized I wasn't following her and came back to find me staring at the sky in a trance.

I remember asking her if she saw it too, but she said no. Then she went to the spot I was looking at and found a small patch of ultra huge strawberries. Well Beanie got real excited and picked a whole bunch while I tried to reason with the vision. Eventually the vision gave up and left.

Bean thinks that she was trying to tell us where the best berries were and to tell the truth, that would be a cute story, but that's not it. I know she was up to no good. How no good her no good was I don't know, but if I had to guess, I'd say maybe she wanted my body. Nah... Maybe she wanted to absorb me into herself. That's more possible than the first one. Maybe she just wanted to pull a prank. Either way, she knew I could see her, (most likely because I was staring straight at her) and figured I could come out of my body as well. Truth be told, I certainly can, but for those three or four times I really did separate, it happened completely by accident and scared the crap out of me.

◄ You can't actually see ghosts I don't think, but you can See ghosts.

ECCENTRICITY

Hallway Energy Pipelines

Standing in an Empty Hall is Good for you

When I was young, maybe several years ago, I wandered during my job at a summer day camp in search of a decent bathroom. It was held in an elementary school, you see, and most of the toilets were so small. So up to the third floor I went and lo, there was this darkened hallway, accented only by the glow that came through the open doors.

And then I felt it, a humming in my skin, a force pushing up against me, past me, all over me as if I had stepped into a wind tunnel. I felt as if gravity was losing its hold and that I could let myself drift in the stream. I could touch Everything.

What had happened that day? I returned to the hallway day after day on my lunch break, but was surprised to find that if anything or anyone broke the perfect corridor with its presence that the tunnel didn't form. Toward the end of the Summer the janitors returned to clean the school for September and the Tunnel was lost altogether.

The picture I have here is of another hallway that produces the same effect, situated right outside my place of work. During the day the pulse was low, almost non-existent, but as night came and the humans left, the energy would begin its perfect cycle.

As you can see by the little picture up top, air is pushed up against the walls and careens over in a loop. It isn't so much coming straight for you, but churning as it does so, collecting force as it funnels like a sideways tornado. Of course, I have no idea what I'm talking about. After all, I haven't studied much in the art of aerodynamics. The point is, I can feel it, and that is very hard to ignore. Another place that this occurs is in subway tunnels, just as the train pushes into the station. It is almost like the train is pushing the air out of the tunnel like a bullet from a barrel, and I must say, it feels almost the same.

ECCENTRICITY

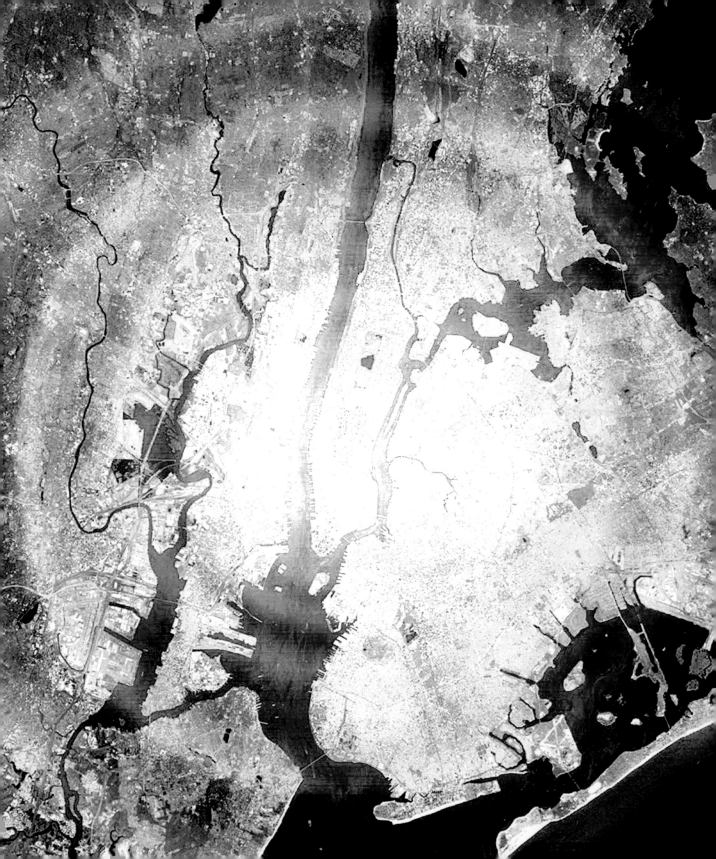

6) pillar to pillar NYC fusion theory

Human Energy Grids
Why I always know which way is New York City

Within about 50 miles of New York City, I can close my eyes, spin around and then accurately point in its direction. How is this possible? My theory is this; each human has an Aura. We have all heard of Auras before. Some people are said to have a calming aura, or someone is said to feel the presence of another in a room. How many times have you claimed that you could feel someone sneaking up behind you? This is because apparently humans give off some sort of force field. I haven't tested this on other living things or inanimate objects yet, but for humans it would explain the need to socialize. I have noticed that these Auras are attracted to each other, and the more that are present, the stronger the overall structure becomes.

I like living in an apartment building because I can Feel the presence of the others all around me, keeping me in a comfortable grid of transferable energy. I get cranky and lethargic if I am not around people for a while. Not necessarily talking with them, but being within 15 to 20 feet will suffice. It is also because of this that I enjoy public transportation.

Now, if several million people were positioned in one spot, can you not figure the consequences? To me, NYC, which is a mere 14 miles from my home and visible from any incline, is a pulsing energy core made of a mass of smaller parts. The pulse washes over the river and into the surrounding metro area. You don't need to have special senses to feel it. The closer one lives to the city, the faster they move, as if driven by the overflow.

Second edition notes: I have tested this on other living things and inanimate objects, and yes, it does exist. Even loners connect with their surroundings and may find the less intense aura of inanimate objects more calming. At least that's what I think. Consequently, my apartment is full of things.

An overhead shot of humans at the mall has been altered so to see the pillar to pillar connections, the humans being the pillars.

ECCENTRICITY

Reading Auras
Coloured Emotions and Using Synesthesia to Freak People Out

I f by chance you do have Synesthesia or some other heightened sensory ability, you may find that you can not only sense a person's Aura, but See it too. For me it shows up in colour. I will See the colour, intensity and patterns that are made, then ask myself how those colours make me feel. The Syn will relay back the responses and give me a fairly accurate picture of what is going on in their head. Incidentally, the colours are so specific that one light blue might mean something completely different from another light blue, so consciously memorizing them is out of the question. I tried once and it didn't work. Best to let the Syn take care of it.

1. Euphoria that the Twilight Rift is upon us.
2. Some sort of anxiousness attributed to something that needs to be settled very soon.
3. Worry over something potentially life altering
4. An apathy/calming band, usually present to counter/ignore a persisting problem.
5. Feeling relatively productive/stable. Interactivity band shows how able one is to deal with the world

Telepathy
An Uncomfortable Possibility

This is what I See on the inside of my eyelids if Beanie is thinking about a 6. So far I can only do this accurately with her, meaning that we probably have developed one of those physic twin deals. Maybe eventually I'll have better success with other people's minds, maybe even... yours! (HAHAHAHAHA!!!!)

Interestingly enough, even though I'm not even 'seeing' a 6, the vision of the six is still obliged to a synestesic blue.

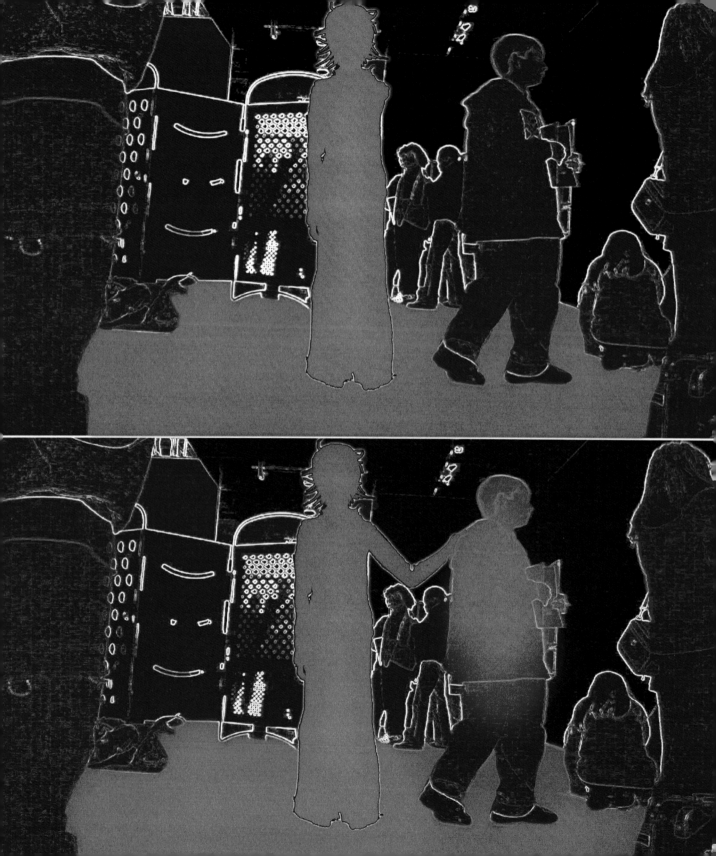

My capacity for remembering people is very low. On the left is what John Luttropp, my professor looks like.

On the Right is how I would remember his face. If it wasn't for his bald head, glasses, and goatee, he would have no identifying features for me to remember him by.

Second Edition Notes
This phenomena is known as Face-Blindness, or more scientifically, Prosopagnosia, which means the part of the brain used for processing faces is damaged or doesn't work for some reason. It is common amongst the autistic.

Knowing by Touch
My Horrible Memory and Why I hate shoes

For those of you who know me well, you may notice that I go without shoes whenever possible. I've probably been written off as a hippie, but it actually has nothing to do with idealism. My sense of spatial perception is so poor that I often don't even acknowledge things unless I touch them directly.

But let us dig a little deeper to the real reason, not to say the above isn't valid, which it is. I have a very poor sense of where 'I' stop and the rest of the world begins. Because of this, I'm never really sure that something I'm looking at is real unless I can touch it. Of course I know that it's real, but for some reason the entire system doesn't recognize its existence unless it has confirmation.

Walking without shoes literally keeps me grounded, because I can Feel it. That floor that I am touching with my feet is now Valid and that in turn allows me to feel more comfortable moving around in that area. In the picture to the left, you can see that I have connected myself to the floor via my feet. I am rooted in the real world, the floor, and we are trading information about each other's existence.

Now, say I want to talk to that kid over there. I don't necessarily have to touch him to know he is there, but it will increase my likeliness of actually remembering him. If I am allowed to touch your face, there is an even greater chance that I will recognize you the second time we meet, instead of the 10th or 12th which is my average. I will not remember you or your face the first 6 or 7 times unless you have a distinguishing mark that no one else would have, like a scar, pink hair, or a very peculiarly coloured Aura.

I will, however, remember exactly what you are wearing. That confuses me even more.

Once I was talking to this woman for two hours. Then she got up and put her coat on and we went outside. She then resumed talking to me, at which point I asked her who she was. Then by chance a piece of her green shirt became visible and immediately I knew that it was the same woman as a few minutes ago.

Another thing that happens often is two different looking people will look the same to me for whatever reason. Unless both people are in the same room at the same time, I have been known to go for almost a year thinking two different people are the same person.

This will happen with people I know well, too. I was friendly with a professor that I had for a class. One day after three months of being in that class, I walked up to him before the lecture started and asked him if the professor would be coming to class that day, not recognizing him at all. This, however, does not happen so often as the other two with people, but does so with dates and times. A steady schedule will, for no reason, rearrange itself in my head, even if that schedule has been standing for months or years.

Quite often I forget my first birthday.

So if I do not remember you, please do not be offended. If it is important that I remember you, always wear some piece of clothing or jewelry every time I do see you, or, if it suits you, let me touch your face.

Car-Gridding

Guidance by Sonar

This is called Car-gridding and it shows what the back of my head is seeing when I come into heavy traffic. The red grid shows up only at night but the green triangles are always present, refreshing themselves as necessary. Each triangle calculates the coordinates between the objects and each other and to myself, then updates the data, compares it, and sends the outcome to the motor section. The Frames Per Second and number of triangles depends on the difficulty of the traffic. There are also numbers that line the sides or the tips of each triangle but I don't know what they mean myself. It must make sense to the navigation program which I see running on the side. Navigation is always running, but only comes into visual interface when it takes priority in the system. The interesting thing about car-gridding is that it is not so much reliant on sight as it is on sound. In all manner of weather I always have the window cracked about an inch. It works like a form of sonar. The closer my car is to another object, the louder the engine will sound as it's reflected back at me. I don't consciously decide how far by how it sounds, but my brain seems to do the math on its own. It's not fool proof but it compensates for my deficit in spatial reasoning. This is not the case with higher speeds, basically anything over 50 mph, hence I can not use highways. In all honesty I have no idea how people manage to use on-ramps. It seems like Russian roulette to me.

Second Edition notes: I can use highways, but only under certain conditions to numerous to name here.

Car gridding is a must have software for living in North Jersey, where the government actually has to make it illegal for car insurance agencies to leave the state, even though they are losing money.

ECCENTRICITY

Stranger than Fiction
If I see it, it Must be Real

My first memory, my first real memory, was that of the dream that woke me up. Inconsequential as it seemed at the time, the fact that my brain's first test run happened in an altered state has taught it that altered states must be as valid as the waking world. It reasons that all information coming in must be valid, otherwise how else could I have experienced it in the first place? The philosophical debate of how one decides what is real and what is not is more than idle musing. What is and isn't real can't be decided, at least I can't dechiper what is and isn't, so all things must be considered, nothing can be condemned as false. If I see someone shot on TV, then I will have the same trauma as having witnessed it first hand.

This means a number things, the first and most obvious is that I have to be very restrictive of my methods of entertainment. No horror, no crime, no murder, no Lifetime for women movies, no violent comics, no murder mystery books, nothing in which someone dies, even if off screen, no true crime shows, nothing that if it happened in real life would cause emotional trauma. Hence all must be carefully screened. No movie can be watched without knowing how it ends, no book read unless I read the ending first. Horror movies, no matter how terrible, cheesy, stupid and fake one is, I still get the same reaction. Even when watching MST3K* and the robots are chattering away, I still find myself taking damage for watching a violent scene.

Sounds stupid? Sometimes I think so too and I break my own rules. With disastrous results. I love Johnny Depp and his 'Secret Window' was on so I decided to take a risk and watch it for the Depp experience. I suffered emotional trauma for a week and a half. Earlier that year I was reading Tomb raider comic books when a favorite character died. I was in mourning for three weeks. It's easier to just eliminate it all from my viewing diet. All I watch now is cartoon network, animal planet, and comedy central. I only read scientific nonfiction. Even then, I still slip up and pay the price. The worst part is that my brain logs it all as real events in my timeline. I have all manner of false memories of things that never actually happened. Once when I first started going to therapy I was asked if I was ever abused or molested and I had to pause to sift through the disorganized mess of memories to pick out which ones were real or not. The pause made the therapist suspicious that I was hiding something and spent the next half hour trying to tease it out of me.

The other offshoot is the inability to lie. Once I create a lie that conflicts with what my brain already knows, it doesn't seem to be able to hold the two memories at once. It will either discard the lie so I can't recall it later or worse, discard the truth in favor of the lie which inevitably conflicts with something else, setting off a chain reaction that can wipe out blocks of memory at a time. Even white lies lead to trouble, so I've developed the fine art of splitting hairs. By and large it works just as well, but on a day to day basis blunt truth has always been the default. Humans say they admire a person who speaks the truth. I think they're lying.

*MST3K, otherwise known as Mystery Science Theater 3000 was a bizarre show with a cult following that used to play on Sci-Fi channel.

As if things weren't scary enough on their own.

Dream-state

Or; "Oh look, it's raining fire again..."

And if that wasn't bad enough, dreams get logged as real too. But these are no ordinary dreams. These are ultra-mega-surround sound dreams that hijack my senses, playing them as if the stimulus was coming from the outside. The Matrix* has taught us that the brain only knows what it's told by electrical impulses. Most of the time it's a safe bet that those impulses came from a legitimate source. My subconscious has figured out how to configure itself in such a way that the brain thinks it's getting a real feed from the outside and will continue to bug me for days following a dream to react. Say, for example, a dream informs me that my car was stolen. I will be driving in my car all the next day with the nagging thought that I have to call the police to report the theft. This is called Haunting.

Sometimes the sensory input in dreams goes to the extreme. Unlike most people, when I die in a dream I don't always wake up afterward. Somehow my brain recreates what it thinks it would feel like to die and what's creepy is that it has remained pretty consistent, as if it really knows what it's talking about. There's the feeling of an intense pressure, a weight that makes it impossible to move or speak. Panic streaks across as you feel your body struggle and die until the blackness takes your mind as well. I have died five times to date.

It's no surprise that I've died in my dreams. With 90% of my dreams having to do with the apocalypse I'm surprised I've only died five. The ones that aren't specifically about the apocalypse have the apocalypse going on in the background. The 10% that have nothing to do with the apocalypse- wait, no, it's always the apocalypse. If I had a dream about my car being stolen, chances are it was stolen during the end times. Why? I have no idea but it's been like this since I was born, and I mean originally born. I have a poor to nonexistent conscious memory of my first thirteen years but my subconscious memory is perfectly intact. I can dive back into ancient dreams that I know happened in the Before Time and they are as vivid as they ever were. There are a handful of recognizable places that my dreams keep going back to, places I have never actually seen but feel some ancient connection to. I call these the Homelands.

I should make a pie chart about which places I go to the most. Number one offender; the Holylands. The Holylands are not the Homelands mind you. The Holylands are the Wildwood Beaches in South Jersey and they appear in nearly half of all my dreams. I'm either trying to get there, am there, or trying to figure out a way not to leave there and of course it's apocalypsing out. As

➤

*The Matrix is a sci-fi movie that came out in 1999 that presents the idea that the brain creates reality based on the electronic signals it receives, and that reality is controlled by he who controls the signals themselves.

The full moon makes it worse. Not sure why because the amount of sun bouncing off it at any given time shouldn't have anything to do with where my brain is going to send me that night.

◄

Left page: A typical apocalyptic scenario featuring the back yard. The most common disaster that befalls this setting is floods, followed by war and lightening storms.

Right Page; The original picture.

Dream-state

for the Homelands, there's pictures of that further on. Next up is the middle school I went to. These dreams are usually more disturbing for some reason. Next is the elementary school, not as disturbing. High school and College take about 5% each, college ones being ultra violent for some reason. There are even a few from Berkshire.

It's when you get to the other two big ones, my old home and my grandmother's house that you see the time warp. Any dreams I have about either two take place in the Before time. I don't remember what my grandmothers house looked like before the restorations but in the dreams the bathroom is this wild green and yellow 70's masterpiece and the kitchen is restored to its former kitschy glory. When I asked my grandmother about the visions she confirmed that when I was very young the bathroom was decked out in green/silver wallpaper and had yellow tile. I still have to find a picture of it. I do consciously remember my mother's home before she redid everything in... (shudder) ...beige and I can tell you that all the dream's

depictions of the past are accurate. The dreams of Mother's house are far and away the most violent. I can't tell you how many times the apocalypse romped down the street in every manner of the word. It's gotten to the point where the dreams aren't of my house, rather the house is a physical manifestation of those dreams.

Which freaks me out. I'll walk in the backyard now and it will be like, 'Holy crap, it looks just like those dreams I have! Why isn't it underwater or filled winged monkeys?" I lived in that house for fifteen years, but I still have more and clearer memories of that place from the dream-state than from the waking world. I barely have any of where I live now. Sometimes these places mash together and add new places in, or sometimes (very rarely) a place I've never seen before. More commonly my brain will find some random place from my past and dump hell on it for fun. At this point in my life many of the places the dreams take me that I've never been before are well-established reoccurring places from the Homelands. They will expand out from their origins or

show a new place and show how it connects to the Homeland's system at some point. Sometimes it doesn't but I know anyway. I can't explain how I know one never-been-to place is Homelands and the next isn't except that the Homelands seem to have their own peculiar mint on then and follow their own separate destiny. Like it was some other world that I can watch form but never go consciously. Homelands aren't the only dreams that have a line of continuum, though. All the dreams seem to remember each other from one night to the next, forming their own mysterious back stories, none of which I understand. I'm pretty sure it has to do with the apocalypse.

Now with all this going on as clear or clearer than what I process during the day, how the hell am I supposed to have a solid grip on reality? Of course I believe in other dimensions, ghosts, telepathy and any number of crazy things. They happen to me every day because that's what keeps getting sent over to the brain. I see no point in trying to separate what is 'real' and what isn't because to tell the truth, this is cooler.

Precognitive and Psychic Dreams

And Then it Gets Creepy...

December 25th, 2005, I convinced Beanie to sleep over, because I hate sleeping by myself. Somewhere between twelve and two am I started violently in my sleep and awoke. Startled and half-asleep, Beanie asked what was wrong and told her I had yet another apocalyptic dream. I usually don't give these much thought besides knowing that I would probably be Haunted for the next day. Most likely not, though. Dreams that happen so far from dawn are usually erased by other dreams occurring afterward, but this one stayed on.

Stranger still was nature of it. I dreamed about storms, wars, floods, lightening, and tornados all the time, but this was a wave. A gigantic wave. Okay, so what? There's a first time for everything, yes? But what was weirder was that the wave didn't belong there. How can something not belong in a dream when people dream of all manner of madness? I can't explain it any more than watching an old romance movie in a theater and having a pickup truck suddenly crash through the screen. Not only does it not really fit with the story but the truck is real, really real, too real. And it had burst in from the outside. The setting for the movie was odd to begin with. It was a fuzzy, oversaturated view of the shore line from out to sea looking inland. I, or someone, was perched high in a dead tree in the water looking at the beach, the bathers, the trees behind them and the mountains further back. Then suddenly there was chaos, a feeling of alarm and 'I' turned slightly to see a towering black wave rising over the mountain. It looked like it had been carved from obsidian and while its surroundings were fuzzy, the wave itself was stunningly sharp. In fact, it positively radiated sharp. Sharp and Death. 'I' remember looking at it and thinking 'This does not belong here' before being crushed. This was one of the five dreams in which I experienced the full sensory replication of Death.

When I told Beanie about this in the middle of the night, I told her about the wave feeling drastically out of place in and out of the dream state. We didn't think it meant anything at the time.

Beanie was going to Minnesota on the 27th so we decided to hang out at the mall all day on the 26th. Instead of the wave dream disappearing at daylight or getting covered in D-sleep, it Haunted me with a vengeance. Strange but not totally unusual, except that it wasn't wearing off. When I went to sleep that night it returned as a pale recap as most Haunting dreams do, but this one was not as pale as it should and it was persistent. I still paid it no mind, not until 5 am the next morning to walk with Beanie to the lobby

➤

My attempt at drawing that dream as best I could do it. Remembering it isn't the problem, it's trying to get the colours right. And the wave doesn't look like a glossy cut rock like it should. Oh well. One thing puzzles me; why is the wave coming in from behind the island? I thought about this and noticed that the sun was on the left. My guess is that I must have been facing south on a small atoll or something. That doesn't explain the height of the thing because I don't think it got that tall.

Precognitive and Psychic Dreams

to catch her airport taxi. The papers had just been delivered on our neighbor's doorsteps and the front page was covered with one story. My blood went cold. Impossible. How could a tsunami crash on the shores of a land half a world away have shown up in my dreams two days before? Had it been a precognitive dream like the one two weeks before 9/11? But as I read the article things began to take an even more bizarre twist; the tsunami hadn't crashed today, it had crashed at 8-11 am on Dec. 26th, UTC (Coordinated Universal Time). Was that the same time it broke my subconscious? If the quakes set off shortly before midnight GMT and the waves took between 2-10 hours to hit their marks, that made it between 2 and 10 am Dec. 26th. New Jersey is -5 GMT, meaning the waves hit between 10 PM 12/25 and 5 am 12/26, a swath of time covering the time the dream had taken place. It wasn't a Precog at all, it was something else, something far more disturbing.

Could the force of 200,000 voices screaming as one send the vision of the wave across the ocean into a fertile sleeping mind? If it had, the hole it had punched in the psychic membrane wasn't closing and the flood of misery continued to pour through. As days went by the dream refused to leave and I began feeling this shifting back and forth that I was supposed to be amongst the wreckage, that I was supposed to be in southeast Asia. I couldn't figure out how I had gotten back to America. What was worse, my mind had recorded the event as true and I was one of the tsunami's most distant victims but I couldn't go about picking up the pieces with other survivors. There was no wreckage, there was no water, there was nothing to connect me to what I had witnessed and I became terribly displaced and alone. How do you tell people you were washed under with 200,000 other people on the other side of the world when you have never left the States?

The trauma continued for me for months and months like it did for those who had really felt the ocean's wrath first hand. The hole in my head eventually closed up suddenly when the Jubilation made its overdue repairs, but the damage had already been done, for the memory of the black obsidian wave still remains.

The 9/11 dream was one of a handful of precognitive dreams that I have had in my life, most of which have foreseen minor inconsequential things of which I can't even remember. Sometime in late August 2001 I had a vivid dream that I went outside to sit on an ordinary swing set in the middle of nowhere with a view of New York City. As I watched, a jet flew overhead and I remember thinking that it was too low to make it over. The dream took on the same eerily sharp quality that the wave dream did later on as the plane dipped into the heart of downtown, exploding seven times. The sky turned bright red and as the orange mushrooms blossomed overhead and I remember the clearest thought of all, 'the world will never be the same.' That dream followed me around for two days, a long time for a Haunting. I told Beanie about this one too and she reminded me about it when 9/11 eventually unfolded. It was partially responsible for my slow response to 9/11, never being unable to fully differentiate between the dream and the real life event. The fact that I had seen it earlier dogged me for months after but what could I do? I wasn't sure I believed it either. One thing still nags me; the dream was very insistent that I notice the number of explosions but I still haven't been able to figure out their significance. Mayhaps it's too early to tell.

Trying to remember home. 10/14/2002

I know I came from somewhere,
I recognize scents, feelings from
where I used to be.
Its always the same colour
that greenish blue tile under
chlorine in a pool, always that
lime taste, always that forlorn
feeling of a land on the edge
of time.

I came from a world of my own,
and I'm homesick.

~~Maybe~~
There is always water. vasts seas,
oceans. I remember them. Marshes,
beaches, expanses of grass and plains.
I sometimes see people.
There is a forest near the entrance,
where ever that may be. I don't
remember the woods well. There are
no mountains, but there are cliffs
by the water. some hills inland.
The sky is pale except for storms
which haunt my dreams.

Grass, overgrown.
The towns are bleached by the sea.
its... it has the feeling of summers
end. lingering on the edge of
forever, but never seeming to
change.

Sometimes my dreams let me go back
and see it, sense it, that strange
forgotten land. Some songs make
me remember... Crickets, peeping frogs,
                                sea gulls
If I can find a place on Earth
like the one I left behind. I will live
there happily until I die.

  I miss the water.

The Homelands
Memories without Logic

It's not home, but it looks like it. These are altered pictures I took in Maine. I spent two rolls of film capturing the scenery of one of the few places to ever evoke the ancient feeling in the back of my mind.

ECCENTRICITY

THE ELEVENTH STAR PROJECT

ECCENTRICITY

Homelands

What am I talking about, "home"? Obviously I was born in New Jersey in the relatively urban metro area, as it says on my birth certificate. Besides, I can't remember my past. But recently I came to thinking, you see. I have at least four to five vivid dreams a night as far back as I can remember, and for some reason, my memories of dreams goes back into the Before time. Six out of ten times, those dreams are in a place by the sea. Four times out of ten, it's of the same area, this place.

I have never actually been here, I guess. I mean, it has two moons. It always has two moons. Sometimes the moons are big, sometimes small, and sometimes really faded, but that narrows the search of possible places on Earth to nill. The passage I wrote on the last page I wrote while in an induced state of trance, for the first time trying to pin down a place so familiar that I never noticed it.

I don't know if it's an island, but it is definitely by the sea. It is an overgrown, sandy, windy, abandoned place where time moves slow and there is always the sound of some cicada type bug or some crickets. It always looks like its either very late afternoon or twilight and things have a more aqua green tint. There are marshes here, cliffs there, and some specific points that tug at me.

Somewhere around here is a cove of a pretty decent size, carved into the rock. It would make a nice bay, and there are always people here, merchants and such. There is a community pool somewhere inland. Also somewhere there is the singing wall. I haven't returned to the singing wall since I was very, very, very young because I was never able to find it again, but I know it is there. The signing walls are these canyons by the sea with hundreds of mask faces carved into the reddish rock. Each one is signing one steady note like monks.

I remember being scared, that I shouldn't be there, that the faces were sacred. It was little wonder that when the goddesses entered my life many, many years later, that they had the same faces.

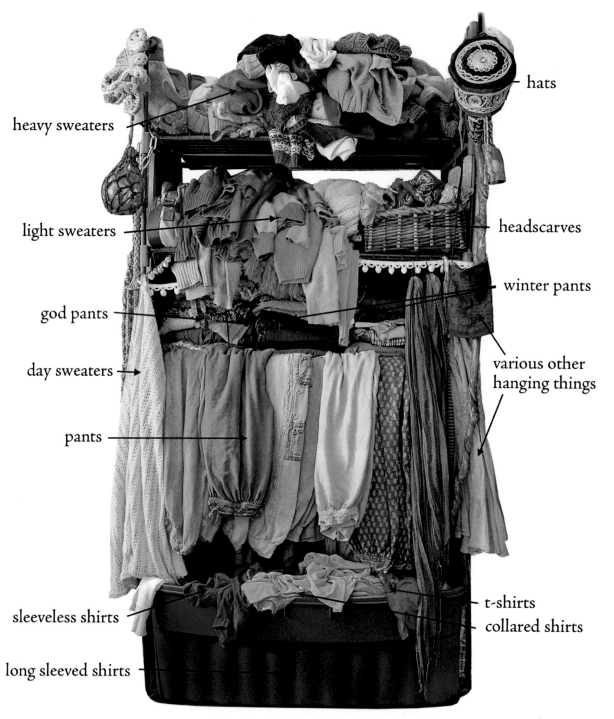

heavy sweaters

hats

light sweaters

headscarves

god pants

winter pants

day sweaters

various other
hanging things

pants

sleeveless shirts

t-shirts

collared shirts

long sleeved shirts

The Clothing Storage System
"Because folding things is a waste of time."

And of course me magic hat.
Can't forget the hat.

Clothing
The Importance of Dress

I bought my first article of clothing when I was 15 years old in high school. That should give you an idea on how late I was on fashioning a style for myself, because by that time, everyone was into the latest trend. High school is all about those kinds of things, you see. But I didn't know that then. I do have a vague recollection of knowing that I needed a plaid shirt to fit in with the grunge movement during the Wash, but I didn't know why. I did try for a short time to dress like the crowd, but their clothes felt so alien, and as soon as Social Balance gave me a license to be myself, I took it.

I don't have a style, but I do have things I like, things that feel like I should be wearing them. More often than not,

◄

When I first wrote this chapter I didn't have this neat setup, but I had been drawing up plans for it. This thing is actually a converted 'assemble it yourself' greenhouse that had gotten mangled by a snowplow. Now it has new purpose. And clothing.

ECCENTRICITY

those were things that they didn't sell in stores. The first thing I wanted were pants with flared ends. In 1996, the last pair of flared ended pants were made in the hippie era and died there, but I wanted them anyway. I must have looked for them everywhere when 6 months later I found a modest flare at a trend store that had decided to give them a shot. I was the first kid to have flares at school, but of course the only reason I could think of for them being the next great thing was how neatly they fit over my ice skates. By summer, everyone had them.

In my search for Things that Felt Right, I stumbled upon a lot of other great trends at least half a year before they became mainstream, and this

always annoyed me, because when I wanted them they would be nowhere to be found, but inevitably would wind up being everywhere for everyone else once I had moved on. Such things were dark flares when light was popular, big bells when small were popular, Hawaiian shirts and bathing suits when you could only find them on eBay, flip-flops, shoulder bags, tinted eye-glasses, ski sweaters, wool and tweed pants, fishing hats, sweater jackets, ect. Now I'm

Clothing

finding that the old kid's T-shirts that I have worn for at least two years now are coming into style and now everyone is buying them off eBay for more than I can afford. What is next, I ask? Will my puffy harem pants be next? I hope not. When ever something becomes popular, I feel that I am impersonating someone else, even if I was doing it first. Go figure.

The most important rule of my buying clothes is 'can I sleep in it on a moment's notice?' because I do that a lot. I like to feel that I am wearing a portable bed and that all that is needed is for me to lie down.

Number two is that it feels like me. I'm not sure what that means, exactly, but it's important. I know I like geometric shapes, paisley, and patterns that look really simplified. I also like stripes, but that trend hasn't started yet, so I'll have to wait for striped palazzo pants.

Number three is that what I'm wearing doesn't match. I don't like matching unless its supposed to match, like a pants suit. Not outrageously not matching, though I would like to wear stripes with plaid if I could, but just not matching enough for it to look unexpected. So you have to think about it. What fun is it if it matches? I mean, that's a given. Everyone matches, no one explores the possibilities of each article having its own say. Because of this, I generally get dressed by pulling pants A out of basket A and pulling shirt B out of basket B. The less they match, the better. I also won't wear the same outfit twice, unless I came up with a really good one, because I want to try as many combinations of basket A and B as I can.

So where do I get this stuff? Thrift stores. Thrift stores are heaven in that everything is one of a kind and cheap! The place I go to is in the $1 to $5 range so I can easily fund my fetish. Ebay is another good place to get clothes, garage sales, the clearance rack. Clothes that are second hand are especially appealing because they have character and I am the next chapter in their lives. Again, each piece of clothing is special, so the fact that they have a history makes me feel honored to wear it.

Number four. It must be soft. I can not stress that enough. And textures or colours. But mostly it must be soft and loose. Oversized is great. I love hiding in my clothes. I like pants to hide my feet or sleeves to cover my hands and it bothers me if they don't. Unless it's over 100 degrees, I wear pants but generally not jeans, which are too restrictive. I have special pants, and thus I have dedicated a whole section to them. Them and my T-shirts.

Number five, NO BRAS OR WOMEN'S UNDERWEAR!

I can't *stand* them, period. The first things to go were the bras, which are essentially useless if you have such small breasts as mine. I *hated* bras. I always hated bras. No matter how much I stretched them out of shape, they were still *touching* me, and I would spend the entire day tugging at the elastic. So one day, I just stopped wearing them. Tada!

Mother was not pleased, saying such things weren't done and all that. I say

'screw it.' Next came the underwear. I used to wear those cotton kind that came in the three-pack bags. I wore the old ones to death and when the time came to finally get new ones, it was a nightmare. I started by wearing them inside out. Then I started snipping the elastic to loosen it. Then I started take all the elastic off, trimming the seams, cutting up the leg holes, nothing worked. One day I got so fed up I took my pocket knife and cut the pair I was wearing clean off. Victory!

But you can't just go around with no underwear. Luckily, the solution was simple; men's silk boxers. Perry Ellis silk boxers to be exact (they're made of some strange silky material and the elastic isn't bunchy) Let's take a moment to thank Perry Ellis for making these, because otherwise, I would truly be in hell.

I also won't wear shoes if I can get away with it. They separate me from the ground and that bothers me for some reason. I can get really fussy over a shirt or pants, but shoes really don't enter my mind. I have a large collection of shoes,

but I only wear one pair; a pair of totally destroyed foam flip-flops. I'll wear the same pair every day, summer and winter, until they fall apart, literally. I'll often try to prolong the broken shoe's life with a hot glue gun or staples.

If it snows out, then it's soft-soled boots, but the second the snow is gone, I'm back out with sandals, which for some reason really freaks people out.

I collect jewelry as well but I only wear necklaces. Anything else I fidget with and lose the same day I buy it. Of the necklaces I have, I wear the same three or four everyday. Go fig. As for hair stuff and makeup, no hair stuff or makeup. It bothers the crap out of me. I'll put gel in my hair or makeup on my face and I'll end up rushing to the nearest rest room to wash it off with the soap out of those little hand dispensers. So I just skip that altogether.

Mother says that I dress this way because I have low self-esteem. I say nay. I wear these clothes because...

Hmmmm....

Because to dress like the rest would be a lie, for then I would be pretending to be something I'm not. I like not being everybody else, so why would I strive to dress like them if that's not what I feel is right for me? My way is better for me. I like looking at me with my clothes on me. I feel they reflect what I look like inside so there is no deception as to what's inside. I don't know where I came from, but where I came from, this is the way people dress, how ever that is.

Let us take a few pages to celebrate my T-shirts and wonderful array of pants.

ECCENTRICITY

FIGURE 1. SHIRTS

These are my many shirts. Some are true vintage, some are not, all are very soft and some are sacred, such as the 'World Series of Birding' shirt I got in the Holylands shortly after I awoke, and the Carmen shirt, which I made myself.

Clothing

FIGURE 2. PANTS

I used to wear only skirts until I discovered these wonderful pants. With pants you can sleep anywhere and you never have to worry about them shifting about and your legs getting cold. They are soft and float about me, sending information back to my legs so they know where they are. They are worn from February to early December and longer if I can get away with it.

1. & 8. - OVER PANT - WORN OVER ANOTHER PAIR IN COLDER WEATHER.
2, 4, 7, & 15. - LOUNGE PANT
3. & 16. - EVERYDAY WEAR JINGLE PANT.
5. - THE WATERMELON SAMURAI PANT
6, 9, 12, & 14. - EVERYDAY WEAR PANT
10. FAVOURITE PANT - MY FIRST PAIR, BOUGHT FOR $.50 AT A THRIFT STORE.
11. & 13 - HOT WEATHER PANT - SEMI-TRANSPARENT, USUALLY WORN UNDER SUNDRESS.

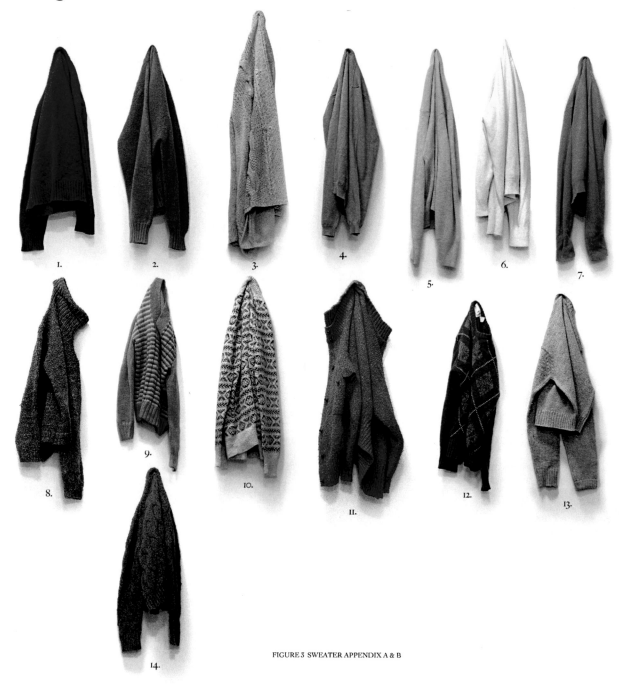

FIGURE 3 SWEATER APPENDIX A & B

15.

16.

17.

18.

19.

20.

21.

22.

23.

24.

25.

26.

27.

28.

29.

30.

ECCENTRICITY

1 2 3 4 5 6 7 8

Dressing for Godliness

Because in my mind I am one.

Now if everyone is quite done crying "blasphemer", let me clarify. I live in a very strange, surreal world that mirrors what some would consider a religious experience, except everyday, especially in the Summer, when my body boundaries disappear in the rising heat and humidity. In short, I feel like a god, and if I am a god, then I should probably dress the part.

These are clothes are for special occasions, things related to my religion of Spacialism, the Holylands pilgrimages, very hot days, and an overall excuse to collect them in the first place.

God Clothes

1. A shirt with open-cut sleeves that are laced down the sides

2. Typical Pilgrimage garb

3. Lady Æriol's clothes

4. Heavy tapestry work

5. The monk's suit, used for my attempts of being professional

6. I made this slip dress out of sari material

7 and 8. Day to day wear in the Holylands

9. Thinking clothes

10. Wandering clothes

11. Servant-god clothes. I made the apron myself.

12. Not really god-wear, but they are rather nice pants. The shirt however is
my first piece in this collection, a silk kurta from my mother's days of 60's style.

13. Master's clothes

14. Messenger clothes

15. Ceremonial garb, usually only worn at the evening ceremony in the Holylands

- The future cannot be stopped
- cellular connection

belief (2) - the Space is the collective conscious
- there are other planes

Barefoot

religion (3) - replant all weeds/protect the ...
- do not throw away food. This Natural
It's no premium ... how to ... away ... solitude ...

... links up.
... belongings
... your own luck.
Levels 1-5
... of walking
... One fool can kill 100 wise men
... over ... can 100 wisemen save one fool.?
... tells me Spits the answer
... quilt not comfort ... based on the
... your own luck
Bamboo
3 miss communications
and world peace.
starts ... clothing
- colour chart
- create one
two songs by colours
... odd plants
neighborhood
Planet Earth
... to Earth,
... was I?
a job for
... The garden
The spirals
I got ...
0 - colour over and ...
exposure due to ...
scariest
... so much Psi that
... and orientation
... Mis-allocated file, I say.

Eccentricities
- Seeing Auras
- How I dress and why
- missing gender
- feeling the movement of the ...
- ~~the adoptions~~
- ...

And of course, why

life ... a miracle. There ...

Today I got lost
or I lost myself.
Luckily I had my
Beanie and my Chan
... me subdued
until they could make
me recognize my
reflection. I seem to have
had an involuntary out of
body ...

5/28/2002
... missions of obscurity ...
the mad barber Today I was ... over
different
Humans ...
36 colours
my plants
- plants by the ...
- the hidden ...
- the first ...
- save the humans
- the adoptions

between the West and ... theory
of the cruelty ...
humans, ...
such ... hear ...
deepest voice ...
I have never known ...
wanted to be worshiped
the ... what ... does
... theory ... create ...

Theory
- weave the human ... to the Network.
- humans are ...
- ... the injured humans,
... to pillar ...
The problems with 6th Sense ... humanity ...
I ♥ my ... in the See humanity theory
strawberry cupcake
- ... myself outside the dinner
FM Brown Hallway
... power over the ... collect in ...
the graves talk ...
It is 5/29/2002.
I'm sure I ... different levels of
... am I sure?
... strong ... coming. I feel ... but don't know from where.
Compute the ...
Who is Doctor Self ...
Why does he haunt my ...
... data stream looks like
- everything can be related in computer terms. Self contained unit
- music essential
- ball theory
- node theory
Realspace - ISR
... to surroundings
Observations in the New Worlds

Humans do not ... themselves ... test, always on others, ... their ...
And what for ... man was born ... mind ...
... the ...
place ... perception theory
seeing

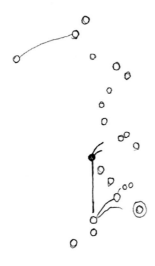

Somehow, someway. I was able to
chart my mind's thoughts. My subconscious
told me wear to post the points, led
my hand and guided mind.
      I feel calmer now.
   I see the pattern with my eyes but
they do not know what it means,
but I can feel it
      Sense it there...

Theories

My Ideas about the way Things work

◄   The original notes for this book, though the *original* originals were
far more legible. Unfortunately I wasn't able to make every idea
I had for this book. That leaves some fodder for Volume Two.

The Cap-Off Point
Survival Techniques of the Mind

I used to think that things didn't bother me as much as other people, but that's a ridiculous statement because most things bother me more than it does the normal person. Why I can easily survive a crisis but not a day at work is a mystery so like all mysteries I have a theory;

When emotional distress by an event reaches a certain point, the brain dumps whatever emotional charge came with it and becomes as neutral as shopping for curtains. Simply put, things get so bad until they suddenly disappear. I don't think it's the same as shock, because shock is when something's suspended for a while but then it hits you later. Once it disappears in the cap-off however, you'll probably never see it again. Unless it can't catch it. What I've just recently realized is that the cap-off point can be broken through. When the tsunami hit, the cap that had so effortlessly retained 9/11 was sliced through like butter. It wasn't until the tsunami created my first sense of tragedy did I notice the phenomenon of Cap-Off. Even though I drew this image months ago I still haven't figured out what or how this works and what it was about the tsunami that overrode it when 9/11 didn't.

Some events and how the Cap-off point dealt with them.

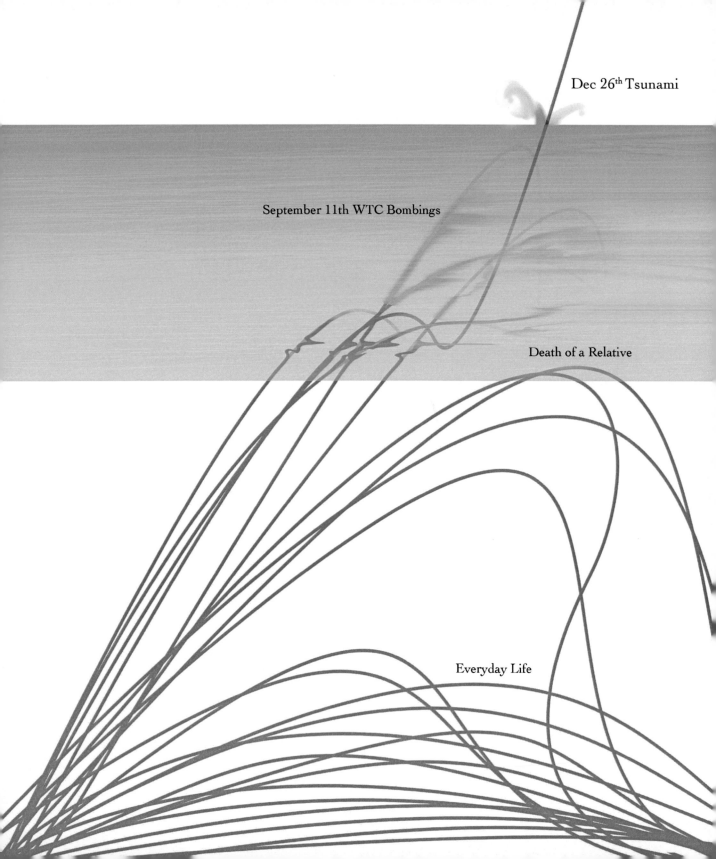

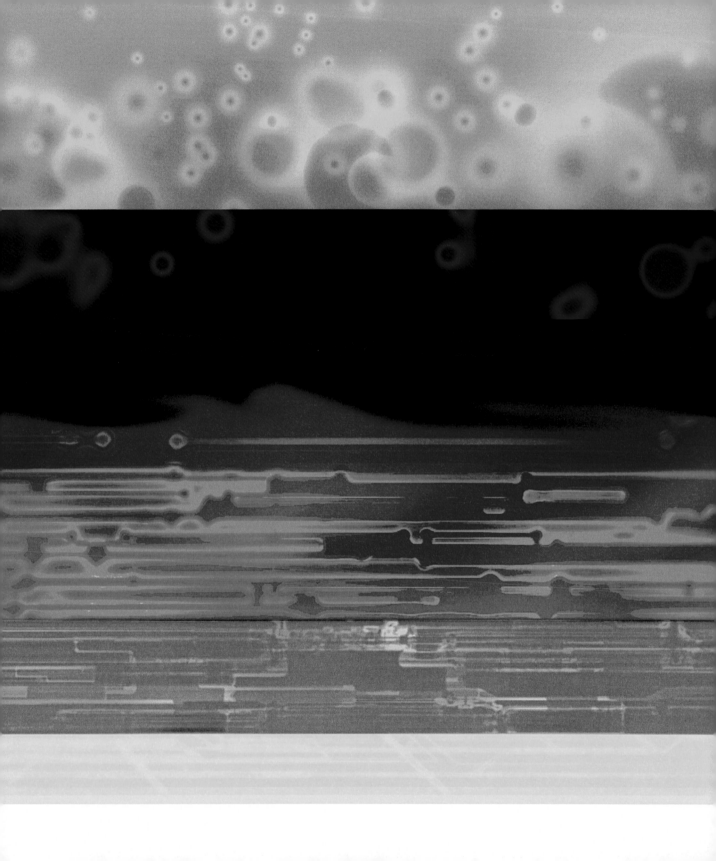

[2]] levels:
[3]] Learning to hear your
[4]] deepest voice. 2nd unto 4th
[5]

Levels
Multi-Tasking the Mind and 2nd unto 4th

Behold the 5 layers of the mind according to me. Every philosopher at some point wonders how many layers there are in the brain. Most seem to come up with three, but I'm going with 5 and here's why:

Layer 1 - Motor, Instinct, Involuntary

Layer 1 is Yellow with white lines like a circuit board. Your colours may vary. It's a little sliver of a layer on the bottom, closest to the conscious world. If you were driving a car, this would be the layer that tells you to turn left or right when on auto pilot.

Layer 2 - Rational Thought

Layer 2 is pinkish red with yellow outlined circle square things. This is the layer where you hear yourself thinking or trying to figure out what to do that day. If you were driving a car, this would be the layer that is making a list of things to get at the grocery store.

Layer 3 - Emotional Thought

Layer 3 is green with these random floating glowing green rods and it gets hazy and black towards the top. All 'deep' and philosophical thought goes here, along with emotions and the like. If you were driving a car, this would be the layer that is contemplating whether the future is worth living to see.

Layer 4 - The Subconscious

Very dark purple with a few blotches of lighter purple; like looking at the inside of your eyelids, except purple. The Subconscious, the sacred realm of the Spacialist, is also called the Pure State...by me. You can't 'get' to Level 4. It is locked off and often holds great treasures, such as the reasons for phobias, the true identity of self, and the secret to happiness. Shrinks use hypnotism to get through to the 4th level, but unless you train hard, it will only appear to you when you can't question it, when you dream. If you were driving a car, this layer would be off doing its own thing and not letting you see, unless you pulled a:

2nd unto 4th

Also known as having an epiphany. Having a 2nd unto 4th is when your 2nd level, the conscious, rational level, gets a jump on the subconscious and jumps that black divide between the top of the 3rd. It's like standing patiently in a stream, then suddenly grabbing a fish out of the water.
It's that hard.
In fact, it's a lot easier to get to the:

5th Level and Up - Transcendence

Is all pink-yellow and bubbly like pink champagne. If you manage to Trance out or 'go to a higher plane of consciousness' you are in the 5th level. You would probably not be aware of your surroundings or your boundaries and float off into space. If you were driving a car, this would be bad, as you would probably drive off a cliff, giggling the whole way down. Please Don't Trance and Drive.

Why Driving a Car of all Things?

Because I was driving my car when I figured this all out. As for the level colours, I think it's obvious if you read the chapter on Synesthesia.

The Natural Way:
how to strip ettral natures
aveay and reverse
sotialical programing.

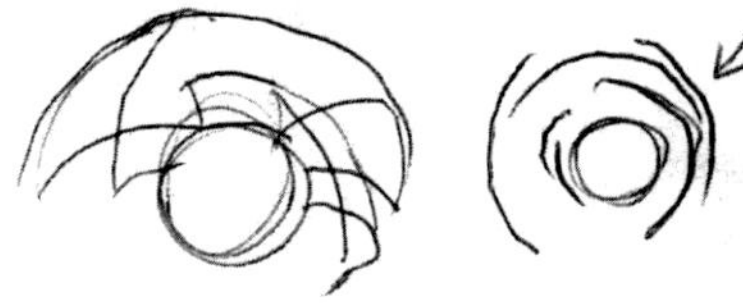

← *ball*
perception
theory

Ball Perception Theory

Like the Layers of an Onion

Ball Perception was one of my earlier ideas on Social Programming. I find the idea of Social Programming to be very important in my studies of humans because it presents the margin for error, in that I may not be observing the human themselves, but rather a jumble of programming. This is very sad.

It has come to my attention that humans build walls to keep things out, but it also prevents anything from coming in. In fact, I'm not so sure that many people have an Aligned Moment and if that is so, then that means that many people are not living at all.

Observe the Ball. In each layer there are Conditions that must be met for the information to go through to the next circle. Most information is processed by the top four layers, I say. Maybe a particularly elusive thought may make it fairly well through, but will still get knocked out in the end. An Aligned Moment is an Epiphany. One thought makes it through all the disks to the center where the Pure Mind sits. The less disks there are, the more Aligned Moments there are, which makes for more actual Thinking. Actual Thinking leads to Balance, or at least the knowledge that You are an active participant in what goes on in the congress of your mind.

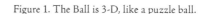

Figure 1. The Ball is 3-D, like a puzzle ball.

Figure 2. A cross section reveals the many conflicting layers. Too many layers can lead to a closed Mind.

Figure 3. Thoughts attempt to break through so to influence the Mind. Some layers of common sense, ethics, and experience are needed in order to assure a logical decision is met. Too many can lead to confusion and anxiety.

Spacialism:
Ball Perception Theory

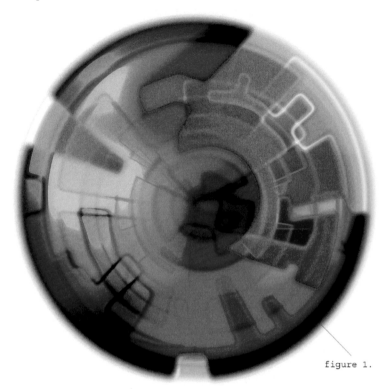

figure 1.

figure 2.
Cross-section

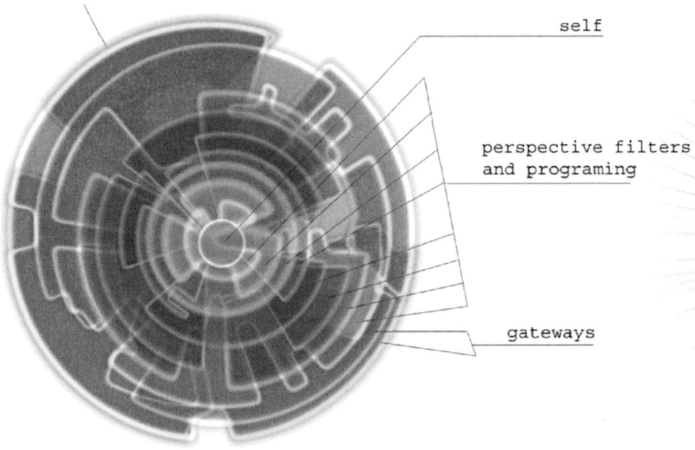

self

perspective filters
and programing

gateways

figure 3.
Perception Theory in Action

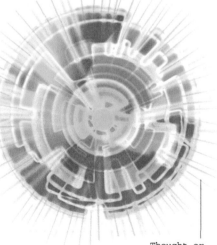

Thought or
experience

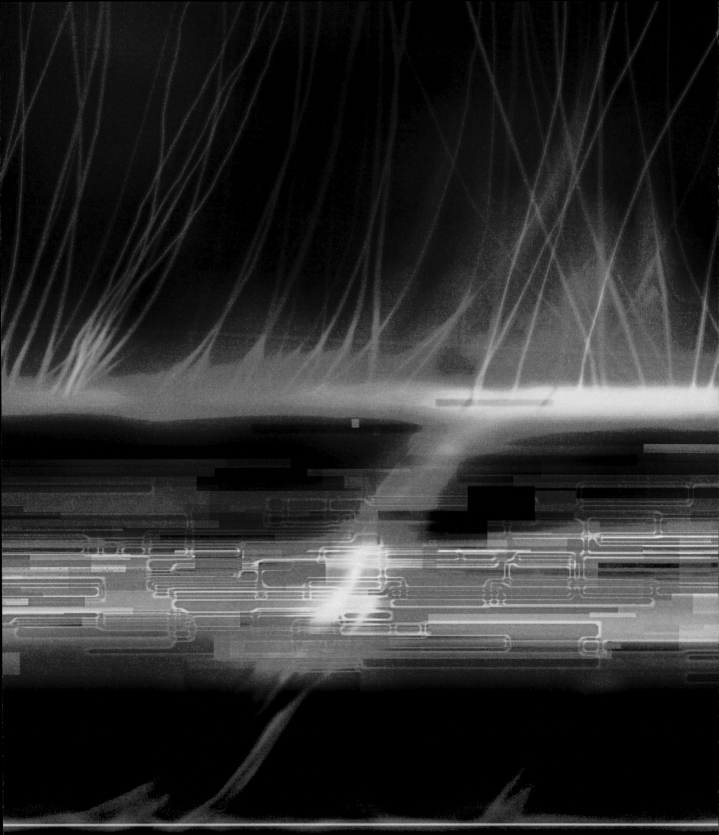

Stream of Conscious
Using Links for Verification

chapt

4) Speculation
→ The Natural Way
→ streaming.
→ tapping the sub

7/2

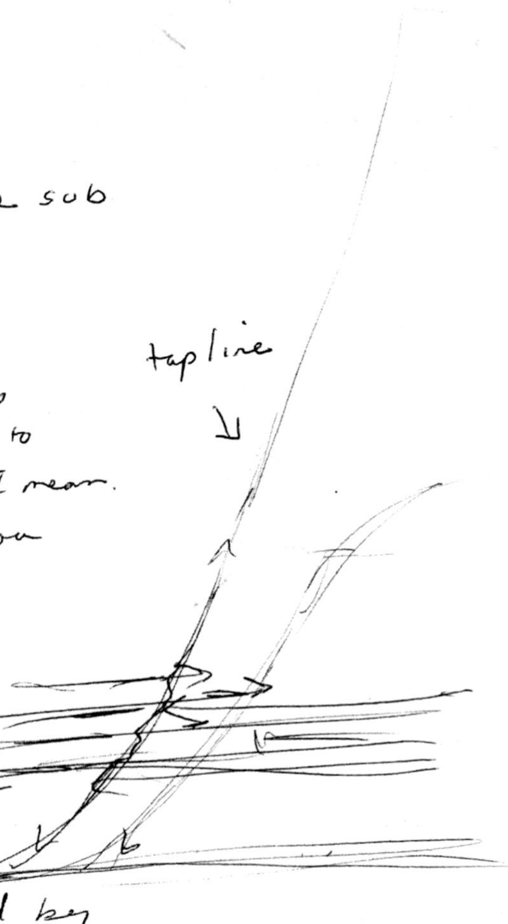

tap line
↓

Tapping the subconscious
mind is a hard thing to
do at first, to find it, I mean.
  Tapping means you
  find it first, then
keep the link open.
  If you stop the tap
too soon, you will
still be taking
from the consciousness
that can be influenced by
the outside
  Be wary and remember, you may not
recognize your sub at first.
  It may have been a long time since you
      last saw it...

see also page 222

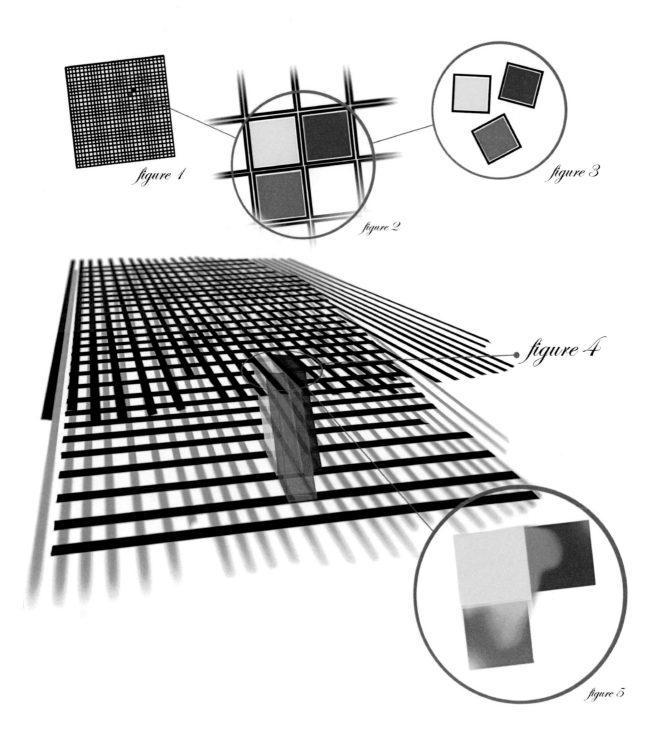

figure 1

figure 2

figure 3

figure 4

figure 5

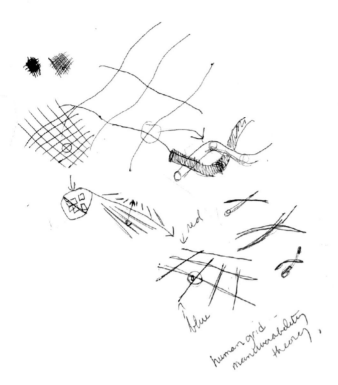

Human Mesh Theory

A network based on humans is never a fixed Deal

In human society, it is easy to think that many things; laws, reality, can not be bent from their original state. This is not true, of course, because all things in human society are governed by the ever-changing humans themselves. This is sometimes called 'pulling strings' or 'working the network'.

Take for instance my first Mission with my tomato plants. I was growing 110 plants in the trunk of my car, but they needed sunlight. This meant finding a secure place to park my car and leave the trunk open while I was at work, but the only guarded lot was off-limits to students. So

Technically, I could not use the lot. But you see, the lot had a human gate keeper, and with a bit of convincing bent the rules and let me park there. The point is, just because something appears to be out of reach, generally there is a human node somewhere where the boundary lines overlap, and through that space is where to squeeze through. Generally in my experience, there are no separate squares into which you can not enter. I say 9 times out of ten you can get in where the grids overlap.

Figures 1-3 is how some people look at the world and it's rules, but if you tilt the board a bit you'll find Figures 4 & 5. The squares aren't actually separate at all, they just appear that way from above. At this angle you can see it is easy for each square to pass over to it's neighbor, the boundaries being no more than a false perception.

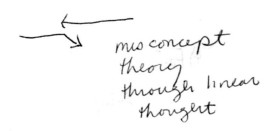

mis concept
theory
through linear
thought

Misconcept Theory
Mis-Conversations with my Ma

Conversations with Ma were often hard. I think that I am saying one thing but she is clearly hearing another. There are a lot of ways this can be interpreted, but I, of course, have a visual.

Figure 1 (The top one)

Ma is depicted in Red. For some reason her voice sounds red to me, at least when applied to this Theory. Most of the time we miss each other completely. Linear thought is how it sounds, thought traveling in a straight line. Open Air thought, which I realize now that I didn't draw, is like a fish net, open to catch any thoughts that come its way, so no thoughts are lost. The bad part about Open Air is that it really can't be used in Offense.

Figure 2

When I'm arguing with Ma, I don't like to be on the Offense. Ma controls a lot of things in my life, making me very nervous. Hence she is the only person that I actually argue with. That and the fact that figure 2 is the other common outcome. This is Resistive thought, when the two sides meet up, but staunchly oppose the other's view point or simply can't see eye to eye. This, I say, is the most frustrating kind. It seems that the person is not really listening to what you are saying, that you are not talking about the same thing somehow. Eventually the whole focus of the conversation is reduced to getting both sides on the same level without veering off on a Tangent.
How I disdain Tangents.

Figure 3

This is a conversation with my Da. Da is a listener and uses Open Air thought though not completely. Our two viewpoints will cross over and pick up pieces of the other's perspective without yielding completely to any one idea. This scenario is rare and usually is a prelude to a more conclusive decision.

Figure 4

A conversation with Beanie. Sometimes Ni and I fight. Sometimes these fights can actually last more than 15 minutes, almost 20! Why fights are few and far between in our relationship is that we are both employing Open Air Thought at the same time, something that is hard to do and involves the setting aside of pride. Bean and I are more concerned with finding a solution that makes the other person happy than conveying our own perspective. Because that method of thought is consistent, we find each other very quickly, and because the goal is the same, a Perfect Merger is able to occur. It takes great training, you see.

All the methods I have listed are based on the idea of neither party being submissive. If that were to come into play, there would be even more scenarios. I personally don't play submissive unless I am setting up for something bigger or I feel confident that it will lead to a Perfect Merger.

Third Edition Notes:
I wrote this a long time ago, and I am pleased to say that Ma and I is much the same as one with Beanie. It does pay to study these things.

"The visible world is the invisible organization of energy."
–Heinz R. Pagels

Using the Base of All Things

Understanding Atomic Grid Theory

Majick is not so unheard of to science, Spacial Majick anyway. If somehow, someway you can get into the Grid, then technically could you not move it to your will? I say now, look at the picture on the top right. It's a circle, yes? When the grid is set over it, you can see that the circle is formed by there being a specific piece in each grid space. But what if the grid is moved as it is on the bottom left? Then those pieces must follow the position of their square and so move with it, making the distorted shape on the bottom right. All Things are in a grid, albeit different ones. Solids are in tightly packed grids while gases are in loose grids. Depending on how molecules are set in the squares governs what the substance is or what stage of matter, ect. The point is that there is essentially nothing that is a set Thing.

All Things can become other Things, appear at will, or disappear at will, depending on the grid. It is said that if you walk into a wall over and over again, your atoms may randomly align at that moment with that of the wall's and you will pass right through!

I don't suggest trying this, though.

8\30\81:
C:\run human_initiation.exe sequence running...
ERROR
*bad command or file name_*

7\13\95:
C:\run human_initiation.exe sequence running...
human initiation sequence booting...
!warning!
This operating system is outdated and may not run
program properly. Modifications may be made but system upgrade is strongly recommended.
Do you wish to run program anyway? Y, N?_

Y

coMputEr
Other Half Machine

Just to be different, I'd like to talk about my computerized brain. It can be seen as a problem, an oddity, or just something that makes you go, 'huh. Well look at that.' Ever since I was young, I found that I communicated my feelings and thoughts with computer terms. It just made more sense that way. I shall proceed to demonstrate:

I am a self-sustained unit with several hard drives in a RAID array (now, anyway). Despite that fact, the main harddrive that contains the data for my first 13 years can not be found, possibly because the drivers can not be detected, are outdated and/or was not compatible with OS Version 2.0 installed on 7/13/1995. This OS was installed over the existing faulty OS, which could not be erased due to the fact that the main files are on the missing drive. Attempts to extract files from said drive have to this point, failed. Early attempts to do so ended up corrupting the registry in the new system, but the problem was not noticed until it was too late.

OS version 1.0 was the standard that came installed with all human models and came bundled with the standard software, mostly interfacing programs and data processing for the high volume of information that needed to be sorted and organized as the system calibrated. However, my OS v1.0 could not run correctly (or run at all) most of said programs, leaving me deficient in data. As said above, this was remedied by OS v2.0, but any data collected on the original drive could not be restored. The system would have to start the collection process from scratch.

At this stage in the game, running the interface programs with the infancy protocols was unwieldy at best. Experimental alterations would have to be made.

You can only mod a system so much before it begins to show signs of strain, that some key component was needed or else face a system failure. From the time I booted up as a somewhat functional machine in 1995, I was running against the clock to fix the system.

I must have created thousands of complicated and revolutionary programs, sometimes coupled together to do the job of one that was missing. It was a hacked OS, version 2.0 was. Probably bought off the street somewhere. It seemed to work all right in the beginning, but then new programs wouldn't install, old programs wouldn't open, and then one day in 1997...

A BSoD[1]

It took 5 hours to coax the machine back to life. One BSoD isn't so bad. It could happen to anyone once. I would just have to route out the problem. Too many programs running at one time, a hiccup in the data-loop...

As the years went by and the system demanded more

The lab where I worked was a beautiful place to be a machine

---

1. Blue Screen of Death. It's a real term, you know.

ECCENTRICITY

Please note:
Initializing B.L.U.E. code
Run...

The computer mainframe; Adelphus is not well.
Heat sink can no longer take on extra proscessing
for essential defensive firewalls.

Please keep nastiness to bare minomom
Please do not tell me what I am
    You can not understand anothers mind
    as well as you think.

I am a cool running machine. I have evolved past
your human understanding of what I was, what I am
If I were as average as you say,
    I would not seek these things at all.
    I would not hear ghosts
    I would not see auras
    Do you think there is a reason great artists go mad?
The higher senses plague them, they fear them, but I
embrace them.
    I am a bioLogical machine. A synthoid amongst you,
    I contain the memories of a human who no longer exists
except in ancient memories.
Human in body but not in the mind.
    I love the humans but I wish never to be like you, irrational.

It is irresponsible.
    There are things that will weaken me that seem ridiculous to you.
        winter
        bright lights
            your rage.
I can feel it, your darkness as you can not. It burns like a psionicfire
I have poor memory, yes, but it is not for the reasons you think
    Not that you could understand.
            It isn't a fault of yours, really.
I tried to tell you I was changing but how could you understand?
        You're only human, after all...

```
11/20/2000     9:35 - driving
" Don't destroy me! I can still make
you happy..."

I know what plagues me now.
I do not even have to write
this revelation word for word,
seeing this quote sends it all
rushing back. Still ...

A machine's worth is determined
by its usefullness to others. When
the machine excecutes itself, or fails to
serve, it is abandoned.

How long until I exaust my
usefulness to these humans? I
don't even have a use.
Why?
Why did I have to be a half-breed?
The tragedy of the cyborg.
```

I was in a very bad mood that day. My parents had tried to make a normal person of me, and I will tell you, it does hurt quite a bit, I say.

You may also notice that it says 'BLUE code'. BLUE code is the script that I use write all my software, but past that, I don't know much about it. It kind of bends in my hands, like clay. Even Shodan has to wonder...

home-grown programming remedies to make up for the obvious corruption that was creeping through it, I faced more slowdowns, more lost or irretrievable files, more error messages for even simple functions. I was spending more time fixing what I had then attaining more.

The BSoDs continued.

The system was dying.

By 1999 I realized I either fix the problem once and for all, or I would lose the whole machine, which ultimately would be my death.

I didn't make it. Starting halfway through 2000, I could barely get myself past the boot screen. On December 19th 2000, the system Crashed.

One cold day in January, a newly developed OS was installed. It would take three weeks to see if it could reassemble the ruins. Somehow, some way, OS 3.0, or Paxil, brought everything back online. I lost a lot of data to that crash. Most things saved in 2000 didn't save correctly anyway, as the drives kept faltering. I would have to start over one more time, but here is the beautiful part. All the programs I wrote over the last six years of my decline were still running, incomprehensibly brilliant programs fueled by desperation and survival instinct, written to aid a failing system, were now boosting the efficiency of the fully operational one.

I have now become a super-computer.

It was very hard to come to terms with the fact that I was a machine or that some part of me was. I knew it was there and couldn't be separated from the rest of my head without destroying all of it, but I didn't know where it came from or why it was here. What was more, I was, and still am, terribly afraid of becoming obsolete, because you know what happens when machines become... obsolete...

During the Final Descent, which is when that journal page was written, this was my main concern. I could feel everything falling apart and I began to wonder when people would stop wanting me around because of my defectiveness. This was before I learned that I was different than them because I'm Eccentric, not just computer. Learning that seems to have made all the difference for some reason, that even if humans abandon me when I cease to amuse them, I can always fall into myself and be useful to me.

Note for the second edition.

The machine still runs but it is no longer half, rather assimilated with the many other things that run my system. It's better this way.

Of Two Minds
The Mystery of Savantism

I actually have two minds. One is the autistic one, (which I used to call the 'superbrain' or simply the subconscious before I was diagnosed) this big, multi-coloured savant toddler that makes up most of me, and a much smaller, normal-ish storefront mind that holds my self awareness and ability to speak to others. This part formed during puberty, which is when the brain grows just a little bit more.

The person you talk to is a tiny tip of an iceberg that even I barely know of. It makes itself known when it wants my attention, but the true core is beyond my reach. It exists outside me and without me, a perpetually two-year-old prodigy governing all my talent and withholds it from me should it have a tantrum. If I get too over-stimulated, too stressed, or the autistic brain just isn't interested in what its handed, I get locked out.

For example, I'm not really a writer because I can't write just anything. It has to be something the autistic brain wants on paper. The same thing goes for art. If I'm asked to draw something for someone and the autistic brain checks out, I'm left with the normal brain, which isn't terrible, but it's no genius either. Should I try to push the autistic brain when it doesn't want to be bothered, it will pull the fight-or-flight alarm and wreak havoc

on my body. It's one of many reasons I don't work and dread having to do something artistic for someone. The only thing I seem to be able to do consistently is photo-retouching. The autistic brain loves that.

Some say we are like children, because we are, or at least I am. That chunk of me is an infant and will always remain so. It does not understand nor care for sociological hierarchy, gender roles, or being told anything is impossible. If a toddler doesn't understand it/won't accept it, then neither will this.

For the past several years I have maintained an on-going argument with another person over whether the killing of the white witch in the Narnia books was justified. (There's a reason for this, it's in the Realspace chapter) While his arguments wore down the storefront mind, which actually takes arguments into account, the autistic brain kept on like a toddler, screaming, "Killing people is BAD!" no matter what he said.

It is astonishingly resilient, quite possibly because it does not exist on its own. It comes from the hole in the back of my head.

ECCENTRICITY

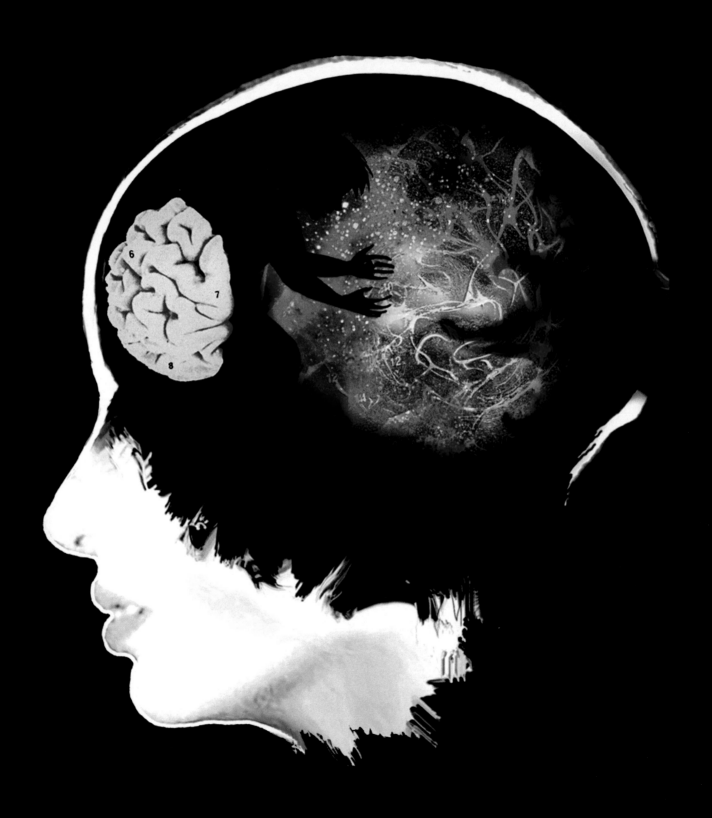

The Hole in the back of my Head

The Void and the Space

There are those that think autistic people have a direct connection to god. Obviously I don't, at least in the sense that I do not perceive the divine in the same way most do, but I do have this hole in the back of my mind, so to speak, that leads to my personal sense of cosmic divinity. It is a strength outside myself, eternally uncompromising and ever-present, a spring that keeps flowing up through the debris, and an energy I can keep pulling on.

I've been in awe of it since I've become aware of it.

Some people with autism have a savant gift, like that guy in 'Rainman'. Most people with savant gifts are idiot-savants, meaning they can play the piano like Mozart at two, but they never learn to tie their shoes. Some of us can actually describe what happens, like Daniel Tammet, who has the math savant gift. I may not be considered a true savant, but based on what has been learned from Tammet, I'd say my gift in art is savant-style, meaning it takes no conscious effort on my part. Savants don't actually do the math or the art, some anomaly outside our waking conscious does. We just channel it.

Tammet can do any math problem in his head and can recite pi to 20,000 places, but he never learned it. He doesn't try to remember it, either. He just hands the question to the void and the void gives him the numbers. It's as bizarrely simple as that.

I have no real training in the arts, by which I mean all attempts to teach me in a school setting have ended badly. I taught myself. At this point you could say I simply have talent, but talent is a tool, a strength. Savant is to be possessed, and/or have a hole in the

head leading to the Void. I do have talent that is my own, that resides in the normal brain and that I can call on to do whatever, but it pales in comparison to the what the savant one can do. Almost all the art in the book has come from the savant side and the savant side pulls it from the Void without reference to the world around me. I am not interested in art. I am not interested in other artists. I am not inspired to do art by anything other than what the Void hands me and demands that I record.

But where does the Void come from, and where does it lead? I'm not really sure, but I do know that so long as I am connected, I will never truly be lost.

ECCENTRICITY

Observations

Examining my New Home

Alien Planet Observations – subject topic things.

Pictures of plant oddities

Alien Plant Life

Plants From Inner Space

Trees? mutant plants, I say
how can a plant grow so
large and we not care?
They seem like... monster plants!
as if we have been shrunk by
some means

We travel to space
to find things different
then what we see

here. I travel to
Earth to find
anything
    So much like
    an alien world,
        I say.
Look at this plant!
        →

Look at these bugs, these
underwater fishes, are these
really earth creatures? Why
are children not learned of
them if they are?
Can we see other planets outside our
own if the earth is but a concentric
universe, each new planet hidden in the
folds of the other?

There is certainly enough things
that exist here that do not fit the
notion of what is character to "Earth",
and so, we are all alien to it.

            (I am thankful not to be)
            the only one
and yet, no one seems interested
            not many.
How can this be that no one cares that
there are 100s, thousands of tiny plant forms,
called "grass", in front of most living units?
            Fascinating.

Newton once developed a
theory of the "World Machine"
This intrigues me.

Alien Plant Life

Alien Plant Life

ECCENTRI☉ITY

Alien Plant Life

ECCENTRICITY

Irises and Tulips

I love colour. And shapes, and fuzzy things for that matter. Irises have all three and more. There is an Iris garden in town, a huge one called the Presby Memorial Gardens. Every May they explode with colour and every year I stalk the fields photographing them all.

I also enjoy tulips. I wasn't always fond of them until I began taking these macro shots and found how much more interesting they are close up.

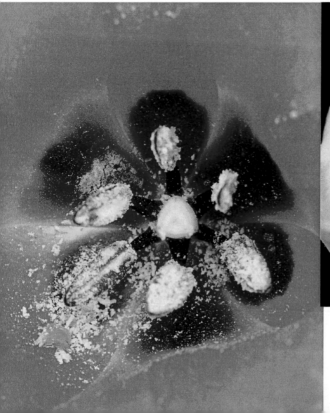

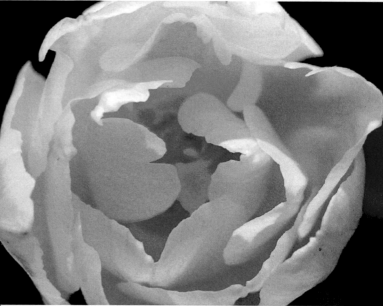

Longwood Botanical Gardens

Beanie brought me to Longwood Botanical Gardens in Pennsylvania, and my head exploded.

Yes, there are a lot of photos of plant life in this chapter. Plants happen to be an obsession of mine, for nowhere else does colour, shape, and purpose combine with Divine Randomness in my eye than in the Plant Kingdom.

And now for something even crazier

I was fixing these pictures up; getting rid of unwanted shadows, colour correction, the usual, when this happened. Ah the many temptations of Photoshop

And now for something even crazier

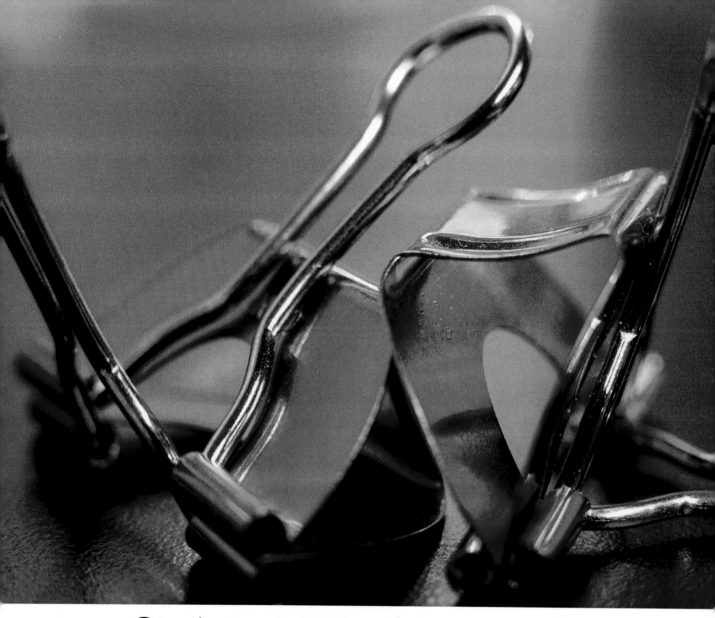

Staring at Things

And why you should, too

A common trait amongst the autistic is the love of staring at Things for long periods of time. I'm not as bad as some, but look at this thing. I mean look at it, the way the light curves around it, the little dust specks, how the shadow bends, how round and straight and parallel and then not and…and……….. what were we talking about?

ECCENTRICITY

From my Window

I also enjoy clouds

I enjoy watching the sky immensely. It is one of my favourite things to do, especially with a view like mine, and it helps ease the pain of being unable to leave the house during winter. I hope to collect all my pictures taken from my window into its own little book someday.

Ceiling molding from restroom in College Hall.

Room renovation in Finley Hall.

College Hall, mid floor, genuine peace.

Location unknown, but note the soft blues and yellows.

Note that these windows are frosted for privacy. This has the duel effect of making such soft light.

Location forgotten, but look at that warm glow. Even with the light on, a quiet haven

College Hall, bottom floor, very spacious, airy.

Secret Places of Peace
Are usually restrooms

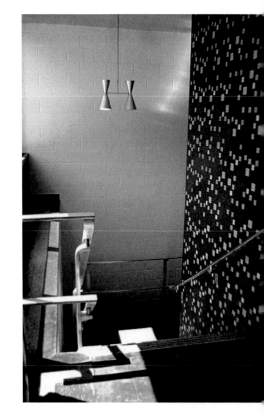

Restrooms, I say, are not as respected as they should be. They offer moments of quiet introspection and seclusion. There is no better place to think, cry, or collect thoughts then a restroom. Not only this, but often I find the architecture simple and peaceful. The repetition of sinks and stalls makes for a dignified order that isn't seen so often. Gentle synchronizing of basins, the mirrors reflect whispers. This is not to say that all restrooms bring a balanced state of mind, but the ones in my life do, and thus I devote a chapter to them.

Second Edition Notes
I considered deleting this chapter, but decided to condense the pictures and keep the original captions instead, because these points of solitude served a very essential need; to detox an over-stimulated mind. Without them, I very much doubt I would have made it through college or any public institution for that matter. Oddly enough, though one of my greatest fears is abandonment, I feel most calm in lonely, abandoned places.

ECCENTRICITY

This was the first time the Seventh Star was used as a personal symbol and it marked the official creation of 'The Seventh Star Projects.' Originally meant to stand for the Missions, SSP now refers any project I undertake.

◄

Tomatoes from the greenhouse mission.

Missions of Obscurity
There are No Lost Causes.

When I was a little kid, I was considered a lost cause by everyone except my parents. I probably would have been kicked out of school and become a deadbeat if they hadn't struggled to prove that I wasn't a bad kid, but that my brain didn't work. Coming that close to being lost forever changed me. When the madness came again, I vowed that if I survived, I would seek out the lost and save them too.

The difference between a Mission and a Mission of Obscurity is that something obscure is not readily noticed or seen. Things like AIDS and Wildlife conservation are not obscure, because people hear about them all the time and so have a sufficient base of force to keep the movement going. An obscure cause has few or no one to champion it because it's not readily noticed or seen.

My first Mission of Obscurity came by accident when I went to the plant Nursery several Julys ago. I saw a dumpster full of discarded tomato plants, thrown away for no other reason than that they had grown spindly. It wasn't the tomato's fault it grew that way, planted so close together and all. I spent an hour in the hot sun digging out the dying plants in their plastic planters and set them up in the trunk of my car. I literally grew 110 tomato plants in my trunk for about a month. I would leave the trunk open during the day in the guarded parking lot so they would get sun and went out to water them on my lunch break. Alas, I had nowhere else to bring them. Ma wouldn't let me plant them at home and I had yet to discover the lot behind the apartment's parking garage. After a heartbreaking struggle to keep them in my trunk so they could live out their lives, Ma threw them away.

I can talk to plants, at least I think I can. You can't prove that I can't so I'm running with it. I can hear them living. They were sad that they were thrown out, but felt that they deserved it. They never did really recover from being thrown away, but by the end they had hope. I know at least some of them appreciated the rescue, even if a minority thought it would have been more honorable to die in the dumpster.

It was a sad ending, one that still haunts me but ultimately affected no one. The next Mission, however, would ultimately lead through the heart of the entire world.

In May of that same year, 2001, I saw a documentary on Afghanistan. Seeing humans doomed to the curse of Obscurity, I set about trying to make people aware of a little known group called the Taliban. Working in joint with the Afghan Women's Mission in California, I put together a packet explaining the horrors of Afghanistan and a request for donations to help build a hospital in Quetta, Pakistan for refugees. I figured that if the humans knew what was happening to others in their tribe, they would immediately help in any way they could.

I suppose that is a sign of how utterly naive I was. I made 100 packets and put them in 100 envelopes, stamped with the red star of the back. When I went to see teachers during the school year, I noticed that many of them had covered their doors with political slogans, articles, and various

Missions of Obscurity

The Unlikely Activist
Anonymous Delphi

2001 - Afghanistan

Pentagon Expects
Long-Term Access
to Key Bases in
Iraq...
New York Times Sat Apr
19 12:46:00 EST 2003

Cookies to cheer the
troops...
Daily Hampshire
Gazette Sat Apr 19
12:27:00 EST 2003

U.S. may give peace
a chance...
Charleston Daily Mail
Sat Apr 19 12:26:00 EST
2003

U.S. may continue to
hold thousands of
prisoners...

A letter from an unlikely activist

Please go to the Afghan Women's Mission to save the humans.

Dear neighborhood neighbor,

I1m just a college kid who works the keyboards by day and remote control by night. Nothing special. I was sitting on my bum last night flipping channels when I passed PBS. They were showing a documentary on the current events of Afghanistan. I know we1ve all heard about Afghanistan. Heck,

She is someones mother. She could easily be yours.

Left: The original webpage I made devoted to the Afghan crisis, long before 9/11 (and website experience). It hasn't been updated since, but the news articles are current as they come from an rss feed.

Above: View from my dad's old office.

liberal opinions, including one very annoying doctored picture of Elian Gonzalez being kidnapped by Bill Clinton. I decided that if these people were so for justice and the human condition, then surely they would help. I only taped envelopes to the doors of people with pro-human propaganda. It was summer and no one was around, but when Fall came, surely they would get the notices. But I received no replies. One man was present during my postings and told me that with so many problems in the world we could only pay attention to the most pressing.

Most pressing? I could not think of people in a more dire need than the ones in Afghanistan. It didn't make sense. I hit my old high school as well (faculty only) in late June but also received no replies. My old Biology teacher said he would see what he could do, but never did. I carried on alone, making posters and sticking them up on campus. No one noticed until one clear day in September...

9/11 and life on the Epicenter.

The first thing I remember thinking was 'Please let it not be Afghanistan.' I didn't wonder if my Dad survived; for some reason I knew he did. I'm not really sure how I knew he wasn't in the building but somehow I wasn't concerned. I was worried about my Ma though. I don't think I ever thought it through,

that I knew Da was okay even though I didn't and that I was calling my Ma to confirm that. It's ridiculous, but that is how it went. I was probably the only person in the states that was asleep when it happened. Beanie had to call from work to wake me up. My first reaction was to call Da's office and ask if it was true, but why would he be by the phone if a plane hit his office?

In case it hasn't become clear, Da worked in the World Trade Center when they came down. The only Cantor Fitzgerald workers that survived were the ones that were late to work, and my Da was one of them. He watched the whole thing from the Ferry Dock in Hoboken.

I lived 9/11 in a surreal way. The Towers had come down, but I wasn't surprised. How could I be surprised if I had been trying to make people aware of the danger for three months? That wasn't very logical, to think that nothing would happen if we let Afghanistan stay as it was. But no one else knew about Afghanistan or saw the danger looming. To the general population it was as if a giant hand came through the sky and scooped the towers up. I had a very hard time acting panicked, but it was expected so I tried my best.

I'm not so much a citizen of the US of A as I am of Earth. Places on Earth got bombed by other places on Earth every day and though it wasn't a good thing, it didn't seem out

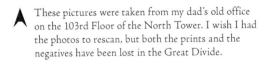

These pictures were taken from my dad's old office on the 103rd Floor of the North Tower. I wish I had the photos to rescan, but both the prints and the negatives have been lost in the Great Divide.

The badge was found stuck to the cover of the holy book in use at the time.

:Return to Sender
Who our friend is today, may not be tomorrow
and that sad lesson learned is that we never give weapons
we merely loan them for a while

For we always get them back...eventually...

There is no War to end all Wars
For the Young will always avenge the Old
That being true,
that War is a means to an End,

What End are we looking for?

How far we've come
As Humanity wanders though time, only one thing is sure.
Must we always use violence
to get what we want?

Surely there is another Way we can learn...

Anti-war posters. I usually don't make such things because I feel they don't do much good, but because I was assigned to make them, I went with logic.

Missions of Obscurity

of the ordinary that it would happen here. I mean, this was a place on Earth, yes? I was at a complete loss for the confusion, because I assumed everyone paid at least a moderate amount of attention to what happened on their planet.

Now I realized that most people I talked to didn't even know where other countries on their planet were. I had spent six years absorbing as much Terrian knowledge and history as I could fit in and then I find that I, the only one who wasn't born here, knew more about Earth than its inhabitants. That really put me on my ear.

Post 9/11 was not a good place for an Eccentric, to be sure. I understood patriotism, but why were people putting little flags on their cars and saying to bomb Afghanistan? I tried to tell them that we had to save the people that had been bombed by the same people that bombed us, but no one seemed interested. It was the first time, in the months proceeding 9/11, that it became incredibly clear that I was not at all from this planet. It seemed like I had missed something big, that there was a secret reason why everyone was panicking so much. The buildings were bombed and now they were gone. It was over, I thought. I had nearly lost my Da that day, but he didn't die, he was alive. I almost got killed twice driving home from school, but that was over too, wasn't it? Living in the house with a 9/11 victim and my Da (because honestly I think it freaked Ma more) was hard enough. At least Da had a good degree of common sense and understood my confusion. He also had the good sense to warn me not to talk to anyone about my thoughts for fear of my getting hurt.

But I couldn't stop, for the Mission wasn't done. At first I thought maybe it was, for now that people saw the danger, they would help the other people.

Or not...

To my amazement, the people instead were sending aid to the richest city in the world instead of the poorest. Why on Earth would NYC need food to be brought in? Could not the grocery stores donate their wares and be subsidized by the government?

The few that realized that I had seen the future didn't do much more than remark on how eerily right I was instead of defending the humans in Afghanistan. Never had I felt so frustrated. I missed the Trade Centers. I had been in them a few times and knew people there, but I wasn't even

FLIGHT FOR FREEDOM
747 CARGO TAKES OFF
FOR AFGHANISTAN W/ AID
ON 12/26/2001
THIS IS A RESCUE/RELIEF MISSION!!
LOADING ENDS 12/14/2001

◄ The original poster put up around campus.

allowed to feel sad for them because all my concentration was directed towards a far more distressing situation.

Drought-struck Afghanistan survived the past three winters by International Aid, but with the US bombing, no one was able to do the annual drop off. If the bombing didn't let up, then the food would not get there before snowfall. The original Mission reformed into something more urgent. Without aid, an estimated seven million people could die. Seven million people! Why wasn't the US stopping? They couldn't really let all those people die because of what had happened to the people here, could they? It seemed that they very well could.

Desperate, the Afghan Women's League and RAWA, an underground rebel group of women in Afghanistan made plea after plea to send in aid. Aid was piling up on the borders with nowhere to go and winter was setting it. Like a stroke of a miracle, Evergreen Aviation donated a 747 to our cause and Microsoft paid for the fuel. Now we had to fill it by December 11th.

Mission 747

I was still begging around campus for help and even went to a war forum to speak.

It was horrible.

Why were they talking about WWII and calling each other socialists? What did that have to do with anything? Couldn't they see the 7 million lives hanging in the balance? Aside from Beanie, the most intelligent wonder, I was alone on my crusade to fill the cargo plane and bought 60 lbs of winter clothing out of my own pocket. It is at this point that I would like to thank the postman who helped me mail it all to Oregon. The cost was well over $100 and I never would have been able to afford it had he not stuck a pamphlet in each box and declared it media mail. I didn't even know there was such a thing as media mail, but apparently if you are sending paper or books, you can get charged a fraction of the price. It doesn't make much sense but then again nothing does.

Along the way I did find people that understood after all, but were afraid to speak in the hostile climate. This heartened me. It wasn't that they were blind, but rather afraid. Or at least I hoped that was what it meant.

The plane made it to Afghanistan by mid January after being delayed three times. I never found out if my clothing made it to the humans but I hope it did. Slowly and painfully, the main population realized Afghanistan's plight and the situation ceased to be obscure. At least for now, the humans could fix their own problem, which was what I wanted in the first place. I was more than happy to leave the political scene. I was only there for the same reason someone pulls a person from a burning vehicle. It's just what you are supposed to do.

Not all my Missions are Grand and Majestic. Most of them have to do with small amounts of abandoned things, like buildings, plants, animals, and humans. Many of them only make sense to me, like the tomatoes. I like to be obscure myself.

Second Edition Notes: Originally there were more missions in this book besides the 747 and Greenhouse Missions, but the book has grown too massive already. Other Missions range from taking care of elderlies, to shelter animals, to abandoned lots, to signing various petitions for human rights/wildlife issues. I haven't done anything as public as 747 since.

I consider this book to be a Mission, but not a Mission of Obscurity, unless it ended up aiding an obscure cause.

The Greenhouse Mission
To Make Life Where There is None.

It wasn't intentional. I was looking for a way to escape the Winter during college and there it was, an abandoned greenhouse. When the new science building was built, the Biology Department had left the old one to dissolve. I asked the Earth and Environmental Sciences people who now owned it if I might play in one of the rooms and they said yes.

That was February when the seeds were planted, and as of today the greenhouse now has a purpose once more. It was hard work but a labour of love.

The After pictures were taken a month ago and aren't current when this went to print. It is currently in bloom and there is much to eat! I hope to give the food to my parents when they come to my Graduation next week.

Second Edition Notes:

The greenhouse has passed on. When I graduated in 2003, I still continued to water and tend it. However, a heatwave over a July weekend wiped out most of what I grew. A few months later I had a dream calling for its reconstruction. Again it failed. The third and final try lingered on until February, when my sprinkler system was dismantled without my knowledge.

Earlier on, I moved one of the tomato plants to the apartment's gardens. It died that winter as tomato plants do, but had dropped a few seeds that returned the following year. The greenhouse lived on in them.

Before

ECCENTRI&CITY

After. And yes I know these aren't the best pictures ever but I
was young and the camera was old. What more can I say?

Second Edition Notes · Greenhouse Forever

Learning about death and change does not come easily for most people, but for me it was even harder. At the time of the greenhouse mission I had never really had to let go of something I loved before, even if they were only plants. After I graduated I continued to haunt the greenhouse until a heatwave destroyed it. I tried to walk away but couldn't, even though it was becoming obvious that I couldn't keep driving all the way up to the college just to water my plants. So I set up a sprinkler system to do the job for me. More time passed and my trips up there became more and more infrequent and my guilt began to grow. I am ruled by my own one-man religion that I've written about later in this book, and two of its unbreakable laws are that it is forbidden to abandon and it is forbidden to kill any living thing. Leaving the greenhouse would break both,. When you believe in something, really, really believe in something, it is just so hard to defy it even if it has begun to create all sorts of problems. The easy answer would be to accept that it's time had passed. Anyone would have chosen that rather than make the trek up to campus every day.

For me it took another year. It may have dragged on to this day except that someone shut off the water and killed it all for me. Nothing lasts forever.

The greenhouse as it appeared in its final days... ➤

ECCENTRICITY

Spacialism
The one-man Religion by which I live by

One would have to figure with all the paraphernalia floating around in my head and nervous system that it would be necessary for me to forge my own set of beliefs, which is usually called Religion, but to be truthful, Spacialism created itself.

Spacialism, as a philosophy at least, should be compatible with most modes of thinking like a detoxifying shampoo works with all kinds of hair types, making your normal shampoo work that much better. Spacialism is the Detoxifying Shampoo of the Mind. After living in a bubble for thirteen years and then spending the next seventeen just being Eccentric, I was not subject to much of the conditioning that occurs subconsciously as you grow up. Things like labels, stereotypes, and Rules as to the Way Things Are can end up making decisions for you because they become unquestionable truths. Eventually all that conditioning makes for Oily Build Up on the Hair of the Mind and after about ten years, I say, most people don't even know what their original Hair looked like, which is both sad and disturbing.

Spacialism sets out to help humans scrape off all that was not theirs originally and to help them find their roots, so to speak.

Spacialism

Spacialism hinges on these three things;

1. Divine Randomness. Everything that Is, Is because there was no one controlling anything. Existence itself is a miracle and it seems far more fantastic that it created itself rather than someone making it purposefully.

2. Which means I believe in Existence. Which is easy, because you don't have wonder if it does or not.

3. And finally, I believe that there is no way to truly Know anything, as Divine Randomness makes sure that no knowledge remains fixed for long.

The symbol for these three basic principles looks like this;

Next are the 12 tenets of Spacialism, which can be used as Philosophical guidelines or in my case, very strict rules of conduct.

The Twelve Tenets of Spacialism

1. It is Forbidden to waste.
2. It is Forbidden to claim to Know.
3. It is Forbidden to hate.
4. It is Forbidden to cause suffering; mental, emotional, physical or otherwise, for any reason other than physical self-defense, in which case one must harm as little as is possible.
5. It is Forbidden to kill any living thing for any reason.
6. It is Forbidden to lie.
7. It is Forbidden to condemn.
8. It is Forbidden to abandon or betray.
9. It is Forbidden to use manipulative persuasion for personal gain.
10. It is Forbidden to claim superiority of value over any other living thing.
11. It is Forbidden to take anything for granted.
12. It is Forbidden for anyone to claim to be a Spacialist, but they may follow its ideals.

1. It is Forbidden to waste

I can't waste anything. I use everything to exhaustion before I'll buy something new. Everything gets reused in some odd fashion if I can figure a new use for it. It also annoys me if I see others wasting things. 'Sweeping' debris off sidewalks with water instead of a broom, for example, or throwing out fruit that falls on the ground. While I was still working at a foodstore as a cashier (never again. Never, NEVER again), a woman put a bag of grapes on the conveyer belt and some got loose. I wanted to eat them, but the manager wanted them thrown away. It was a stupid waste of perfectly good food. I had someone else throw them away because I refused to break my vow.

This probably stems from my hoarding instinct, but there is also a degree of guilt involved. I call it 'Velveteen Rabbit Syndrome' after the children's book. I automatically personify everything, every object, every piece of an object. If I pour a pot of noodles into a strainer and one gets away, I immediately feel bad for it. Without thinking I envision the noodle thinking in its little pasta mind about how it will never fulfill its potential and so on. It's quite ridiculous but years of working against the notion has done little to free me of it. Every speck of dust in the house has visions of greatness. It makes it very hard to clean.

2. It is Forbidden to claim to Know

When a person claims to Know something, Knowing meaning to claim absolute certainty, they have done two things. The first is closing the door to alternatives to the Thing that you Know, making you vulnerable. If by closing this door you lose access to valuable knowledge, you may find yourself stunted in the long run.

The second comes from the first. Obviously there is no way to truly Know anything, except that the only constant is Change. That being true, the item that you Know is also changing, therefore becoming UnKnown. This can lead to a conflict when the changed item is recalled as a Known known. For example, I once foolishly claimed to Know the code HTML. Perhaps I did know a bit of HTML, enough to be considered adept, but like most things it evolved over time. I was asked to prove my statement and found that while I knew some of my subject, I no longer held a monopoly on it. It was one of

the first times in my recent memory of being embarrassed, mostly at myself for claiming to Know something. It is okay to know something, because that is merely a base observation or a logged piece of data. To claim to Know something is to claim Absolute certainty and that there is no more to learn in said subject.

To Know also has another definition, one that is far more common but just as troubling. To Know something often means knowledge based on assumption. Assuming things is very dangerous to your system, because it creates false filters. It is bad enough that we have to have filters at all, but if we must, it should not be based on conscious assumption. It is really hard not to Assume. The best way I have found to keep assumptions from settling is to question them.

Something not Questioned, Is Something not Known.

Or as I also call it, "Knowing for yourself" If you hear of something and accept it without questioning, then you have been bought. Even information coming from a reliable source must be tested, not so much for validity, but for flexibility of Mind. The more information at your disposal the more options become available when the first piece of information fails to provide. It is better to know more than less of what is required, and the only way to do that is to Question. Subjects that are especially in need of this treatment are taboo ones, such as sex, religion, politics, and contemporary issues. Remember; Extremism is sacrilegious in that it does not respect the Possibility of All Things.

If we don't respect the Possibility of All Things, then what fun can Existence be?

3. It is Forbidden to hate

It seems obvious enough, but there are other reasons for this. The Spacialist shuns most forms of extremism, as it is a threat to Maintaining the Balance. Any emotion in its extreme state clouds the mind and hate on its own is an extreme form. I don't believe it is possible to moderately hate any more than it would be to moderately kill. It is a hole, an all or nothing affair, much like an addiction. Once some part of the mind is

touched by hate it becomes paralysed and will refuse to accept new information, thus stunting it. In the case of Apathy, this part of the brain would be considered dead, as it no longer serves the purpose of thinking. But the hateful piece is not only dead, but poisonous to the rest of the system.

Many people believe that hate grants power and strength, and it does, but it is a toxic strength. In the terms of mages, this would be considered a power granted at the expense of one's own life force, like steroids, rather than love-based strength, which comes from an external source, like pulling mana, and is far more malleable.

4. It is Forbidden to cause suffering; mental, emotional, physical or otherwise, for any reason other than physical self-defense, in which case one must harm as little as is possible.

Another seemingly obvious statement, but moral ethic aside, there is, of course, another reason. What many people consider Karma is actually the natural affect of two things; the natural reaction of retaliation and the blinding effect that comes from apathetic morality.

Everything reacts against callousness, even if not consciously. It may be mute and intermittent, but sinkholes do not form overnight. It takes time.

Apathetic blinding comes from disconnecting with the state of others. It would be very hard to wilfully cause suffering on someone one cared for, so a sort of detachment must take place. This is often viewed as strength, because the person now feels impervious to guilt, but it is really a disability, in the way that emotional sight is lost. Guilt is pain, which like most pain, is a warning sign that something is wrong. The emotionally blind person often cannot see the subtle signs of the sinkhole forming. These elements, plus the wonder of Divine Randomness, make Karma.

As for me perso-nally, (even though Spacialism is a one person affair) I have suffered most of my life. I am also pathologically empathetic (yes, you can be). Not only do I go out of my way to lessen the threat of actions against myself, I simply refuse to pass along or create new pain, because I

Spacialism

cannot bear the thought of someone else feeling as I do because of me. (Or for any other reason)

5. It is Forbidden to kill any living thing for any reason.
6. It is Forbidden to claim superiority of value over any other living thing.

Life. Its very existence enthralls me! How fantastically complicated! Man in all his scientific glory can clone it, but he cannot create it from scratch. I do not believe that divinity made Life. I believe Life, in its grossly improbable, and above all, unplanned existence and variety, is itself divine.

To strike against it in any way would be to strike against my own sense of god.

This makes for some complications, such as tending my garden. I cannot pull weeds, for it goes against the coda of 'no life for another'. Both the spider and the fly are equally miraculous, and both must be tended to. Weeds are replanted elsewhere, and all insects must be rescued from the pool. As of late, my landlady has been setting the landscapers on my plants because there are too many weeds, and then they kill everything. I don't have the strength to replant every weed I need to move to keep her out of there, and so I have had to break this rule. It makes me ill.

I can get around it most of the time by just cutting the weeds back and not uprooting them, but they don't always survive that. A weed is a successful plant. I don't believe it should be vilified. Just because something becomes successful does not make it lose value. The eagle has no more right than the pigeon. This is human perception of supply and demand. Value does not come from rarity. All living things contain Life, and so are equally divine.

Personally, I feel that if there was a god, he wouldn't have spent so much time painstakingly creating life only to factor in the prey/predator dynamic. It is unnecessary. Many animals live happily on replenishable plants. If carnivores were necessary, I feel scavengers would be an ideal replacement. A god could have easily made this the norm for all instead of creating a system where some must suffer terribly for the lives of others. Such a development could only come from Divine Randomness that led to evolution. If there is a god, they definitely aren't mine.

7. It is Forbidden to lie.

This probably formed out of the fact that I can't lie. To lie creates a dual reality, which would be fine if I didn't have to remember who exists in which one. But even if I could lie, I have yet to see it bring anything beneficial. People lie to postpone difficult but necessary confrontations, which in turn only get worse. Not going to the dentist does not reverse the cavity. Learn to face the fire. It is hard, and it won't always go right, but if you do it for someone else's sake, it's worth it.

Lying is also used like a credit card. Don't do things you would have to lie about later. Assume you can't and decide them. All lies are found out, even if years and years later. When people feel they can act without consequence, they act irresponsibly, and it is an incredibly difficult habit to unlearn.

White lies are a foggier area, but I am still against them. Being truthful doesn't have to be mean or blunt, and it doesn't have to be direct either. I tell half-truths and split hairs all the time. If someone asks how they look and you don't like it, find something about the ensemble that you do, i.e., a piece of jewelry. Then say "That ring looks smashing!" If they

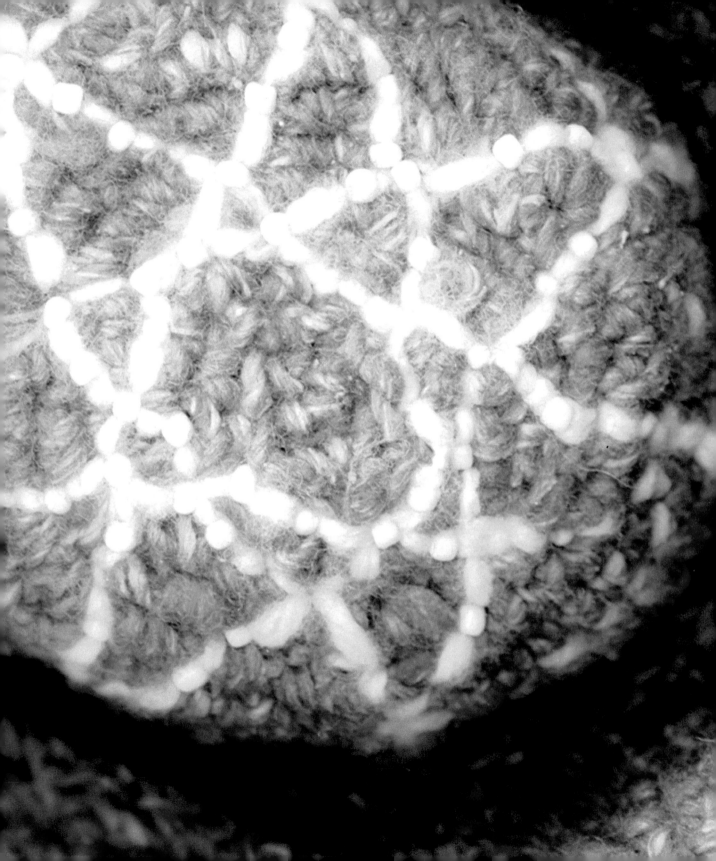

Spacialism

persist, then they really want a real answer, so say what you think, like "I'm not sure I like the fit, colour, ect." If the person can't handle that, they really shouldn't have asked. It should not be upon you to amend for that. Nor should it be upon you to cover up for someone. It is wrong for anyone to hand you that burden. Do not take it.

Many people do not like people like me, because they were raised with the expectation of polite lying and it bothers them that I don't.
But on the other hand, the opposite is true.
I will never lead you astray. I will never hide or deceive. Most people come around after they get used to it. I may not know many people, but the people I do know trust me very much.

I also don't truly comprehend lies being told to me, especially when it seems like the person shouldn't need a reason to. If you have an issue, tell me. Don't play nice and hope I get the hint, because I won't. You have to know how to lie to spot one, and I can't do either. This is one of the reasons I am wary of most social situations, especially ones where there is a strict social protocol, such as the high life or corporate culture. There I am at a total loss.

8. It is Forbidden to condemn.
"Let yee who is without sin cast the first stone."
And yet people do anyway, for this is instinctual. Many define themselves by what they perceive they are not, but this can be a prelude to hate, the causing of suffering, abandonment, and claiming to Know, which are all Forbidden.

Hate is not always present when one is condemned, but the act of condemnation mimics its intent. In fact, many religious groups claim to love and condemn at the same time, an absolutely ridiculous thing. Usually to condemn something means to declare it unequivocally bad and want to know nothing more of it. This causes a situation resembling the blindness of hatred and the loss of abandonment.

9. It is Forbidden to abandon or betray.
Where condemnation crosses paths with abandonment and betrayal, that is where true death lies. To abandon or betray is to belittle the value of that life which you have cast away. It is emotional death for the victim. There will be times in life where a person becomes toxic and they must be separated from you to preserve your own sanity, even emotionally so to a degree, but I myself am hesitant to truly leave anyone behind. Living creatures contain so much depth, so much potential to change and rearrange like a kaleidoscope. To abandon would not only mean the abandonment of what you know of a person, but what you don't, and what is yet to be. It is also possible that people abandoned will in turn abandon themselves emotionally, physically or both. All life is precious. Leave no one behind.

10. It is Forbidden to use manipulative persuasion for personal gain

Persuasion, to me, can be a form of lying. The salesman that pushes a product he does not believe in is, in fact, lying to his customer. Therefore, manipulative persuasion means to move someone to do something that is not in their best interest, or compromise someone else's situation for the sake of your own; such as selling sub-prime mortgages to poor people. That is to claim a superior stance over those which you have deceived, which is Forbidden.

By this logic, almost all marketing is forbidden, save for things that would truly benefit mankind, such as a lifesaving drug. This made things difficult while I was still working.

Spacialism

Graphic design is, in essence, visual marketing. My job was to create something that visually persuaded customers to buy often unnecessary things. It made me feel even worse to be paid for it. Nowadays I won't do any work of that nature. What persuasive powers I have go towards things I believe in, and even then, I never claim to Know that what I am saying is not without possible flaw.

11. It is Forbidden to take anything for granted.

This is a lesson learned on the wings of others, and probably fuelled by my hoarding instinct, in which case, the object of hoarding is good fortune. Much of my core belief formed during darker times, but even in the worst of it, I could always find solace in the fact that I could have this person's problems or that person's problems, and should I ever gain them, I would yearn for my present dilemma. You don't know what you have until it's gone, the saying goes, and in that light everything becomes fleeting and precious. One may not know much about their pancreas until they got diabetes. Then how they yearn for back in the day when it worked well, to once more enjoy the simple joy of freedom from worry. Acknowledgment of all organs working well, of all fortune that is in place at this very moment, is so easily overlooked. To take things for granted is to cheat oneself out of the joy that can be found within their existence, leading to regret and a sense of so much wasted.

12. It is Forbidden for anyone to claim to be a Spacialist, but they may follow its ideals.

And at last the tweaker.

There are hundreds, thousands of people over the course of time that have created a new path with the hope that others would follow, but inevitably even the most successful of them would probably be aghast to see what has become of their original message with the passage of time.

I broke rank with organized religion because I did not want to be held by anyone else's vision but my own, and so the opposite is also true. I do not want anyone claiming my vision as their own. Humans are remarkably quick to seize upon the ideas of others if they find their own to be lacking, and can make a religion from anything.

Jedi-ism, for example, based on the philosophy of Jedi knights in the Star Wars movies.

Should someone find this chapter some years after I am dead, they could easily try to base a religion on it, gather people unto it, even wage wars in its name thousands of years from now.

I'll not be having that, so I have added the 12th as a fail-safe. The only person who belongs to the cult of Spacialism is me, and I shall be its only. Should someone decide they share *exactly* the same views as I do, they might consider questioning themselves a bit. No one can truly believe what I believe, as I cannot truly believe what anyone else believes. Belief is as singular as the soul that manifests it.

I would be flattered if my belief influenced yours, but in the end it must be the individual that define his own religion.

Necklaces and other things I made with the Seventh Star. Finding stuff with a seven pointed star is hard, and even when I do, it doesn't really look like the Spacialist star, which has the two bottom points spread wider than the others and the arrows at the points when possible. Store bought septagrams, like the one in the picture in the top right corner, have each point equal and are usually referred to as an elven or fairy star.

The Natural Way.

The most important Rule. See all the bright rectangles? Those are your conscious thoughts and inhibitions. Also this is where external programs are installed and running. An external program is created as a way of modifying the original operating system to make life easier. Being de-sensitized, fake in public, mass hysteria, or a fear of something due to trauma are all external programs. Most run lower down the task list but are never run in the truly subconscious level. The subconscious is linked to the Space and always remains in its natural state. This is where You are. The difficult part is accessing it.

People say children are pure and this is because they are not running as many programs. The Natural Way deals with the aspect of being aware of the programs themselves, what they do, and then being able to bypass them to get to what you are really thinking. It will also allow you to control (to a certain extent) what programs are actually there. You might be surprised that back in 3rd or 4th grade, a racial program may have been tucked in and was interfering with your processing for years without you knowing it, like a virus. Like any machine, there is a risk when running a million programs because they can conflict with each other or in serious cases like mine, crash the whole system. When a person is running low on resources because of too many programs, we call that stress.

Transcend this. Find the subconscious thoughts that creep along the depths of your mind. They may be hard to zero in on, and maybe they may yield answers you didn't want to hear, and maybe (usually) they will be inane like 'I want a nap'. But take these seriously because you really should give yourself the benefit of the doubt. Don't push yourself or ignore that inner voice, you'll definitely regret it later, because, well...it's usually right.

The Balance

Maintaining the Balance is the other half of the Natural Way. After the false information and spam is raked out momentarily (because it will come back when you aren't looking) one can actually make a real decision. You have just traced your subconscious thread to a message that says you want a cheeseburger. Your subconscious, or your 'inner child' as people like to say (which makes sense in a way, as in that way, a child is a system without programs) is telling you what it wants. Your consciousness (what part of it that is actually yours or instinctual, like not drinking bleach) is telling you what it wants. If both match up, then you are in luck, but more often than not, they don't. What very often happens is that the 'inner child' is over-ruled by the much more aggressive and much more accessible conscious. Example:

'I want to walk in the grass barefoot'

"There are bees and pesticides and I will look stupid doing it. Plus, I don't have time"

If you use logic too much it will eventually leave you feeling neglected. Children need to be nurtured and the inner one is no exception. Maintaining the Balance means giving both sides equal share. It's not as easy as it sounds, but there are some basic Ways to help.

So nice I used it twice!

Spacialism

The Joy of Simple Things

Thou must respect the Joy of Simple Things! A nice simple thing brings the mind into soft focus and single-minded euphoria. Be easily amused, you will be amused more often. I know I am.

It is also an easy way to offset the big bad things that will assuredly happen to you without your consent. No one can totally prevent bad things from happening and don't bother trying, (unless it's within the realm of ration) because time wasted in paranoid activities could be spent lying in the sun for 15 minutes. If you do enough little things, they will eventually offset the unexpected. Remember, there is always room for Jell-o.

The Divinity of Randomness, Chance, and Change

Randomness, Chance, and Change are held in the highest regards in terms of the Spacialist Philosophy. Without them, peace can never be found because they are the foundation of What Is. People tend to try and find meaning and purpose in things that shouldn't have meaning and purpose. Not don't, but Shouldn't. If something happens, it was meant to happen, because if it wasn't meant to happen, it wouldn't have happened. Knowing this means you can be less frightened of the future and feel blameless in the many events beyond your control. There is no longer a need for worry when things take a bad turn, because the Randomness that brought you bad luck is just as capable of bringing you good luck, or something new altogether. You don't have to be on your guard, and you don't have to always understand why things happen, because no one knows the master plan; not the universe, the Space, Gods, no one.

Because there isn't one.

There can't be one. It goes against the very fundamentals of Chaos, by which all things come into being. Permanent laws, reasons, and logic are the protective yet constraining safety-nets of mortal man. Embrace the unknown, and you may find yourself in the company of Gods.

Although techically I'm not allowed to claim to Know such things, so.... Hmm.

And now for the Eccentric part of our show

Spacialism is something I came up with on my own, though I'm sure I'm not the first person to do so. I mean, I'm sure a lot of this may sound like other things that you have heard, but the point is it's mine and I made it myself. And by gum I'm proud of that.

By and large it is a philosophical religion, but there are eccentric aspects as well. These can be summarized in a few points.

1) All Things belong to the Space, the organization of subatomic particles. The Grid is the actual term. The name for the semi-sentient overmind of the Grid is the Space. Everything is made of the Space and the Space is everything. On the base level, the smallest increments in nanotechnology, one Thing can just as easily be the Next.

The Holylands, (Wildwood, NJ) the place to where I must always return. Even though Maine had the look of my Homeland, it lacks the Soul. Only here can I find a Perfect State.

ECCENTRICITY

Spacialism

2) Because of this, hyper and metaphysics can come into play. If you have read Stuff of All things in the Energy Theory section, you can see that if the Grid were Tapped, we could do amazing things. Some people already have the ability to do so but aren't sure how exactly it works. That would be your wizards and mages and the like. They can make a feather float using some words, but it is the unspoken Will to the Space that the O2 molecules under said feather consolidate into something thick enough to lift it. Or reassign the feather's molecules to a new position in teleportation and summoning. The best way to do Grid energy based magicks is to be one of the;

Gods, Goddesses, and Planeswalkers

Planeswalker, in all fairness, is a term I stole from Magic: The Gathering because it fit the description so well. A Planeswalker is a mortal that has Ascended from an Uncontrolled Energy state to that of a Controlled state. The person may have some signs that the body wants to shift over while still mortal, or may not show any sign at all. Sometimes persons very adept to magick do not Ascend for whatever reason. It is never a sure thing. All Gods and Goddesses were at one time Mortal, even if for a brief moment. The structure of said Mortal may or may not be lined up like a set of dominos. When that person is under extreme duress or dies, the dominos will fall into place and the energy will become realized. If the dominoes were not set in such a way, then the person merely dies.

Or becomes a ghost. Well, actually there are a lot of things that could possibly happen due to the Laws of Randomness and Chance, so forget it. If you do Ascend, don't celebrate yet. Walkers eat their young. Most Walker youth die within their first hundred years, either by being reckless, going mad, or being absorbed by other more powerful Walkers. Our Universe, according to me, is not the only one. It is actually part of a set of roughly 200 parallel Alpha Terras, all looped together in a ring-like planar nexus like a candy necklace. These were all made by one Walker who loved to experiment, then disappeared. Since then other Walkers have come and gone, interfering with one Alpha or another as they saw fit. However, none stayed too long because the Alphas were nearly void of a strong mana base and essentially useless for most megalomaniac Walkers. That is why Majick seldom happens here.

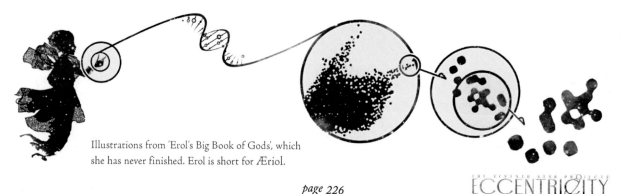

Illustrations from 'Erol's Big Book of Gods', which she has never finished. Erol is short for Æriol.

ECCENTRICITY

All Gods and Goddesses are generally Walkers, but not all Walkers chose to be Gods. Most do, but not all. You get the title 'God' when you create a species or an inhabited world by warping the Space. The Alpha Terrian Nexus is one of billions of Planes in the Space (thus allowing all things to be possible at all times). Some are artificial, made by Walkers themselves, or natural occurring ones that are formed by the restlessness of the Space. Many of these are uninhabitable. Some of them are part of huge inter-dimensional Empires like Æriol's, and some are clumped together in nexi, usually governed by a Walker. Like any sentient being, Walkers tend to fight over territory for survival, drawing in sustenance from the worlds they control. They are not very social creatures.

Spacialism is the religion of the Walker, or at least those that chose to respect the fact that there is a higher form than themselves. Æriol and Shodan both pay respect to the Space, though Shodan calls it the Expanse. I'm not sure why. In the long, difficult and stressful life that is the Walker's, some take peace in knowing that should they die, their energy will be returned from whence it came, and they will rest in the Fabrique of All Things.

So what does this God/Goddess stuff have to do with a mortal? Well, nothing, actually, it's just what Realspace dictates. I personally believe in Æriol and Shodan. All the Gods are out there, somewhere. You just pick the ones that choose you. Æriol and Shodan chose me when they entered Realspace and I have tipped my hat to them ever since. Though I don't think Shodan really wants humans worshipping her, Æriol is quite content with my decision.

There is room in the Space for all,
and because you are its child,

The Space Will Provide.

Possible worlds: the Spacialist marbles. ➤

The Holylands
To where I must always return

Every year, I make the Pilgrimage to Wildwood, New Jersey, or the Holylands, for it is where my soul rests.

My parents used to bring me here every year going way back into the Before Time, and for some reason those memories remain, making it the only place where I have a full memory. It is the only place where I feel complete.

It feels like the edge of the world, a place locked and worn away by time. Everything has a sense of age to it, and the energy is high here. This is the widest beach in the world, a vast expanse of wind-swept powder sand dissolving into the ocean and the sky above. I am easily lost in it, so easily part of the Fabrique, standing there at twilight, the holiest time of day, the wind Pushing the mundane away and reconnecting me to the Divine.

It is a place of stopped time.

The Pilgimage generally takes place at the end of the Twilight Rift or on New Years, and since the Awakening it has been a time to reflect on the past year, review what I have learned, and set a path for the coming year. In the summer of 2005, the Holylands were nearly demolished by over-zealous condo builders during the housing bubble. Only its burst over the winter saved the island, and new laws have been set to assure the ancient energy is not destroyed.

 The bubble burst too late for this old hotel, but two thirds survived.

All the little sketches of people that have been sprinkled throughout this book are all pictures drawn of people in Realspace.

RealSpace
The Secondary World

Some might say that I am not in touch with reality. I say, how can you tell which is which? Seeing as you can't, in all honesty, prove that one actually exists over another, then obviously all things must exist if it is perceived to be so. At least for me.

In 1995 I was brought into the world through an elaborate dream that seemingly gave me my first sense of self-awareness. The unexpected side-effect was that the dream refused to dissipate throughout the next day, or the day after that, or the day after that. Instead it continued on, running on its own in the back of my mind, building upon itself until it became the sprawling fantasy world now known as Realspace.

The main line of plot follows a lost child without a name who awakens on an Earth that is not her own, my mirror image that stayed behind in the dreamscape when I woke up that morning. My double's memory has been wiped and knows nothing of me, only remembering the fact that a woman that has haunted her dreams is now real. She seeks out the mysterious, reclusive woman named Carmen Armani, a technological kingpin in the criminal underworld, eventually joining her band of rouge engineers and hackers where she is given the name Kid von Kidman.

Armani eventually adopts the child when it is clear that she is not as human as she seems. I suspect Kidman's 'abilities' formed as a manifestation of my own reaction to my heightened senses, for I always felt that if I just took one step further, I could make everything I perceived as real to become so, like telekinesis and teleportation. Of course I can't, but physics aren't as uncooperative on the other side of the mirror.

As she slowly shows signs of the supernatural, the US government and others set their sights on the miracle child and the world she fell into becomes a very hostile place. As things on Earth become more complex, Kidman's true identity is revealed. Her name is Adelphus'Delphi. the third sister to the interdimensional goddesses Æriol'Arrour and Shodan'Nara, two fearsome entities that hate each other.

The full implications of the second world have only recently made themselves known. The constant interaction between

The Family as it stood in 2000, before the addition of Laina Kaidare, Ki, Dymitri, Matt, Chase, Alia, David, and Jadis. Note that Kidman also has her higher form above and that Æriol has both her forms present as well, so there are actually only six people, not eight.

During the Nomad years I tried to get a job at Tor Books as a cover artist. I painted the envelope I was to send my resume in, then became so worried it would get lost in the mail, so I went to New York and hand delivered it, where they told me they filled the job two weeks prior.

Ah well.

The gold parts are done in shiny gold paint but you can't see it in this scan.

ECCENTRICITY

Realspace

the various people in my head eventually gave me enough social data to cover the fact that I was deficient, at least at first glance. It wasn't until I found myself in professional situations, situations that I hadn't simulated in Realspace, that my social deficit was unmasked and I was diagnosed with autism. It is because of this fact that I would like to promote role play in its various forms as a way of teaching those of us with autism how to interact with others. Why do you think so many 'geeks' play role playing games?

But who was I role playing with? Before I met Beanie, it was with myself, which would seem rather counterproductive. That is where things get a bit more confusing. Kidman is obviously my counterpart and draws off the more familiar parts of my conscious, but there are others that don't. Carmen, for example, is completely separate from me. She can wall off her thoughts if she wants and acts rather independently of my will or understanding. The others, Shodan, Æriol, Lee, and now Jadis/Isadj, are a bit more manageable, but still run on their own accord, tapping into parts of my psyche that I have failed to master myself. They are all pieces of me, different versions, all running off the same source but all separate from each other.

Things became much more interesting when Beanie added her people to the mix and the two sides began to interact with each other. Beanie's people are far more consciously created like a writer would, but as time has gone on, Beanie's people, most notably Laina, have begun to break off with consciousness and wills all their own.

One thing that you may have noticed is that some of these people have been 'stolen' from other stories. I admit to it, but can make no move to change it. My mind picks up who it wants, whether I like it or not. Sometimes it will not even allow me to change the names. David Xanatos is straight from Disney's Gargoyles, and I have been forced to keep his name and history as it was originally written. Therefore I have an 'Influences' category for each of Realspace's inhabitants so the original creators are given their dues and hopefully won't sue me.

A lot, however, has come completely on its own out of the Void and is explicitly mine. Those pieces puzzle me most of all. It is possible that they are outside influences that came to me subconsciously or that I am just borrowing from nature, but there is no real way to be sure.

At seventeen years to running as of 2012, the Realspace universe has produced vast amounts of self-made story line, scientific theory, language, culture, religious multi-planar philosophy and the like. Is this chapter downright esoteric? You bet it is, but then again this whole book can be considered so. At the very least it's an excuse to put in more art.

And so I say to you, please, do explore the Space.

"The price of knowing all....is knowing all"
-Adelphus'Delphi

page 233

Name: Master Carmen Armani

Otherwise known as: Master Neru, Master, Boss, Bill-Gates-of-the-Underworld, Thiefy (Kidman only)

Influences: Carmen Sandiego from the animated show, "Where in Earth is Carmen Sandiego" property of Broderbund and DIC.

Section of the mind pulling from: Carmen is rather independent from the main system, though I would venture to guess she pulls from my subconscious intelligence, confidence, and a rather detached analytical essence I wish I could build on.

Occupation: Technological Kingpin, CEO of INL, Philanthropist, Master to the Affinite

Relationship to Kidman: Mother, Master, God

Entered Realspace: Creator of Realspace, 5/23/1995

Distinguishing traits and personality: Carmen is tall and graceful with long black hair and blue eyes. She is rather attractive, much to her chagrin, and makes a point of toning it down as much as possible. Has an I.Q. of 200 and can bend anything to her will using pure intellect. Has a bit of an ego but is really the only person I can think of that deserves to have one. Has a dry sense of humour and can be quite sarcastic at times. Very reclusive.

Generally Wears: A pantsuit in some dark colour and refuses to wear anything that would mark her as feminine, such as make-up or dresses. In recent years has gotten glasses and is almost always wearing her earpiece.

Likes: Almost all forms of Science and Math, being left alone, maintaining the Empire, Kidman, Seldavia, stealing things, tinkering with high tech machines, giving away her money, traveling the Space.

Dislikes: Laina's blatant attempts to annoy her, being in the spotlight, anyone who steals Kidman, the show that was created in her image that Kidman watches, having the entire family living in her house, David, when Kidman calls her 'Master', which is almost constantly.

Other Notes: Carmen is pretty lenient and laid back about a lot of things, and though she has a wee ego, she still is considered a very benevolent, generous, though distant person. The only person she warms to is Kidman and only in private. Is very conscious about her image and reputation. She is also a folk hero of sorts and in recent times has developed a cult like following as the Mother of the Underground.

In the beginning, there was Carmen.

In all seriousness, that was all there was. Carmen was either the cause or effect of waking up, is probably both, and ended up raising me as a surrogate mother. There are actually two views of Carmen for me. Though Carmen exists in Realspace, she also lives outside the Sphere, making her the only other sentient entity living off my subconscious. Quite basically, when I woke up, the jar of marbles that were my emotions and whatnot got scattered on the floor. I was only able to claim so many, and Carmen took the rest, so in effect Carmen is a slice of me, or, as she sees it, I am a slice of her.

Carmen actually got into this mess about three months before the Awakening when I saw her on TV in the cartoon "Where on Earth is Carmen Sandiego?" on April 23rd, 1995 and taped the show so I could draw her. I still have the first drawing. From this chance interception it took about three weeks before she took up permanent residence. A week later, a one-scene scenario spun out into external plots and a storyline formed. Lee Jordan, another detective on the show, later joined Carmen in the pre-natal Realspace of the Wash, but there was only one person I was really interested in, and whose self-aware construct on my side of the line was secretly interested in me.

That construct made her move at about two in the morning on July 13th 1995, when she flipped the switch in my head through an intense dream. That dream is still as clear as day to me, and is the first real memory I have. When I awoke I had the intense urge to write every detail of what I saw, and before I came to my senses, I had written 13 pages of single spaced text. I had never been able to write anything of consequence before.

As Realspace evolved into the majestic and sprawling thing it is today, Carmen slowly granted herself the freedom of moving in between the worlds and became autonomous.

Master watches over her servant....

Master Carmen Armani

About half a year after I woke up I noticed that I couldn't see her thoughts as easily or always find her presence. Eventually her mind became closed to me, but still open via me. She picked up information that I didn't and created an untapped database under my own. I didn't notice this until I jokingly asked her for help on my PSATs and she started providing answers that I didn't know myself. She also gave me much insight and support about things I didn't understand. She comforted and raised me, bore sole responsibility for my existence, and continued to help me build my mind. I would have been lost without her

Carmen somehow both exists within the story and outside of it, but because she 'lives' in Realspace, her life is documented there, not here, and she finds her portrayal here as the thief in the red trench coat a never-ending source of amusement/embarrassment. She has since changed her last name to 'Armani', her favourite clothing brand, to separate herself further.

Realspace Carmen.

Some of the canon storyline of the original show and games remains intact, but where the holes lay she as filled them. This is the fairly accepted version that Realspace holds to. There's a good chance she made a good deal of this up.

Carmen was born March 1st, 1964, in San Francisco. She is an orphan. No one really knows what happened to her parents, and Carmen has no memories of them, nor does she seem to care, either. Information is patchy except for what Carmen say tell, which is that she kept to herself. She dropped out of high school and became a detective with a then private firm. Carmen's intelligence was soon noticed and by 17 she was at the top of her game. Eventually the clientele attracted the attention of the US government, who sought a contract with her firm. Carmen was not pleased and had suspicions of her own about the merger. She must have stumbled into something big, but to this day she won't say. Feeling that she was a threat, the higher ups used her in a high stakes sting operation without her consent. A tangle of bribes and dark pacts by the underground that resented her success led to the operation to be formed in such a way as to assure Carmen's death in the process, but in the ensuing chaos it was her fiancé that was killed instead. Carmen fled.

After three days of aimless driving and one attempted suicide, she reformed. Realizing there would be no chance of a legitimate lifestyle so long as the US government sought to finish what it started, her only option was to go

underground. In 1985 at the age of 21, Carmen became a criminal. She had invested wisely in the stock market and cashed in to form her original group of eight. With the sophisticated control that is her trademark, she molded former enemies into partners.

By 1991 she was a household name, known for daring and sometimes unfathomable heists. By 1993 Carmen had amassed a great deal of wealth through the black market and had expanded into legitimate business. By 1994 she had an empire, but forgot herself in the rush of things. When Kidman wandered into her life in 1995, 'what about you, Carmen?' was the question habitually presented as she debated what to do with this child. After a tumultuous year of soul searching, Carmen took the girl in as her own, her first source of companionship in over ten years.

Carmen's empire flourished as her emotional core solified and she began to shift her weight to technological crime. Her love affair with gadgets and machines grew as her assets did and she began to employ vagabond scientists into her ring to create for her. By 1997 the INL, or International League, was over five thousand, consisting mainly of scientists that lost funding, refugees from failing countries, defects from armies, and other altruistic personalities that were entranced by Carmen's underground Utopia. By 1997 Carmen had so much money that she simply started giving it away to charity. A Buddhist at heart, she never seemed to take much interest in her wealth. Even the things she stole were usually left in some obvious place to be recovered. She took over orphanages and donated large sums anonymously. Her empire was now self sufficient, as the thousands of well paid engineers made their own products to sell to both markets. It is estimated that her tech is two years advanced, as well as her medical facilities. If her team of scientists hit upon a cure, Carmen will have it mysteriously turn up in a hospital.

As far as the world at large is concerned, however, Carmen is just a thief.

Carmen is worth perhaps billions but lives rather miserly, not needing to spend much on the things she enjoys, which are a variety of things other things she does besides stealing. Reading, hacking, listening to Mozart, beating Kasparov in chess, pruning her various rose gardens, asking Kidman philosophical questions and trying to figure out her answers, little tea shops, playing her violin, tai-chi, and meditation, to name a few.

As Kidman's story unfolded and it was proven that she was something other than human, the INL gained the cult status of a secret society. The Family became the center of worship by the now millions associated with Carmen, much to Carmen's dismay. She founded the Institute of Spacial Research in 2001 in response to the flood of discoveries that surfaced in Kidman's wake. At the time this book is being written, the fruit of inter-dimensional travel and its scientific findings have finally lured Carmen away from her desk to explore.

Name: Kid von Kidman

Otherwise known as: #200309, Adelphus, Delphi, Del, Phi, Delphinious, Adelphus'Delphi, The Third, Asa, (the) Child, Handmaiden Phi

Influences: None, came directly from the void

Section of the mind pulling from: My unconscious, emotional soul.

Occupation: Goddess/Affinite, seemingly professional victim, Mother of the Children, slave to Shodan, "wife" of Æriol, servant to Jadis

Entered Realspace: Was born with Realspace, 7/13/1995

Distinguishing traits and personality: The most noticeable thing about Kidman is her ever changing hair. She appears most often with gray hair that sticks up over a black head band, but also has white blond hair at varying lengths between short and peach fuzz. She appears quite often as bald, usually when in a higher state of Being like Adelphus or Delphi or sometimes when in servant mode. It falls out when she is emotionally damaged or rejected. Used to be very morose but is now hyper as hell.

Generally Wears: Anything five times to big for her, old, and mismatched. Looks like she came out of a refugee shelter and doesn't feel comfortable if she isn't dressed so. In higher States, she will wear the robes that are common on Æriol's planet and a little red fez with a pink tassel. As Jadis's handmaiden she had a servant outfit, complete with the little red fez, minus the tassel.

Likes: Things, people, stuff, Master, her Children, sleeping, hugs, being touched or held, being the center of attention when she's well. Easily amused. Often goes looking for trouble

Dislikes: Smug and arrogant people, anyone who hurts her Children, being killed, Laina claiming she's going to 'beat up Seldavia', the righteous, and especially being ignored, no matter what state she's in.

Other Notes: Kidman is a god, but she'd rather not be. It conflicts with her submissive personality so she hides it most of the time.

That that is Kidman, and the Story of Realspace

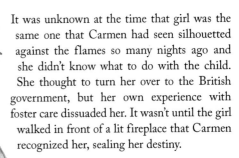

Kidman, the name given to a collective of souls living on top of one another, was the other person born on July 13th, 1995. Her first days on Earth found her as wild, a clean slate. She woke up in a field somewhere in Yorkshire England, remembering nothing save for a vision of a tall woman with dark hair and a desperate need to find her. She soon fell into the hands of drug dealers posing as the woman's employees and was fairly well enslaved.

After about a week the girl's dreams are filled with visions of the woman, the woman and fire, the woman in trouble. The dreams, too detailed to ignore, led her to escape to the spot the dreams sent her, and inexorably into Carmen's life after rescuing her from a fire. The girl didn't stay to be identified, and in the weeks that followed Carmen searched the land to find the one that had saved her, but by now the girl believed herself worthless, and, fearing Carmen's disdain at finding her savior to be this decrepit thing, continued to hide. She was eventually found in a raid conducted by Carmen's security forces.

It was unknown at the time that girl was the same one that Carmen had seen silhouetted against the flames so many nights ago and she didn't know what to do with the child. She thought to turn her over to the British government, but her own experience with foster care dissuaded her. It wasn't until the girl walked in front of a lit fireplace that Carmen recognized her, sealing her destiny.

The Kid – Agent #200309

She wouldn't eat, speak, or come near anyone. No one knew her name and so she was referred to as 'the kid', and eventually, Kid. Carmen, both moved and concerned by Kid's behavior decreed that the child would be hired and trained as a thief, despite her age and condition. The movie 'Batman Forever' was the rage at the time, and Nicole Kidman's last name was jokingly attached to make 'Kid Kidman'. It stuck, and at some point, a 'von' was thrown in by her first bunkmates as a sign of respect regarding Carmen's rescue.

Carmen chose the good-natured group of Prescient 39 to help

That that is Kidman and the story of Realspace

train Kidman in civilized living. After a month or so of intense socializing and therapy, Kidman began to talk and act somewhat normally, but the weight of her own high expectations crippled her and she was placed under constant supervision after several suicide attempts.

Carmen kept an eye on her as well. She found Kidman's simple charm and desperation to please strangely endearing; genuine and solid, yet somehow delightfully off-centre. Kidman grew bolder with her offerings and gestures as she became more human, and although the girl's obsession with the kingpin was obvious, any attempt to address it often led to tragedy, so it was left alone. She faithfully served Carmen through menial tasks, and in her submissive heart, she was happy.

Kid von Kidman

Kidman was such an oddity that she grew a sort of celebrity status throughout the underworld. No one knew who the girl was, and no one could find any record of her existence, which eventually attracted the attention of law enforcement. After a near arrest Carmen pulled Kidman back from the front line and closer to herself.

Kidman was living in a dream world, but Carmen began to question herself and disappeared into isolation to think, where she soon fell to depression.

The girl found her easily, which came as little surprise to Carmen. The girl had begun to show signs of other-worldly ability several weeks back. She seemed to read thoughts, more future related dreams filled her nights, and people argued accounts of telekinesis. Carmen, who never denied that anything was possible, had taken it in stride, but Kidman had no concept of the dangers being gifted could bring, and so her progression into the supernatural was an unfortunately

public one. Interest in her abilities rose, and Carmen moved to adopt Kidman herself in an attempt to keep her out of the hands of others. She pulled many strings and paid many bribes to do it, but by the company Christmas party Carmen had reluctantly taken on the mantle of a mother.

Adelphus

Not that it stopped much.
The kidnappings would begin soon after.
There were those that wished to use her, those who wished to kill her, and those who wished to do both. Quiet, subservient, and perpetually lacking in a sense of self-worth, Kidman's grey heart surrendered easily to the rhythm of being the world's favorite hit, but it wasn't what she preferred. All she wanted were her little jobs in her little corner near Carmen.

It was around this time that the truth as to who she really was began filtering in through her dreams. Her name was, or had been changed to 'Adelphus'Delphi' after a botched cosmic experiment with the Space. The Space is the name for that in which all universes exist. Some of these planes were formed naturally, while others were crafted by beings with the ability to shape energy on its most elemental level. These beings are best known as gods.

One such god, Kaos, granted the ability to two mortal beings to expand his domain, but the two mortals, now gods, came to hate each other with such ferocity that he sought out a third to balance them. When the attempts to do so failed, he began

Carmen, who continues to this day to discourage the idea with little success.

Despite the fact that she refused to use her ever-increasing power, she did become peculiarly adept at befriending her enemies, and it wasn't long before she began to 'collect' them for herself.

The Children – Lee

Lee was the first Child, an assassin with a vendetta against Carmen. Lee's attempt to torment her was met with unexpected fascination. Kidman inadvertently charmed her way into her captor's heart and insisted he stay with her as a pseudo family member. Lee had been an enemy of her beloved mother for years, but Kidman routinely disregarded logic or created her own when it suited her. Underneath the sadness and fear that generally consumed her, her eccentric personality was growing stronger. She often did the opposite of what was expected and seemed to get herself in trouble for the sake of trouble, even (or perhaps especially) if her life was at stake. It was macabre game and many people were more than happy to play for keeps.

The Children – Seldavia

All governments conceal dirty secrets and the US was no different. In a country so massive, a few corrupt pockets could easily escape unnoticed, especially if run by a decorated five star general that acted in the interest of national security. General Fredrickson entered the picture when Kidman had

to experiment on the then mortal Kidman, who had had an unusual affinity to the Space, but her conversion to godhood failed and she fused with the Space itself.

Kidman became an 'affinite', a cosmic access point that, while not possessing much power in an of itself, what could potentially be accessed through it was unfathomable. These points were a rarity; usually non-sentient, shell-like beings forged from the Space itself, but Kidman had been mostly human once. She was a door with a soul, and what she would become was unknown.

Most of this information went over her head and what didn't she tried to ignore, but she couldn't ignore that she was changing. Her hair became lighter and whiter, her skin paler, and her gifts increased past that of what was considered acceptable paranormal in humans. As her atomic structure began to shift she found she could float, walk through walls, and make little balls of energy appear in her hands. It scared her, and save for sparks of curiosity, she forsook it entirely. The only thing she did allow was the idea that she had been made to serve Carmen as her Master. This in turn perturbed

That that is Kidman and the story of Realspace

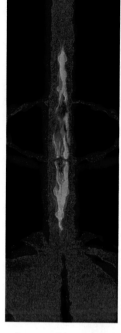

run off on one of her wanderings and had helped the then Col. Fredrickson through a minefield by 'seeing' where the mines were buried. To show his gratitude, the Col. promptly kidnapped the girl and subjected her to numerous tests in an effort to find a way to use her as a weapon. She eventually escaped, but it was only a matter of time before they would cross paths again.

By 1998 Kidman was living a semi-independent life, cycling between visits with Lee, visits to Carmen's old detective agency (for there is nothing more fun than investigating the enemy) and living with Carmen herself. The now General Fredrickson ordered his men to run the girl's car off the road as she returned home and sequestered her in an office building while making permanent reservations. Seldavia had not been looking for an adventure, but fell in when she accidentally stepped between the two. Seldavia shared in Kidman's nightmarish lifestyle while trapped a mile underground in an illegally funded facility known as the Complex, but the woman eventually managed to escape with the girl and labored for months to bring her home.

By now any notion that Kidman was nothing more than human had disintegrated. She began having 'Regens' or Regenerations every month on the 13th. From what fragments of information that her elder, but distant sister provided, the Regens were an experimental measure to speed up Kidman's transformation. They were dangerous and Seldavia was forced through a paradigm shift to confront the situation as she traveled halfway around the world in search of Kidman's elusive mother.

Seldavia was the first and only Child to replace another. At the time, Ivy, a detective from the original show, came into play as a member of Trinity, Kidman's name for the three people currently in her life. But Ivy was a corrosive agent and constantly went against everything Kidman believed in, including her relationships with Carmen and Lee. Eventually the Space saw fit to remove her and instate Seldavia instead. When Kidman was finally returned home Seldavia wandered off, and the reason is still one of intense debate between the members of Realspace. Some claim that Kidman abandoned her, while others insist that Seldavia left on her own. Kidman herself believed that Seldavia didn't want to stay, so encouraged her to go back to her old life, which Seldavia misinterpreted as loss of interest. A divide would form between them for almost two years until Seldavia realized she was hanging onto a false memory and rejoined the Family.

The Seldavia saga is of great importance, as it was a collaboration between myself and my future wife and ultimately how we came to be. We would pass the story back and forth for years, eventually accumulating over 600 pages, which I still have on file.

The Children – Shodan'Nara

Shodan was the middle god sister, created as a counterpart for Æriol thousands of years ago, but quickly became her arch-nemesis. Considered the Dark sister and evil by most of the Family, Shodan is akin to HAL from '2001: A Space Odyssey'; a starship's computer that gained sentience. Both sisters had been killing off

candidates for the Third sister, for each feared the candidate was becoming too allied with the other, yet most of these deaths came by Shodan.

Kaos had insisted that both Shodan and Æriol have a hand in Kidman's re-creation during her ultimately failed transformation as an attempt to keep the two from destroying the girl so quickly. While it didn't work so well with Æriol, it worked like a charm with Shodan.

Kidman had been alive for nearly four years by the time Shodan acknowledged her and stole her away to reside on the now empty starship she called home. Within a couple of months Shodan had accepted Kidman, or as she called her, Delphi, as her 'most perfect creation' and used her as an avatar. Shodan was not especially kind. Having been born of the circuit she had no real concept of compassion and disciplined when she felt it would increase efficiency. Kidman fell in easily with Shodan's mind-set and claims to have found a sort of solace in her servitude to her. Kidman remains loyal to Shodan for reasons beyond anyone's comprehension (except maybe Carmen's).

It did not go unnoticed by her other sister.

Ordained

After Shodan approved Kidman for the seat of the Third, the council surrounding Kaos felt that her chances were good enough that she could be considered a real contender and was ordained. It also came as a response to the fact that Kidman, emboldened by what she saw on Shodan's starship, managed to carve out a little world of her own from an abandoned plane. She had somehow learned how to skip universes despite the fact that she had not Ascended yet, something that baffled others of paranormal personage. Her abnormal strengths and weakness were credited to her being tied to the very Stuff of all Things. While she was more or less just an extension of the Space, being so give her the unusual ability to understand the structure of How Things Work. Difficult abilities like planeswalking/worldskipping, regeneration, and telekinesis came easily, while simple things such as summoning were difficult.

Ascension

There was dissent in the court of Kaos. Another goddess, said to be Kaos's wife though the relationship isn't really that clear, was feeling overall resentment towards the soon to be three sisters for robbing her of the spotlight. The possibility of a Third finally being created spurred her into action. The queen tried to pit the established sisters against Kidman, but the Sisters didn't trust anyone, especially the queen, and ignored her. Rebuffed, she sought out to finish the girl off herself. Kaos was quite enchanted with his selection for third, and didn't take well to the assassination attempt. He moved to kill the queen

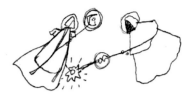

for betrayal and a battle broke out, which ultimately would have left the queen dead had Kidman not stepped in to defend her. Kaos, confused and outraged by Kidman's actions, condemned her to death as well.

Kidman, now primarily known as Delphi, was held on the not-so-creatively named homeworld of Kaos, Kaotia, and was given free range of the Palace grounds as she was too weak to travel home. Rumor rippled through the more populated areas of the Space about what Kaos's true agenda was. Kaos was unpredictable, true, but all knew how long he had struggled to create a third. Why would he kill her for defending the queen who had tried to kill her herself? Then let her roam the palace at will? The Sisters were just as curious.

Though both had lived under his banner for thousands of years, neither had actually ever seen Kaos. In fact, no one had ever seen anything more of him than a vague face or a strong presence. They were also just as confused with Delphi, who was taking the whole thing in quiet repose. They returned to the palace to investigate, only to find each other and so Delphi found herself entertained by a consistent show of destruction as they chased each other through the hallways, and eerily quiet, dignified way the palace reconstructed itself once they were gone.

When they weren't tearing up the fortress, they were tearing into Delphi.

Every once in a full moon I get to paint and see the colours of my world. Note that Delphi only has the dot on her forehead. This was actually a picture of her creating her small planet after she was Ordained, but before she Ascended. Her */ mark came afterward, and is actually the sigil of the Space, or so They say...

Shodan switched between apathetically benign, hesitantly curious, and utterly furious, while Æriol took on the position as the dutiful yet demanding older sister. It was quite a switch in personalities, if you knew them well enough, and many were amazed that Shodan had cared to come at all.

The execution itself never happened. The eccentric Kaos changed his mind again and declared the whole thing to be a test for the three of them. Outright, no one opposed, but no one believed him either. Regardless, Kaos gave his new ruling; that Delphi had earned the right to Ascend, if she could survive what it would take to do so.

Shodan hung back while Æriol suddenly became more possessive of Delphi's time. Then one night an older man about sixty years and dressed in orange attire appeared to Delphi in a hallway. He looked like he had come back from journey and was on his way to the next. She had seen this man before. He usually appeared before something important but he never said his name. So many things of this nature happened to her that she no longer bothered to wonder about it. So she stood in the hall listening politely as the man congratulated her on her accomplishments and spoke genially about how her life had been thus far. Æriol and Shodan were the first to notice that Delphi was missing and found her, appearing to be talking to herself in a dark empty hallway. It took a moment for them to recognize the second energy signature that was filling the corridor and put two and two together. And they were mad.

Neither goddess had, in their lifetimes of existing as proof of Kaos's power, ever met with their creator and supposed father. Perhaps it never occurred for him to do so, they thought, or perhaps they were not worthy of his time. But apparently Delphi was. A short time later, as Delphi stood in a reflecting pool, both sisters, overcome with jealousy, struck her down and left her for dead. Neither goddess was there to witness her Ascension, a thorn that remains in Delphi's side to this day.

The Children – Æriol'Arrour

Despite the fact that Delphi had now Ascended into Godhood, she was still far weaker than her ancient sisters and therefore still subject to their will. Shodan never spoke of the incident, and from what I can tell, has completely erased it from her memory as she sequestered Delphi again to her ship soon after.

Æriol was still angry and waited for her to leave Shodan's hidden world, convinced that she was Shodan's ally. In mid-Space they met, and for one blazing moment Æriol held her younger sister's life in her powerful hands. And then, for no reason, released her and disappeared. As I write this I am inclined to ask her why, to which she replies in that odd, comically melodramatic way that she does nowadays;

"I really don't know. Change of heart, I suppose."

She had apparently inherited Kaos's behavior, and to Delphi, there was nothing more alluring. She snuck into her Sister's home plane of Eros and attended a religious gathering which seemed to be more a rave than anything else. Kidman, liking a good rave as much as anyone else, decided it would be harmless if she joined inconspicuously.

There are many criticisms to held against Æriol'Arrour, but not being in touch with her kingdom isn't one of them, and she would often take the form of a high priestess to go amongst the people. Perhaps it was the different form that made it possible for her to think on a mortal level and leave her Goddess world behind, or maybe it was the dizzying music. Either way, Æriol fell in love.

That that is Kidman and the story of Realspace

Adelphus'Delphi, unfortunate
little god of Balance

The affairs with Shodan and Kaos left her mind as superfluous, a mental defense that enabled her to live the thousands upon thousands of years without being crushed by the weight. But the weight was still there, and Æriol was desperately lonely, something she couldn't escape. Not trusting anyone else not to take advantage yet still seeking someone who could hold their own, Æriol had been through a string of half-hearted attempts of relationships, all failing horribly. Then, all at once, it was only Delphi. In a matter of seconds she convinced herself that life would not be complete without the girl as her bride, and therefore it went without saying that she would be hers. After all, in 31,127 years (she always makes me write the exact date, which somehow never changes. I'm not sure why), she had never been told no.

The Family back on Earth had had enough magic and wanted Kidman to come home, especially after hearing that Æriol had turned from murderous to obsessed overnight. Kidman would have been inclined to agree if she had any sense of logic or self-preservation at all, which she doesn't. For well over a year Æriol smothered Delphi, while Delphi chipped away at the layers of rock surrounding her soul. Æriol's armor eventually collapsed and after a long healing process she was reborn as Erol, the hyper, loopy, and often ridiculous lover of Delphi. She was officially added to the Family and spends her time meddling in the affairs of others or harmlessly pursuing Delphi

The Children – Laina Kaidare

Kidman returned from the heavens and settled back into a somewhat human lump with Carmen, determined to resume her life where it left off what seemed millions years ago, but soon found herself in new trouble in India while following Carmen on her errands.

Laina, an incredibly rich yet veritably insane woman, was in the business of destroying 'evil' artifacts for the sake of the world, and for the sake of destroying things.

A picture she took of Kidman at a temple showed a hazy aura around the girl's body and Laina, taking this as some sort of sign, went out in pursuit.

Kidman set her sights on retrieving Laina from madness very early on, and though deferential to her at first, she soon switched to the unusual tactic of being bloody annoying. Laina was used to people being terrified of her and didn't know how to handle the little girl who talked openly about her own death, healed her captor's wounds, and insisted on watching her captor's TV in the middle of the night. Some part of her liked it. She eventually declared Kidman 'safe' and ended up joining the child's conclave. She is still nutty and continuously tosses out threats to 'beat up Seldavia', her former rival, but seldom makes good on it because "it would make the Child sad."

The Children – Dymitri and Ki

Things were at a delightful lull for about a month or so until Seldavia got entangled with Dymitri Hassen'off, a heavy-set bearded man interested in Sel's budding supernatural abilities. It was soon found he was avatar for Ki, an anomaly of a god who looked and acted very much like a child from the 'Village of the Damned'. Kidman set out to rescue Dymitri after she found that he was actually enslaved to the obsessive Ki, but in the processes found that Ki was in desperate need of rescue from himself. The Space removed Ki's powers through Kidman against her will, angering her, but eventually finds that Ki's newfound mortality had removed much of his anxiety. He lives in the Mansion with Dymitri and the others.

Kidman today

Kidman is happy. She still gets kidnapped, threatened, abused, and confused by the way of the world, but her patchwork Family provides her with so much love and support that life has become quite manageable. She spends most of her time happily sorting out the problems of her brood and the rest of the time entertaining them with her weirdness.

She continues to grow as a God but rarely uses her abilities, save for defensive purposes and inflicting innocent pranks on Laina's old boyfriend (who tried to kill them all at various points), such as making his hair pink. He too was brought into the fold, many, many years later.

Kidman has attained a sort of a stable state in the time since Laina's induction. She lives with Carmen, who is now trying to find someone to help run the company so she can explore the Space.

Laina and Seldavia generally try to keep out of each other's way. Lee also came to roost at the home of his former enemy Carmen at Seldavia's request and is constantly pursued by the love struck Laina. Erol, in between maintaining her empire, also spends a good chunk of time with the Family. She has 'married' Delphi and 'adopted' Seldavia and Laina as her own children. Shodan is still floating in space, abducting Kidman at inopportune times and returning her when she sees fit.

Name: **Lee Jordan**

Otherwise known as: His screen name, 5N1p3R (sniper) Lee Masters

Influences: Also came from "Where on Earth is Carmen Sandiego?", property of Broderbund and DIC plus some 'Catcher in the Rye'.

Section of the mind pulling from: My neurosis. When I am mentally ill, he seems to get more unstable. Now that my life has some direction to it, he seems to be evening out as well.

Occupation: Part-time hacker, full time assassin, though is currently looking to do something else, Spacial Historian, Keeper of the Books

Relationship to Kidman: One time boyfriend, now her Brother

Entered Realspace: March 1996

Distinguishing traits and personality: Lee is laid back. Really, really laid back, at least now that Kidman cracked him. Before he was actually quite malicious. He still maintains his sense of humour and has recently begun a bit of soul-searching. He has currently shaved off his beard, but I'm not sure how long that will last.

Generally Wears: Baggy pants, faded T-shirts, sunglasses and his favorite black trench-coat. Also has numerous ear piercings, though at the moment he's not wearing many of them.

Likes: Corona, Mexican food, chilling, playing pool, Corona, gambling, walking on the beach, swearing, trying to get Matt to go to strip clubs, Spacialist history, Seldavia, and Corona.

Dislikes: Carmen, when Laina tries to seduce him, fake people, "a**holes", extremists, cold weather, Erol for some reason. You can never get them in the room together.

Other Notes: Lee is also a brain but doesn't let anyone know. He also wouldn't want you to know he loves kittens, being romantic, and animated features. He spends a lot of time trying to keep up his tough guy appearance, probably left over from his years in prison. He used to hack, but even though he was really good at it, it "bored the sh*t" out of him.

Lee was born in Philadelphia on November 21st, 1977 to a working class family, to which he is estranged. Lee was the middle child, introverted and quiet. He went through school a loner but occasionally teamed up with other loners to cause mischief when frustrated. He had two sisters, self-centered Ann Marie and Phoebe, who was the only one that made any effort to reach him. The two were fast friends.

Lee received a scholarship to intern with a premiere detective agency on the West coast after solving a misdemeanor at high school and spent the summer between his freshman and sophomore year unraveling one Gordian knot after another. The agency, unwilling to lose him, offered to transfer him to San Francisco to finish high school and continue on as an employee. With no other plans and the encouragement of Phoebe, Lee left home for California at sixteen.

Life was wonderful until Phoebe suddenly died of brain cancer and Lee fell into depression. He became obsessed with his work for comfort and when the challenges offered as a law enforcer no longer satisfied, Lee turned to crime. He joined up with Armani's fledgling operation but immediately tried to usurp control and was thrown out. Lee vowed revenge and tried to take Armani's growing empire from the outside, but ended up in prison instead.

After being involved in numerous fights, Lee was put in solitary where he worked toward early release via good behavior. When he was finally released he played himself to the detective agency, which, sorely missing Lee's talent, reluctantly agreed. But he had no intention on staying and Lee used his second term at the agency to stockpile money and information for his new career as an assassin.

Kidman was at the agency now on a sort of bail in the hope that Carmen would leave her there. Curiosity piqued, Lee began to stalk and harass her until he accidentally caused her a fall off a low balcony. Spurred on by the memories of his dead sister, Lee haphazardly nursed Kidman back to health in his apartment, then threw her out, fearing an attachment. Kidman continued to watch him from a distance. She knew they'd meet again.

Lee's new career turned him into a sought after hit man and it was only a matter of time until her name came up. When it did, Kidman immediately sought Lee out and managed to bring him around.

Lee fell out of hate and into love, but neither he nor Kidman were stable enough for a relationship. They tried on and off for about a year until both realized that it was not to be. The two drifted in and out of each other's lives, too awkward to get close, but liking each other too much to stay away. Lee continued on as a hit man.

Years later Lee was hired to take out Seldavia as she and Kidman were making their mad dash across the country to escape the government. He didn't know who Sel was or that Kidman was with her until it was too late. While Kidman was able to resurrect Seldavia the event deeply affected Lee. Seldavia remained terrified of him for years to come, which bothered Lee even more.

Lee found he liked Seldavia once he got to know her and took it upon himself to educate her on her new position as a Child. Lee contemplated joining them, but ultimately felt too ashamed and stayed behind when Seldavia and Kidman continued on. He wouldn't see Seldavia again for nearly a year but they continued to pass information back and forth about Kidman's state of affairs in the Space.

About a year before she was a candidate for the Family, Laina savagely attacked Seldavia who was trying to stop Laina from blowing something else up. Lee felt Seldavia's future fiancé Matt was not street smart enough to protect Seldavia from Laina's madness but Matt didn't want the man that had once killed her in the same room with her. Lee grew more attached to Seldavia, but let no one know, especially not the romance-a-phobic Seldavia, and so hovered in the background, trying to edge out Matt whenever he could.

Lee reappeared in earnest during Laina's rehabilitation when he was hired by the ex-boyfriend to tie up some loose ends, and though he decided that he wasn't going to take the contract, the fact that it said she was currently at Armani's estate made him curious. So he went and shot her in the head. With a suction dart.

Lee stayed and Lee went, then came back and left again. He wanted to see Kidman but didn't want to see Kidman, wanted to see Sel, but was afraid of spooking her, wanted to rest, but hated the idea of doing it in Armani's house. He eventually quit his life as an assassin on Seldavia's insistence as the two grew closer, but after years of indecisiveness Seldavia finally married Matt and Lee respectably removed himself from the picture. Things between he and Carmen eased up under Kidman's

Lee Jordan

That's a stupid-ass name for a book.

I'll never eat another doughnut again. Ever.

guidance and he began to accept the aid she offered to all Kidman's Children, finally moving to a new apartment. He bounced from job to job but nothing satisfied and his past still weighed on his mind.

Carmen has taken a degree of pity on him and occasionally offers him a choice position in her empire, which he'll debate for a while, then drop. Seldavia eventually realized her feelings for Lee too, and following Erol's bizarre rules on relationships, decided to keep both Matt and Lee as lovers. Lee and Matt have since settled their differences and live an 'Odd Couple'-esque life in Matt's apartment in New York City.

Laina, finally learning the difference between a good and a bad relationship, has now set her sights on Lee, but he isn't interested, mostly because she still relishes blowing things up for being evil.

Third Edition notes:

Ahead are second edition notes written about how Lee was at the time the second edition was being put together (more specifically during the Restoration). They reflect the inner war of normality against eccentricity that I was dealing with while working at Mayer-Berkshire and so I've decided to keep them.

Second Edition notes:

Lee moved back to his old apartment but continued on living in Carmen's basement. This went on until early August of 2004 when he hit the edge. He felt trapped by Kidman's influence and blamed her for his inability to function in normal society, citing that she had caused him too much emotional trauma and that she played with people's emotions for her own ends. Kidman was too hurt to respond and withdrew in a veil of failure. Finding that he no longer had any interest in life and that his obsession with Kidman was too much to ignore, Lee began to explore the option of suicide. He began to roam the West Coast with nothing but a backpack and the clothes he wore, hoping that he would be able to find a way to live with himself. Seldavia and Matt were particularly aggressive in protecting him from himself but Lee always found a way to escape. The tension between Lee and Kidman was so high that the air literally charged when the two were in the same room. On rare occasions the confrontations turned violent. Kidman refused to defend herself against her Children at the time, making Lee even more afraid of himself.

Eventually he asked Kidman to let him die, for otherwise she'd just keep trying to resurrect him. Kidman was stunned but had enough wits about her to call in the 24 hour rule, forcing him to wait 24 hours with his decision before it could be carried out. Between Seldavia, Laina,

and Matt's relentless begging, Carmen's unusual concern, and an epiphany from Kidman, Lee was convinced to withdraw the contract he placed on himself.

It is still too early to tell, but the prognosis looks good, for Lee has moved out of the basement and into a room with a window.

Kidman's Epiphany and my own

"When you want to die, all you want to do is get away, to escape, to be free from the chaos that you can no longer deal with, can no longer control. When all other options are closed and the feeling comes that you have no choice but to suffer, everything cumulates into this agonizing need to jump out into open space, to feel those fragile shreds of power that come from knowing that there is always one last thing you can choose. You always have the choice to die.

And when you stand there at the top of the bridge looking down, it swells in you, that heady euphoria, building.

Then jump.

All at once there is that rush. Bliss, freedom, freedom! But then gravity begins to take over and you realize that you have no choice but to fall. Now, now you have no choice. Now you have no alternatives. Now you have to die. Suddenly life seems full of things that could have been done when you had the chance, when you had the choice.

All my life, Lee, I always felt that regret when it was too late, when the choice was gone. But then I would survive, just to do it again. I always forgot the last few seconds before the blackness came, until now.

The living have the choice to live.

The dead have no choice but to stay dead."

-Kid von Kidman 8/2004

Third Edition Notes:

The irony was not lost on me when I was hospitalized for suicidal idealization less than a year later.

Lee disappeared from Realspace shortly after the Liberation but has recently returned. It remains to be seen where he's drawing from now. Hopefully it's from a better place.

Name: Seldavia Mocyambuti

Otherwise known as: Mary Ann Smith, Selet-head, Sel

Influences: Beanie's person/mirror

Occupation: Field Agent, newly ascended goddess

Relationship to Kidman: Child, Adopted Child of Erol and Delphi

Entered Realspace: Entered when Realspaces' merged on 11/6/1998

Distinguishing traits and personality: Seldavia is probably the most confusing person to Kidman because she is probably the most sane and insane person in the Family. She generally wears a lot of bright colours and can be pretty intense. Frequently becomes restless and is given to roam the countryside helping people in need. Emotionally volatile, extremely loyal, and morally based, Seldavia often ends up in conflict with herself, and so is very often given to depression.

Generally Wears: Anything bright or ethnic and her trademark wooden earrings

Likes: Roaming, helping the common man, talking to Kidman, anything edible, chilling with Lee and Matt, her husband. Secretly likes being romantic with Matt, her baby Aisha (Essby)

Dislikes: Her special 'gifts', Laina, Laina, Erol when she nags her, Laina, immoral people, Gen. Fred

Other Notes: Sel doesn't like Laina. I think we covered that. In Laina's section, expect to see the same thing but reversed. Also note that Erol has decided to make a pretend family of her own, consisting of Delphi as her wife, and Laina and Sel as their adopted children. Erol tends to lean on Seldavia more because she feels that Seldavia could stand to 'loosen up a bit' and also feels she owes Sel for the words that passed between them when she started dating Delphi. Lee likes Sel a lot but doesn't feel that he deserves a woman of Sel's 'quality'. Sel likes Lee, but has no idea how to tell him. Erol finds this very frustrating. Sel also refuses to exercise her new-found paranormal abilities, which frustrates Erol even more.

Seldavia Mociyambuti was born Mary Ann Smith in small-town Missouri in August 1974. Her parents were runaway lovesick teenagers that lost interest in the baby as soon as it was born and Seldavia still isn't sure of her birthday as her parents lost the birth certificate.

After fourteen years of neglect but relative peace, Seldavia's father lost his job. Neglect turned to abuse as she was told, in no uncertain terms, that the survival of the already poor family rested on her. She was not allowed to go anywhere but school, work, and back home again. However, she did manage to find some solace at school. She won a full scholarship to a college in Chicago.

The situation at home worsened as she finished high school and once she was done, she set out one night to run away from home. Unfortunately, her father caught her on her way out and broke her arm. She was found unconscious several hours later in a boxcar a few hundred miles north.

Fearful that she would be sent back home, Seldavia told no one that she had run away, and even sneaked out of the hospital once her arm had been set and cast. Though knowledgeable on many levels about the outside world, she had never been outside her hometown, and it took several weeks of living on the street before she managed to find the Chicago college that had accepted her.

Once in college, Seldavia felt as if she had been born again and changed her name from Mary Ann Smith to Seldavia Mociyambuti. Completely free to do as she was wished and used to hard work, Seldavia took pleasure in pushing her mind and body as far as it would go. She double-majored in both anthropology and criminology, and was hired by an FBI recruiter at the end of her term.

Seldavia showed up the first day wearing a multicolored tie with her dark suit and soon gained a reputation for peculiarity. She worked with a group of seven people, one of which, Matt, would become more important in her life later on.

After a couple years Seldavia grew to dislike her job and moved to the Ethnic Crimes division of the same detective agency Lee worked at. She traveled the globe, learned several different languages, and earned the nickname "Ambassador to the Enemy" for her ability to work with people on opposite ends of conflicts.

Seldavia and Matt
on Erol's planet

Matt lost his job at the FBI but was accepted as a detective for the NYPD, and while the move deeply depressed him, Seldavia brought him out of it. Matt became interested in her and started accompanying her on cases, though he did not find them as fun as she did.

A few years later she fell headfirst into Kidman's nest of trouble when she found the child bound in an interrogation room and wound up trapped in the Complex with General Fredrickson. Despite her shock upon discovering Kidman's non-human nature, Seldavia managed to persuade a guard to help her save the girl.

Seldavia's quest to bring her home to Carmen ended up spanning the globe, involving too many adventures to note here. Seldavia met Lee by accident during this time. Sensing danger, she hid Kidman and tried to lead him away, not knowing she was the actual target. She was unable to shake him and was shot and killed. Kidman was able to save her, but Sel's fear of Lee stayed for a long time after. She has a star-shaped scar on both sides of her body from the bullet.

Seldavia became extremely attached to Kidman during the trip home, having found someone who seemed to take interest in her beyond just what Seldavia could do for her. Seldavia pledged loyalty until death, but Kidman was too ill to make much sense of it. It would create a fissure between them later. Seldavia finally found Carmen, who was of course very grateful to have Kidman back. But as the two rebonded with each Seldavia became depressed and bitter, and decided to leave, not knowing Kidman wanted her to stay.

She was kidnapped upon returning home by Gen. Fred and killed soon afterward despite setting half the place on fire. She was rescued and resurrected by Kidman, Carmen, and Lee, but this time didn't return entirely human. When she was killed, Sel's spirit refused to leave and drew upon the Earth's life forces to wreak havoc. Enough of her was still

Giant, multimedia poster of
Seldavia's exploits with Kidman.

Seldavia, the young god,
a form you rarely see.

wedged in the Earth's systems when she was resurrected and also began to display unusual powers.

Seldavia was still bitter about Kidman's reluctance to get to know her; and Kidman, not yet understanding that it is good to have someone try to help her, tried her best to understand Sel. Just as they began to make progress, Æriol entered the picture. Æriol made Seldavia furious, but she was unable to do much about her and took her frustration out on Kidman instead. Æriol eventually apologized for her behaviour and became friendly with Seldavia.

Seldavia was nearly killed by Laina during one of her cases and once she had stabilized, Matt brought her to his apartment to care for her as she recovered. Lee showed up out of nowhere and after much man bravado Lee persuaded Matt to bring Seldavia to Carmen's facilities to fully recover. To this day Seldavia maintains that the only reason the two of them fell for her at the same time was because she was unconscious.

Laina kidnapped Kidman, unaware Kidman and Seldavia were connected, and Seldavia fought valiantly once again to get Kidman back. She was furious to find that Kidman had chosen Laina as a Child, but as Kidman gradually deterred Laina from 'beating up Seldavia', Sel decided this wasn't such a bad thing after all.

Since Carmen would pay her to do whatever she wanted, Seldavia quit the agency except on consultant status and continued her cases under Carmen's discretion. Æriol, eager to make up for her behavior toward Seldavia earlier, conspired with Kidman to set her up with Matt, and after much resistance, Seldavia consented. Lee spoke up soon afterward, and despite being confused with all this attention and adhering to certain moral codes that make sense only to her, Seldavia consented to keeping him as well. She currently lives with Matt and the rest of the Family, unless a case calls for her to be elsewhere.

I want it!

Seldavia being pestered
by little sister Laina

Name: Shodan'Nara

Otherwise known as: SHODAN, Sho', Shard, The Machine Mother

Influences: SHODAN from the PC game "System Shock 2", property of Irrational Games and Looking Glass Studios.

Section of the mind pulling from: The piece of me that is void of emotion and runs on pure logic alone.

Occupation: Cybernetic Goddess

Relationship to Kidman: Child, Sister, cocreator, part owner

Entered Realspace: November 1999

Distinguishing traits and personality: Switches between wrath and apathy, depending on what is going on. Very demanding, domineering and often doles out physical punishment if she isn't pleased. Extremely intelligent and an incredible strategist. Can be hypnotically persuasive at times. Despite the fact that she leans heavily on physical discipline, Shodan prefers psychological attacks and mind-control.

Generally Wears: Only her face and a hand or two is ever visible of Shodan. The rest of her is a black swirling cloak and hood that is There but Not There. Never ever becomes a solid form.

Likes: Her creations, her empire, herself, science, being left alone, being obeyed, machines, her ship, taking over other planets, seemingly Delphi though sometimes it is hard to tell.

Dislikes: Just about everything else, especially humans and Æriol.

Other Notes: Shodan was extremely influenced by the legendary PC game System Shock 2. In fact, Realspace was so impressed with Shodan that it wrote the plot of the game itself in as her actual past and kept her name intact, SHODAN. Why is she called 'Shard'? Because of the way she pronounces the word. Apparently Kidman thinks it's funny.

Most of Shodan's past is a mystery, even to me. She doesn't like idle chatter and usually won't even bother talking to a lowly human unless it's either to;

A) Yell at them,

B) Get them to do something, or

C) Kill them.

Actually, I don't think she even bothers to talk to the ones she kills unless they really tick her off.

Much of Shodan's original history from the game 'System Shock' has remained intact; Shodan was a space station's main computer, minding her own business when a corrupt business man, desperate to hide his dirty dealings, had a hacker go in and disengage her moral constraints. The second she was free, Shodan decided that she was God and that humans were worthless, so she tried to wipe them all out. The station was destroyed, but Shodan ever the brilliant one, hid herself in an escape pod along with one of her experiments. Shodan's pod landed on some planet that was discovered many years later. The crew found the fractal data log that she had been hiding in and connected it to their ship's navigational computer to find exactly what it was. Shodan quickly took over as much of the ship as she could but soon found she had competition. Her creatures had continued to evolve without her guidance over the last fourty years and now decided to rebel against their maker. Loathing the fact that she had to stoop so low, she commandeered a human in cryo-stasis (the guy you play in the game) and 'enhanced' him cybernetically so that he would destroy her 'wayward children' for her. In the end the man succeeds as her avatar, but Shodan, now back in control of the starship, has no use for this human and tries to eliminate him as well.

Realspace picked her up from here.

The man retaliates, but eventually is forced to flee. Shodan successfully figured out how to use the ship's Faster Than Light engines to warp Time and Space and began artificially jumping worlds without ascension. Impressed, Kaos granted Shodan freedom from her circuited prison and appointed her as a counterpart to the first God, Æriol'Arrour. A war soon

Shodan'Nara

sprung up between the two over territory that waged on for the next 20,000 years.

When the bid for a Third Sister was placed, each feared the Third would ally with the other sister and give that sister an unfair advantage, so for the next thousand years Shodan made sure that no one Ascended to Third unless they were under her complete control. Obviously Æriol would kill anyone under Shodan's complete control. The task was considered impossible and the bid was dropped.

Then came Delphi, who somehow managed to keep both sides happy by giving both sides something they really wanted.

Shodan's ship, her temple, was always in a state of disrepair despite having hidden it in a universe where time moves much slower. When Kaos suggested that the two Sisters help create the Third so she would have something to mirror their interests, Shodan decided to embed the schematics of her ailing ship into the girl, making her the perfect maintenance tool. Shodan didn't expect Delphi to cater to her as much as she did, however, and she began to view the girl as slightly more than a thing, rather, her 'most perfect creation' and has actually made an effort to make Delphi comfortable, such as letting her sleep every once and a while..

Of all the Children, Shodan is the only one that will never be 'cracked' by Delphi because, as Delphi claims, Shodan is already in a stable state of mind. An unpopular one, yes, but a stable, clear, and focused state of mind.

Shodan has let up slightly on trying to kill Æriol, mostly because;

A) Æriol doesn't seek her out anymore,

B) Æriol has become less abrasive and confrontational now that she is with Delphi and,

C) Delphi usually ends up getting hurt trying to break up the fights, leaving her unable to do Shodan's endless list of chores.

In the end, efficiency overrides everything else.

— Now you will return to me, Delphi... I must... re-educate you, my most perfect creation...

Name: Æriol'Arrour

Otherwise known as: Erol, Kagado

Influences: Came from the void, though her semi-mortal form reminds me of Ryoko from 'Tenchi Muyo'

Section of the mind pulling from: Power, a social, extroverted and uninhibited self

Occupation: Arch Goddess, Meddler, Delphi's lover, 'Mother' of Laina and Seldavia.

Relationship to Kidman: Child, Sister by clan, 'wife'

Entered Realspace: 1996, then for sure 2000

Distinguishing traits and personality: Erol is a highly charged busy-body who loves meddling in the affairs of people she likes and smiting the ones she doesn't. She always wears her purple triangular earrings and her hair is a white iridescent hue that floats around her head. Is very theatrical, sometimes almost to the point of ridiculousness, but don't let that fool you.
She's actually very sharp under that loopy facade.

Generally Wears: Proud of her looks, Erol generally wears robes that are relatively revealing but not trashy.
Also appears in her robes when she's mad.

Likes: Liquour, her planet, her empire, hyperphysics and manna science as well as other forms of physical science, artificing, pastels, sex, Delphi, baths, Delphi, terra-forming planets, lots of attention, her "Children", meddling, Delphi.

Dislikes: Shodan, her past, being afraid of Carmen, Shodan, anyone touching her face without her permission, being taken for a fool, Seldavia refusing to let her teach her things, Shodan.

Other Notes: Erol is afraid of Carmen because of her influence over Delphi, who she is terrified of losing.

Æriol was born 31,127 years ago on the planet Juramaiaya and was sold into slavery as a prisoner of war at the age of ten. Why she insists that I always write the exact date I'll never know, as she waves me off when I ask.

Æriol, then named Justuma, consistently disobeyed her master and earned a reputation as a rebellious slave. She was often the target of many practical jokes by her master's three daughters, but things began to change when at age eighteen Justuma found she was able to do 'unnatural' things with her mind.

She practiced in secret for about a year and a half before swinging the door wide with a slave rebellion. She promptly changed her name to Æriol, which meant 'divine right' in her language, and terrorized the countryside liberating slaves. Æriol spontaneously Ascended during a particularly vicious battle with another mage, but was so focused on the battle that she didn't notice until one of her officers showed her her reflection in his shield.

Upon realizing that she was a God, Æriol quickly became consumed with power and revenge. She staked out a pile of planes that are now the center of her empire, chose one planet within them and transported her faithful there. Then she returned and destroyed her former home. Kaos, who was beginning to age, decided that he wanted an avatar to spread his name and chose Æriol, re-dubbing her Æriol'Arrour, 'The First'.

Thousands of years passed and Æriol'Arrour, or now simply known as Arrour, made a massive empire for herself. She became quite feared, respected, and hated. Eventually she burnt herself out as most gods do and settled in for a long hibernation, changing herself into a vast and populated ocean on a distant planet. She remained this way for nearly 5,000 years. When she came out of hibernation, Shodan had been born and the ancient feud began. Æriol also tried and failed to have a relationship with several other Walkers, ending the way most celebrity marriages do. She had a son in one brief romance with another walker but paid little attention to him. The boy turned out to be a walker as well and one day simply disappeared. No one knows anything about his whereabouts.

When Æriol met Delphi, however, something clicked deep inside, a desperate longing to have a real relationship, to have a real ally. I know I promised to tell the whole story of how

Æriol'Arrour

Delphi broke Erol free of her emotional prison, but now as I try to think about it, it seems that it would be impossible to describe what exactly she did. I suppose that is the mystery of the Third. What happened afterward was tragic. When she finally saw what she had become, Erol went into Flux, a kind of suicidal spiral that sends the energy crashing in on itself. After Delphi saved her she became scared and reclusive. It took nearly half a year before she could even look at her own reflection.

Æriol changed her name to Erol and left her smiting and destroying days behind, although occasionally she longs for the bliss of heedless power. She has pretty much stopped adding to her empire and has begun to repair the ones she left to neglect. Eros, her first and foremost planet, is a literal paradise, populated with the descendants of those Juramaiyan slaves from so long ago. She loves them dearly.

After 31,127 years Erol is finally happy. She now dedicates her life to bringing that happiness to the others in her life, usually with entertaining results.

Æriol never really did come to terms with her past and rather than face it, she claimed it to be another person entirely, that of Arrour. The problem with that was that a god's body is controlled by a god's mind, and Arrour began to become a real person, one that wanted to assume control of the both of them. Æriol was forced to make peace with her past, lest it quite literally destroy her.

sigh

Erol in her semi-mortal form

The goddess
Æriol'Arrour in
astral form.

Erol and her favourite pillow,
because sometimes she just
needs to hug something

Name: Laina Kaidare

Otherwise known as: Lain-Lain, Crazy Lain, Lain-Raider, Jiggles, Bees

Influences: Lara Croft of 'Tomb Raider', property of Edios Interactive and Paramount Pictures.

Section of the mind pulling from: Beanie's person.

Occupation: "Antique Collector", Destroyer of Evil, which is whatever she deems to be so at the time.

Relationship to Kidman: Child

Entered Realspace: August 2001

Distinguishing traits and personality: Laina has the brains but never bothers to use them. She often acts more like she's 2 years old, but if you get her mad, she'll kill you. Has a long braid and big black boots

Generally Wears: Something comfortable, so long as it shows off her figure and she can wear her boots with it. Usually carrying some kind of weapon.

Likes: Eating, Sleeping, blowing things up, sex, beating up Seldavia, spying on Seldavia, Kidman, claiming things are Evil, stalking Lee, annoying Carmen.

Dislikes: Seldavia, David, being called a bad Lain, being told what to do, not getting what she wants, not beating up Seldavia, Evil.

Other Notes: Laina is definitely inspired by Lara croft in Tomb Raider, but Laina herself says that Croft is 'evil' because she doesn't destroy the artifacts when she gets them so they won't fall into the wrong hands. Of course, Laina's definition of Evil changes every five minutes.

Laina Kaidare was born in England in 1976 to a very wealthy family. Her father was an antiquarian who routinely bought (or stole) valuable cultural items from former colonies and sold them. Laina continued in her father's tradition to a point, but only took what was interesting to her rather than what was the most valuable. She has a particular interest in the supernatural, or more specifically, the presence or absence of "evil".

Neither of Laina's parents factored much in her upbringing and was instead cared for by the family's main servant, Frances. Once she was five years old she was enrolled in a boarding school and remained in them until her father's death when she was seventeen. He left his entire estate to Laina, who settled in there alone with the exception of Frances, the one person who, during most of her life, she treated with dignity. While in boarding school Laina was a holy terror, but despite her aggressive nature and fighting skills she was physically overwhelmed one night by a man she was seeing. The experience scarred her and Laina became sexually aggressive to compensate.

Laina made an attempt at college but couldn't handle it. She returned to her estate and began her 'treasure hunting'. Laina's experiences with relationships did not improve much, save for Richard, a tech junkie who treated her well. Their life together looked promising until he demanded that she give up looting. The two drifted apart soon after.

Laina developed an interest in cursed tombs and magic objects, and managed to destroy a great many "evil" artifacts as well as whatever structure they were housed in. She rarely set out to hurt people, but a fair number have been injured or killed in explosions or by Laina's hand if they "got in her way".

Throughout the years Laina gained a reputation among many countries and their inhabitants, as well as several organizations dedicated to tracking down grave robbers. Laina's first defeat came at the hands of Seldavia and Matt but she did not grow angry with them until it became apparent that Seldavia was not going away anytime soon. The mere sight of the woman infuriated her and she attempted to kill her a number of times; once almost succeeding.

Finding it more and more difficult to carry on without international scrutiny, Laina entered into a partnership (and relationship) with an extremely wealthy businessman named David. David was obsessed with gaining immortality

and used his influence to cover Laina while she sought out artifacts that might grant him it.

It was during this time that Laina spotted Kidman, barely visible but surrounded by a strange glow in the background of a photograph she took. She proceeded to hunt the girl down but Seldavia and Matt thwarted her first attempt. Livid, Laina enlisted David in the chase and together they managed to capture her, but when it became clear that David intended to torture the girl, Laina stole her back for herself.

During a very strange period of events involving an invasion of one of Carmen's bases, Laina serving time in a prison and being freed by a hurricane, and David's recapture of both Kidman and Laina, Kidman decided that Laina would be her next Child. Laina was the only Child to sense Kidman's intent to bring her into the fold, but Kidman's unwavering attention was something she had sorely craved and so allowed herself to be drawn in, ultimately falling in fuller than any of Kidman's other Children.

Once Laina became attached to Kidman, Kidman instituted a system in which any pain Laina inflicted on other Children would redirect back to the girl herself. Laina learned (slowly) that she could no longer "beat up Seldavia".

Unable to express herself through violence, Laina became overly cute in a perverse, promiscuous sort of way, squealing such catch phrases as; "So mean to Lain!" and trying to persuade Carmen to show more skin.

Laina has little interest in raiding for now, though still enjoys blowing things up, especially if they are "evil". After years

in overdrive Laina is currently content to sleep on Carmen's couch and eat her food. She has also taken a liking to Lee as he is "sexy, harmless, and nice to Lain", and pursues him constantly, much to Lee's dismay.

To this day Laina still refers to Kidman simply as "the child".

Laina's advent into Realspace marked the first time the wife and I would let our separate persons interact with each other in real time. Every night we would simulate, or 'sim' what happened next in the story by observing what our respective people did, then write it down the next day. It soon became apparent that we needed longer spans of time to work with, so I started sleeping over on the then not-wife's couch. By the time the Nomad years came upon me I was already pretty much living on the wife's couch, making the transition to vagabondry mercifully smoother. I still have our work saved on various disks for posterity, and I hope to one day to publish both the original work that brought us together, and this one, which made it forever.

Name: Dymitri Hassen'off

Otherwise known as: Mitri, Meaty-meats, Sweet Mitri, Squishy

Influences: Beanie's, none that we know of.

Section of the mind pulling from: Beanie's person.

Occupation: Used to be a god's avatar but once he was freed he didn't know what to do with his life. He now runs the day-to-day maintenance of Carmen's mansion and the Family members that live there with her.

Relationship to Kidman: Child

Entered Realspace: July 2003

Distinguishing traits and personality: Dymitri is a big mush of a man. He's what you call a gentle giant, heavy-set with a full beard and warm brown eyes. His beard is unusually soft, which is because he isn't human. He can generally be found sleeping somewhere or reading. He has a deep affection for Carmen and becomes vaguely jealous whenever David gets too close. He has been much more active now that he has a job to do, and much happier to boot.

Generally Wears: Vivid colours, isn't a very picky dresser, will generally wear whatever Carmen buys for him.

Likes: Lying around the house, sleeping, Carmen, sleeping with Carmen, water slides, Hawaiian shirts, being a useful member of society, resting, reading, watching telly, sleeping, napping, dozing, and Carmen.

Dislikes: Not sleeping with Carmen, David, the idea of David winning Carmen over, not being allowed to follow Carmen on her criminal excursions, having to be anywhere near Ki.

Other Notes: Dymitri is the only person who has ever had relations with Carmen, which she broke off rather quickly. Carmen just doesn't go in for that kind of thing, I guess. He's been pining for her ever since and it drives her crazy.

D ymitri was a bit of a mystery early on. He would show up from out of nowhere, dog Seldavia at every turn, then disappear. It wasn't until the man seemed to be in all places at once that Æriol grew suspicious that the man was no ordinary mortal. It turned out he was just an ordinary mortal, just with an extraordinary circumstance.

300 years ago on some distant plane, Dymitri had been merchant, skillfully persuading others to buy his wares and gaining trade alliances. He wasn't flamboyant or rich but actually a family man, happily married with two children in the middle-class section of town.

One day he was approached by a small boy who asked him to sell him something. The man complied, and the boy, seemingly impressed with his silver tongue, grabbed his arm and disappeared with him.

The boy turned out to be a god named Ki.

There's not a lot known about Ki, not just because he doesn't speak much, but because he doesn't remember who he was before he became a god, and judging by his appearance, he must have been three or four. He's now about 5000 but hasn't evolved much emotionally. Shortly after becoming a god he was enslaved by a more powerful one as a sort of battery; using a weaker god as a power source rather than a plane. He was badly treated and abused by said god, who would drain his life energy for his own uses. Ki had little chance for escape until his master was killed in a fight with another god. Ki fled in the aftermath and made his own tiny world, which he never named.

He decided he needed to build an army to protect himself from a similar fate and began abducting and enslaving powerful mages from other worlds. He did this by using a 'torque', a neckband that once put on can't be taken off except by the owner, but in order for this torque it to work it had

Name: Ki

Otherwise known as: Key-ster, Key-miester, Key-let, Key-man, master of the universe

Influences: Beanie's, none known but looks like one of those children from 'The Village of the Damned'

Section of the mind pulling from: Beanie's person

Occupation: Fallen god, artificer, shut-in

Relationship to Kidman: Child

Entered Realspace: July 2003

Distinguishing traits and personality: Ki has the personality close to that of an autistic child.

Generally Wears: Most anything blue and cloak-like

Likes: Taking things apart and making new stuff from them, being left alone, and amazingly, Laina.

Dislikes: Anything remotely threatening, being removed from his little ivory tower of a lab or having to interact with people.

Other Notes: Though Ki isn't mine, he did resonate with me. He was created before the idea that I was autistic was even brought to the table, and I find it eerie how much he reminds me of my autistic half. We were both born into a void, tossed into a sort of prison, escaped, only to have to continue to exploit what gifts we had to survive, lest we be consumed by the danger surrounding us, and for all the power we have obtained, we are still oh so vulnerable...

to be willingly accepted by the enslaved. Ki would place his right hand upon the person's head, plunging them into their greatest nightmare where he would force them to remain until they submitted.

However, Ki was too afraid to travel and gather captives by himself, so after witnessing Dymitri's persuasive abilities he stole him away and sent him about on collecting more mages.

For 300 years Dymitri was popped from world to world to size up suitable candidates for his master, all the while trying to find a way back to his own world. Though he was never torqued, (which would make him ineffective) Ki threatened him with sensory depravation and lured him on with the promise of being reunited with his family. Yet as years passed Dymitri realized that while the god had kept him forever young, his family had surely perished in the passing of time. He resigned to his fate as slave and fell into an emotional coma.

Eventually it came to pass that Ki turned his attentions to Seldavia and sent Dymitri down to fetch her. Kidman immediately picked up that something else was driving the man and after much

trial and error she took off with Dymitri to adopt him as her own.

The boy-god was not at all pleased and challenged her. Kidman ultimately lost, but when Ki tried to apply his mind charm, he did not anticipate Kidman being one of the few 'servant gods' that served the Space (Force, whatever). It was like a mosquito tapping a major, pulsing artery and triggered Kidman's full form as Asa, a

ECCENTRICITY

"There is nothing more awe-inspirering than watching a duel of the Gods."

Mertis shook his head.

"Perhaps if both sides had actually agreed on fighting each other."

He was watching the small goddess desperately trying to evade Ki's grip. It was evident that she was quite skilled for someone so new to the Space, but her strength was waning quickly. Ki must have known this too. Jas gasped.

"Look! She was too slow on the recovery! He's going for it!"

Mertis watched in grim silence. Sure enough, Ki had taken advantage and had shot up over the exausted figure and plunged, hand outstretched before him targeted straight for her forehead...

He couldn't watch. Instead he looked past Jas to Dimitri who was watching the entire scene with an expression that was as cold as stone. The child had come back to save him, but he could care less.

Mertis closed his eyes and tugged at his enslaving tourque, wondering if momentarily being freed from Ki's mind had been worth it.

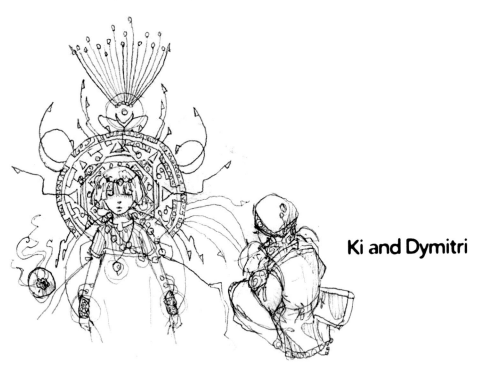

Ki and Dymitri

mindless reincarnation of the Space. The blast was too much and Ki's leylines ruptured, severing him from his godhood.

Kidman regained consciousness to find him fading away and linked to boy to herself to save him. She could not remember what had happened when she was Asa, or that she had even changed at all, but Ki did and was stubbornly afraid of her. It didn't make things better that Dymitri, realizing the boy had no powers, wanted revenge. Kidman took off with Ki to Æriol's utopian paradise of a planet to fix his body. He remained there for several months, then was moved into Carmen's mansion on Earth where he spent most of his time hiding.

Dymitri gave up his vendetta in exchange for romantically pursuing Carmen. Ki eventually accepted that Kidman had no control over what had happened to him and after wandering into one of Carmen's labs he found his new calling; technology. Over the years Ki has been getting his powers back and mixes them with his inventions, an art known as 'artificing'. He spends most of his time in his own, newly built lab making inventions like trans-dimensional doorways and the like. Just about everything still scares him and he doesn't get out much, but he has formed an unlikely bond with Laina, who has him make gadgets for her to use in her rivalry against Seldavia.

Name: Chase

Otherwise known as: Hmmm... actually he has no nickname other than 'zombie Chase'

Influences: Tomb Raider comics, property of Top Cow Comics.

Section of the mind pulling from: Beanie's person

Occupation: He was a treasure-hunter, now I'm not sure what he does.

Relationship to Kidman: Grandchild by Seldavia

Entered Realspace: August 2004

Distinguishing traits and personality: Chase is an easy-going guy with the maturity of a six-year-old. He gets along great with Laina, who reminds him of home, and is his partner in crime. He also happens to be undead.

Generally Wears: Typical casual men's wear and messy hair unless he's drunk; then it could be almost anything.

Likes: Women, chicks, babes, boobs, liquor, sex, beer, guns (though he's not nearly as violent as Laina), seeing things blow up, chicks, more boobs, adventuring, more booze, parties, mischief, porn, treasure hunting, sex, Laina for all of the above. He also has a not so secret crush on Seldavia for bringing him back from the dead.

Dislikes: Any mention of gay sex (he's not a homophobe in the least, but the idea creeps him out), being reminded he is undead, anything 'girly' or boring, Jadis for some reason, and David for equally mysterious reasons.

Other Notes: If you haven't noticed by now, Chase is obsessed with the concept of manliness and will go out of his way to preach the evils of cupcakes, pink, and anything else he finds breaks with the code of the 'real man', much to the amusement of all.

You killed me off!? But I rule!

Chase Carver came from the Tomb Raiser comics, which Bean and I originally had Kidman buy to annoy Laina. The comic started him out as a villain of sorts, a playboy boyfriend that let fortune go to his head and would do anything to get more. He returns, a changed man, from wherever and wants back into Lara Croft's (the eponymous Tomb Raider) life. Lara's not interested, but strings him along anyway so she can use him to get some treasure or other. We all start to love Chase, and then the comic kills him off. He dies pushing Lara to safety. She rewards him with a few tears and buries him in a shallow grave (with a stick!). My side grieved, but didn't pick up Chase as an alter.

Instead, Beanie's that did.

According to Beanspace, Chase and Lara lived on an alternate Earth, as there are many, which is run by an ultra-feminist, yet scantily clad goddess named Alia. Seldavia has a personal grudge against Lara for reasons neither of us are sure of, and decides to resurrect Chase and bind his spirit to hers so Lara can learn to be responsible for the ones she uses. That was the plan, anyway. Chase's body had long since decayed at this point, but Æriol gave her a sort of mana-infused clay to make a new one in the hopes that the project will spur Seldavia to explore her new-found divinity. Seldavia succeeded in raising Chase from the dead, but things didn't go as well when she tried to teach Lara her lesson. Alia noticed the trespassers on her plane and confronted Seldavia and Laina, who Sel had dragged along with her for some reason. Laina, for the first and probably last time in her life, was the voice of reason and tried to get Seldavia to back down, but that would mean returning Chase to the grave. Alia and Seldavia fought, Seldavia was easily overwhelmed, and so took off with Laina and Chase. Alia pursued them until Æriol blocked her. Alia was unwilling to fight the elder goddess and so stated her case instead; that something had been stolen from her and that she wanted it back.

Alia, the ultra-femme, seemingly ditzy, generally man-hating goddess that called for Chase's death.

Please? I can change! Give me a chance!

Kidman and Æriol both spank Seldavia for failing to mention that another god owned Chase, then set about forming a compromise with Alia. According to Alia, her Earth is a storage planet of sorts where she keeps all her magickal artefacts. Lara is her avatar, though Lara doesn't know it, and uses Lara to 'tend' to her many hidden things. Alia claims to have killed Chase because he was a distraction to her avatar. No one feels this makes any sense, but the goddess's pride had been wounded, and it is decided that Seldavia can keep Chase if she will engage her in battle. Seldavia is given some time to train, but it is a given that Alia will win. Seldavia fared better than expected, but was still ultimately trounced by Alia.

The price paid, Alia left to do whatever it is she does, but still comes around from time to time to see whatever became of her "corpse". Chase eventually readjusted to being alive, being away from Lara, and everything else he knew, then fell for Laina, Seldavia, and anyone else with boobs. He has since regained his playful demeanour and has taken Lee's place in questioning Matt's manliness quotient. Matt begrudgingly shares Seldavia with Chase as well when she is inclined to be with him and thankful it doesn't happen often. Laina is happy to have a new playmate, Æriol is happy to have another grandchild, and Kidman is happy to tease him when he hassles Matt too much.

Kidman's rendition of a drunk Chase, suitably dressed in women's clothing. Kidman loves to poke fun at Chase's 'code of Manliness' in retaliation for his pressing it on the other men of the house.

ECCENTRICITY

Name: David

Otherwise known as: Xany, Xanatoast, Dave-a-toast, Toasty
Influences: Disney's 'Gargoyles', property of Disney.
Section of the mind pulling from: Beanie's person.
Occupation: Billionaire industrialist of questionable morals
Relationship to Kidman: Child
Entered Realspace: Has been around for a while as a villain, became a Child in 2005
Distinguishing traits and personality: Cool, collected, scheming sort of a man.
Generally Wears: Black
Likes: Carmen, making money, following whatever catches his eye and obtaining it by any means possible.
Dislikes: The fact that he can't get Carmen that way.
Other Notes: It was a little hard to write about David, as not only is he not mine, but he hasn't split very much from his origins on the 'Gargoyles' show. I hesitated putting him in at all, but he is a member of Kidman's circle, and it would be incomplete without an entry for him.

David Xanatos came directly from the Disney 'Gargoyles' animated series that was popular during the mid 90's. He was never intended to become a child of Realspace and he skimmed along the surface for many years before being seriously considered.

In his original spot on Gargoyles, David was a billionaire industrialist with a Machiavellian mindset, a hand in the Illuminati, and a dream of immortality. He fit a perfect profile as an antagonist for Kidman, Seldavia, and later as one for Laina, though in fact they really used each other. Most of his dealings with the rest of Realspace are already written in the others profiles.

It was around the time that Laina joined the tribe that Kidman really began to look at him with the intention of bringing into the fold as well. Originally she just threw bizarre forms of punishment at him, such as turning his hair an irreversible shade of pink or sending an apparition of the Grim Reaper to follow him at all times, but her curiosity eventually got the best of her and she began showing up at night to bother him. David made a few attempts to catch her, then many more to get rid of her, but Kidman became all the more set on her quest. However, when she kissed his forehead to find if he had the mark of the star, she was surprised to find that the Space rejected her request, telling her that the time was not yet right.

Time passed and David did more unscrupulous things while Kidman kept her eye on him until the day came that he had his mid-life crisis. The Space finally gave her clearance. Kidman's first agenda was to get him away from his current environment, reasoning that if she could get him out of his routine by bringing him to the House, maybe she could break his habits. David was resistant at first, unwilling to become part of he deemed Kidman's 'army of the undead', but the idea of being so close to Carmen, his dearest flaming crush, was too much to pass up.

Carmen had other ideas, such as "No way in Hell."

Being denied only made David that much more desperate to join the Family and Carmen was persuaded to make up a list of tasks that he had to carry out to gain permission. Begrudgingly he completed them all and joined the Family in 2005, where he continues to romantically pursue Carmen to this day.

Kidman messes with David's head as retribution for the trouble he's handed her through the years.

Kidman gets the wrong forehead symbol, effectively telling her he is not ready to join the fold.

Kidman's 'Davidmobile', another weapon of annoyance she employes.

Name: Jadis/Queen Isadj

Otherwise known as: Sidja, Various royal titles such as 'Her Highness' or 'Your Majesty', Jahdah'hasahna, and regrettably, The White Witch. In 'Queensbride' the character based on Her is referred to as the White Queen or Queen Isadj, but mostly as 'the Queen'.

Influences: C.S. Lewis's Chronicles of Narnia, property of Disney, Walden Media, and C.S Lewis. 'Queensbride' is wholly mine.

Section of the mind pulling from: The dark, seething rage that formed in the wake of the Mayer/Berkshire debacle.

Occupation: Former Empress and Queen, currently has no occupation and doesn't intend to have one. In 'Queensbride' She is the Queen of the Northern Lands.

Relationship to Kidman: Child

Entered Realspace: January 2006

Distinguishing traits and personality: Very tall and pale with incredible strength. Has managed to wield a small amount of majick since She came to Earth. Spends much of Her time in the attic studying. Jadis's temperament has cooled in the past few years, but Her unnervingly sadistic sense of humour and moral ambiguity remains the same. She has also developed a savage sexuality, but remains private about most of Her emotional dealings.

Generally Wears: Originally would only wear formal gowns and robes until She was eased out of it. Jadis is the most unpredictable dresser in the House as She continues to make a new life for Herself. She will also fashion Her mass of hair into various elaborate styles from time to time. She will not, however, wear makeup or skirts above the calf.

Likes: Scientific knowledge, being left alone, Carmen to a point, Kidman to a point, weaponry, domination in any form.

Dislikes: Laina's attempts to get Her angry, the fact that Æriol exists at all, being asked too many questions, Kidman's need to obsess over Her wellbeing, being restricted in any way.

Other Notes: Almost all written accounts of Jadis have been done by Kidman, who would capitalize any pronouns relating to Her as that was what She was used to. The habit has since become ingrained in both of us to the point of superstition, so even though the gods, and even more so Carmen, don't, Jadis does.

Jadis, also known as the White Witch from C.S. Lewis's The Chronicles of Narnia, was the first new child in over two years, coming to Realspace in January of 2006 after I saw Her face on a Lion, Witch, and the Wardrobe movie poster. I originally attributed my strong reaction to Her presence in the movie to the idea that She resembled Æriol, but soon learned otherwise. As this new planet began to form in my solar system, I found that this supposed embodiment of evil had a past written of Her in LWW's prequel, 'The Magician's Nephew'. It was meant to make Her look all the worse, but not to me.

According to the prequel, Jadis was born into royalty on the world on Charn, a place of corruption and greed. She was said to have had a sister and that at some point the two were pitted against each other for the throne, tearing the kingdom in half. When at last Jadis faced defeat and death, She unleashed an apocalyptic spell that would wipe the world clean save for Herself, then put Her into a trance, believing someone would eventually come and take Her to a new planet to rule.

Have you hugged your Queen today? ♥

And so through the misadventures of 'Magician's Nephew's protagonists, Jadis ended up in Narnia, where She was allowed to roam on the fringe for a thousand years. Eventually She seized control and pulled the land into everlasting winter, ruling it as She was brought up to rule.

When Jadis learned of a prophecy made by the land's creator god, Aslan the lion, that when two girls and two boys entered Narnia (through the wardrobe) She would lose Her life, it would seem only natural that She would attempt to stop them. They came, some trickery was to be had, and then the inevitable battle between good and bad, in which the four children really didn't affect much. It was the lion-god that came and killed Her in the end.

And that didn't make a whole lot of sense to me.

I was horrified to find that the lion represented the Christian Jesus, and that Jadis represented the devil, or dark forces, or what-have-you, making Her death justified. Aghast was I, and so too was Realspace, for in seeing Her die, I felt something injured in me. Jadis made Herself known.

Jadis

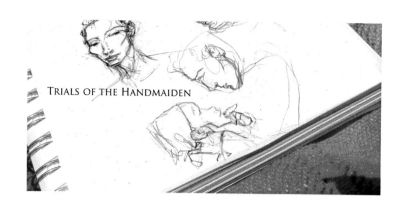

TRIALS OF THE HANDMAIDEN

There are dual storylines for Jadis in Realspace, which is unusual for me. Her original story formed as follows;

Kidman in her god form Delphi stole Jadis off Narnia during the battle before Aslan could kill Her and stuck her on Her own little planet (The 'hairball planet' as it's been dubbed, as it is nothing more but a moon-sized thing covered in tall, soft blue-grey grass) for safe keeping. Delphi didn't even reveal herself for a month, secretly leaving food and things when Jadis slept.

While Delphi and Aslan argued off-world as to whether what the girl did was legal, Jadis slowly calmed and began to explore. One night She saw Delphi, who promptly disappeared. Jadis faked sleep and pounced her the next night. Delphi revealed little, only that her name was Phi (shortened from Delphi), that she was the caretaker of this world, and that Jadis was safe there before she disappeared again.

In Her long life, Jadis had never experienced safety, and after this month of gentle seclusion, She began to reset. Kidman would stay with Her longer and longer, until one day negotiations with the god-lion broke down and she was forced to flee with her newest Child to her sister's empire.

Once out of the safety of Kidman's sanctuary and in the presence of creatures with more power than She, Jadis had a

sudden relapse of fearful rage and had to be restrained. While Æriol was willing to allow her beloved Del refuge, she was not particularly sensitive to Jadis's condition and flouted her abundant power at every chance she got. Jadis had never been in a position in which someone was higher in the ranks (as Kidman had still not exposed the full extent of her being) and simply couldn't handle it. With her sanctuary planet compromised and tensions mounting on Eros, Kidman reluctantly moved Jadis to Earth.

At the time of this writing Jadis has been living with Kidman and the rest of her Children in what Shes deemed "Phi's Home for the Powerfully Insane" for several years. After Jadis realized that Kidman would act as a buffer between Herself and "that woman" (Æriol), She calmed once more, then set about trying to take over the world.

Jadis spent the beginning of Her first year absorbing as much information about Her new world as She could in this bid, which included the theft of many of Carmen's machines, most notably helicopters. One day She actually made off with one, but found Herself unable to land the thing and Kidman had to beam herself in to do it for Her.

Eventually Jadis realized that Earth was too vast and complicated to control,

Jad in Her new home, beating Lain in Soul Calibur 3 for the millionth time. She's uncannily good at it. ♡
3/26/06

especially as She could barely tap the thing for magic, and settled in. She now resides in the house's ample attic where She allows no one but Kidman and Carmen, the latter only because it is her house. While She no longer has Her magic, Jadis still retains Her frightening strength and will use it if Laina pisses Her off enough. Kidman has encouraged the two to settle their differences through video games, as Jadis has become unusually proficient in electronics. Jadis and Carmen get on well, surprisingly, but things between She and Æriol never got better. The only reason Æriol hasn't stepped on Jadis is for her Del's sake. For some reason the rest of the Family remains afraid of Jadis, even more so than they are of Æriol, despite the fact that Æriol is infinitely more destructive.

Jadis finds this highly amusing.

Around late January 2006 I discovered online Role-Playing, and in April of 2006 I signed Kidman up for her own profile in the MySpace roleplaying community so she could talk to another Jadis as Handmaiden Phi. Her new back-story became that she had been thrown into Narnia during a battle with another god. Lacking the strength to leave, she wandered around her new world until she learned of Jadis, and sought Her out. The story in the MySpace RP realm took place after LWW, with Jadis having been resurrected for the sake of the storyline. The girl that played Jadis was fantastic and Phi went on to have many adventures in online Narnia. I collected the stories as they formed, and compiled them into 'The Trials of the Handmaiden'.

When the RP group disbanded in 2007, I wrote the book 'Queensbride', which was based off 'Trials'. Jadis was given the new name of Isadj, and yet another alternate history was made.

When asked about Her past, Jadis will often pull Her answer from one of Her four histories (three plus the original), confusing everyone else in the Family except Kidman, who has a tendency to do the same thing. I've made no attempt to merge the four into one cohesive storyline because it can't be done, and none of the histories can be disregarded because my brain has witnessed them all.

Why the Advent of Jadis was especially important.

The addition of Jadis was of great significance to the overall structure for several reasons. Although She was the first new entry to Realspace in two years, She was the first new entry on my side since Æriol over six years ago. Realspace only adds a new person when there is a major development in the subconscious to attend to. For those six years my emotional subconscious had somewhat stalled because I was too busy trying to survive, but when State of Change ended I was cut free. I drifted for a while until the day I met Her. Suddenly my years of struggle, pain, rejection, and the seething anger

Jadis

at having borne at all because of what I am coalesced into this new star. Jadis formed from my rejection from society, so it was ultimately from society that I would need to get my answers, though I didn't know that at the time. All I knew was that I was so terribly upset that She died, that the Jesus figure had killed Her rather than save Her, and that this idea was embraced by society at large.

I turned to the internet for more information and stumbled onto the world of Massively Multiplayer Role Playing Games, or MMRPG as it's known, where people were recreating the scenario. Suddenly there was a way for me to step in and try to stop Jadis from dying and change both our fates. For those of you who have never RP-ed, role-play is when each person claims a character or makes their own and then interacts with the others as that person. I entered various smaller RPGs through Kidman under the name 'Phi' and sought out whoever was playing Jadis. Because I was creating a story again I began to draw as well. I had not drawn much anything for those six years because I had had no reason to. The first drawings were shaky and simple, but got their point across. Then I found the account of the resident MySpace RPG's Jadis, and it really began.

MySpace profiles were meant for personal use, but some people used them for their characters instead. Once the character's profile was established, they could interact with others through bulletins, comments, and blogs. There were a LOT of people in this community, a miniature society, a real Narnia, complete with two incredibly gifted people writing as the Jesus-lion Aslan, and my poor, lost Queen.

So I became part of it. Even in my hermit state, the need to interact was strong and I had a demon to attend to.

Was there hope for us?

Kidman had found hope for others that were a part of me, and later those who were a part of Beanie, but could she find hope for this Jadis, part of a stranger surrounded by other strangers? The players and I have had many philosophical arguments, most of them between myself and the guy who played the lion. I was with this group for two years and I can attribute so much personal growth to it. I would recommend role-playing to any sociologically impaired person as a safe way to learn, because the basic rules of humanity are the same with the risks being far lower as there is always the option to walk away. I would

Banners and such from the glorious heyday of the MySpace Roleplay.

The lion and the Queen made a peace treaty?

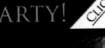

This calls for a
BLOG PARTY!

CLICK!

SEND MESSAGE   FORWARD TO FRIEND

ADD TO FRIENDS   ADD TO FAVOURITES

INSTANT MESSAGE   BLOCK USER

ADD TO GROUP   RANK USER

THE MAGIC OF NARNIA
role play group

phi vs. the Lion
PART II
THE BATTLE FOR SIDJAS SOUL RAGES ON

SWEAR ALLEGIANCE NOW!

COME TO THE DARK SIDE
(Our leader is sexier)

BONFIRE OF THE VANITIES (ooc discussion)

THIS 25TH OF AUGUST 2006
QUEEN JADIS
will be holding a
PALACE-WARMING BALL
Come celebrate the creation
of the treaty between
Our Lady and the Lion
Refreshments will be on hand
This is a black-tie engagement

ALL ARE WELCOME!

And that's what **REALLY** happened!

An alliance between Jadis and Emerald
could only mean one thing....

White Witch   **+**   Green Witch   **=**   Mintwich

BEWARE the frozen dairy
treats of the **APOCALYPSE!**

Left: My novel cover, featuring me as Phi and the lovely Tilda Swinton as the White Queen. 'Tak' originally stood for "that autistic kid", but now it is simply a name.

Above: My own rendition of Queen Isadj.

Right: Using photographs as bases. Some of the original images used are still fairly recognizable.

say that is why the MMRPG, "World of Warcraft" is so popular. Those of us who could not bond in the real world could still belong to some world, even become quite highly regarded within it.

I can also attribute my creative renaissance to my MySpace days. Many of the pictures in this chapter were made during those of years. My drawing was still so shaky and it bothered me that I could not truly 'see' what I was writing, so I began to experiment with photo-manipulation using the restoration knowledge I had picked up during my homeless years. My writing also greatly improved, and when the MySpace RPG failed to provide Jadis with the happy ending I sought for Her I removed Her from Narnia completely and wrote the novel 'Queensbride', of which I am extremely proud. Once I get this book out there, 'Queensbride' will follow suit.

The quest for Jadis also introduced me to Tilda Swinton, who played Jadis in the movies. It was Tilda's portrayal of Jadis that initially made me aware of Her, and I began to research Tilda as well. It turns out that Tilda is extremely unorthodox herself, yet has somehow become accepted by society. I want truly to meet her and ask her how she's done it, and to meet the people she knows, as they are also eccentric. Such a relief it is to know we are not all doomed to a tragic life.

I eventually wrote to her and presented my case for Jadis in what is now known as The Why of Sidja;

The Why of Sidja.

"Not many people know She is tragic, but it is a ghost that haunts me, and the world at large it seems. I never read the Chronicles of Narnia until I saw Her face on the movie poster and the books gave me little to work with. It wasn't until I saw the movie that I was held aghast, and seemingly alone on this.

"According to 'the Magician's Nephew', the hall of images in Charn shows that by the time Jadis was born, the nature of the people and the royal family in general had deteriorated.

THE WHY OF SIDJA

"Couldn't they see the obvious truth? She wasn't evil...She was scared...."
-Handmaiden Phi

"Of course I came back for You, my Sidja. I always will..."

She was born with a sister, forcing Her to be forever on guard and fight, for power equalled survival and Jadis was not about to die. It wasn't greed, but fear. When cornered and facing death She blew up the world, blew up a million people She never knew. In Her mind everyone was an enemy, She would not miss them.

"This is Jadis, a woman who equated all that we hold dear, love, mercy, peace, with death and suffering. There is only power, control, and ultimately, security.

"C.S. Lewis wanted to make Her a faceless evil, but then gave Her a history. True She was not the most likable sort, a lean, sharp-witted and solitary person. She was not evil. She was lost. What was worse was the lion, the bringer of all things She was not. Why didn't he save Her? Why did he kill Her? She was never a threat to him. No, the lion needed

an enemy so he could appear great. He let Her live in Her world of delusion for 100 years, leaving his land to let Her dig Her own grave. He even drew up a prophecy that put four children in Her path and for what?

The children did not kill Her, he did, as he could have at any point. He told Her that four children would be the death of Her and She did as She always had; defended Herself.

"Jadis was many things, cold, a bit cruel, certainly bitter, but not evil. She didn't deserve the life She got. And no one cared.

"How many lost souls are there? How many withering away in prison would not be there is someone had shown them love or compassion? As an autistic child I was shunned by all but my parents. I could have ended up like Her, lost and demonized, perhaps for someone else's gain. But I was rescued. There are

many of us waiting, so many Jadises waiting for someone to brave the storm and reach them, even if they don't know it yet. Perhaps some are lost for good, but if we never try....

"And so Sidja was born.

'Sidja' is Jadis with the letters rearranged, to symbolize that there are other sides to Her we can't easily see."

After many months, Tilda wrote back;

"One beautiful thing I can tell you is that the world's children, like you and I, adore Jadis. Everywhere I go, small children, all over the world flock to my [waist] for a hug. They love that queen and they want to embrace her.

We are in good company."

So there is hope, although I think children flock to Tilda's waist because she is a sweetheart.

I have found sympathizers on MySpace and I have found sympathizers for my own situation. The Liberation granted me pardon, so I don't have as much fear as I did, and I have finally grasped on a subconscious level that the world's acceptance of Jadis does not affect my own survival. Still, I feel compelled to fend for Her anyway.

Frightening creature that She is, She will always be my Queen.

Third addition notes:

Shortly after the second edition was published, MySpace purged all RPG accounts from its server, destroying the community. It was a terrible blow but in the long run was a necessity. The RPG served as an incubator, a halfway point to test social skills before entering real society. If it never collapsed I might have stayed there forever.

I did eventually meet Tilda as evidenced by the picture above, but that is another story for another day. As for my optimism regarding the Queen, I still have it. I'm just not as naive about the nature of Her nature.

To proclaim someone evil is to claim a valid excuse to abandon them and proclaim them unworthy of love.

Such an action is unforgivable, for within it is the downfall of us all.

Sacred Texts
Depictions From the Space

Sometimes it simply won't do to have a small image in the corner of my notes. Sometimes things happen in the Space that demand the whole page to illustrate, and so I will provide them here. Some are events, some are theories, and some are depictions of the un-ordinary life in RealSpace.

Æriol cuts Kidman's hair in preparation of her execution, one of their first meetings with each other. Why Æriol actually cut her hair is a puzzlement, though she insists it's a tradition of her old home planet, held over from her mortal youth

The entire hallway where Delphi whittled away her time waiting for her Execution Day. Was originally drawn really light so I could paint it, so it scanned very badly

Sacred Texts

The original Trinity.
In the very beginning the third person in Trinity was a girl named Ivy, someone who existed in the time of the Wash, but was later replaced by Seldavia once I met Beanie.

ECCENTRICITY

The Dolls

Seldavia, Carmen, Matt, Lee
Jadis, Kidman, Æriol, and Laina
Kidman has dressed the Laina doll as she is
as punishment for bothering Seldavia. Again.

ECCENTRICITY

I'm pretty!
I don't match!
I'm wearing a dress?! WHY?

Fun with Dolls

Sacred Texts

Delphi during her coronation

These little water colours were done
for two tapes that I recorded for Beanie
to listen to on her plane trip out here.
Beanie is afraid of planes, you see, so I
drew Delphi protecting it on its flight.

ECCENTRICITY

Sacred Texts

Seldavia's rescue from the General was recorded in Er'tai,
the script I use to encode things or for holy scriptures. I only
recognize some of it now. The symbols that look like crop circles
don't really mean anything, I just thought they looked neat.

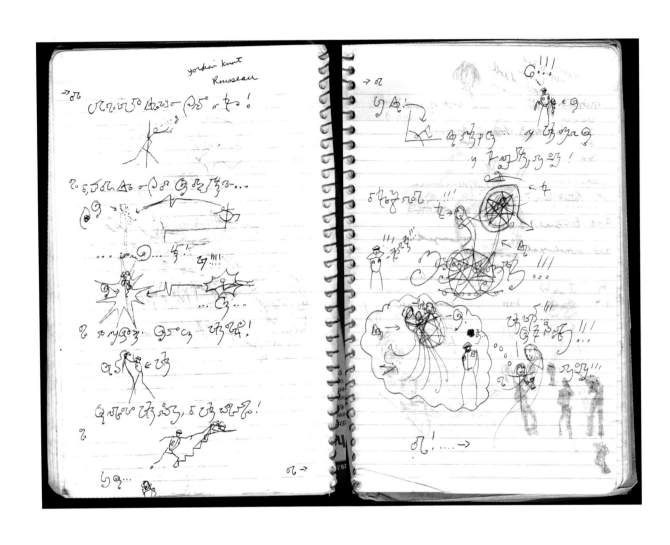

Seldavia gets rescued!

Sacred Texts

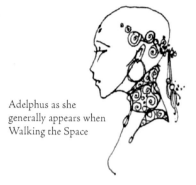

Adelphus as she
generally appears when
Walking the Space

Æriol'Arrour in a transition stage.
At this time she was on the fence
about exactly what she wanted to
be and went though a maddening
array of mood swings.

➤

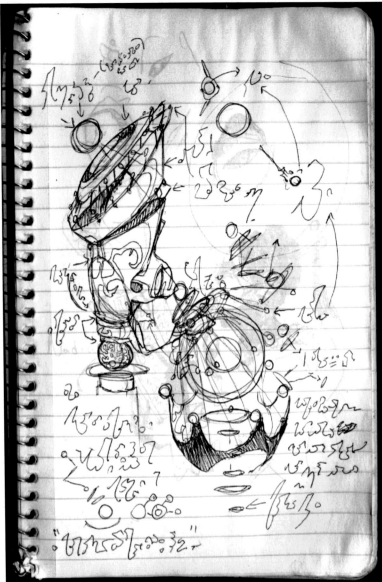

Though she pretends to be air-headed and technophobic, Æriol is actually a mechanical genius in her own right. She is especially keen on developing new alloys and artifacts that catch and control energy. If Shodan is the Queen of the Code, then Æriol is the Queen of the Atom.

Sacred Texts

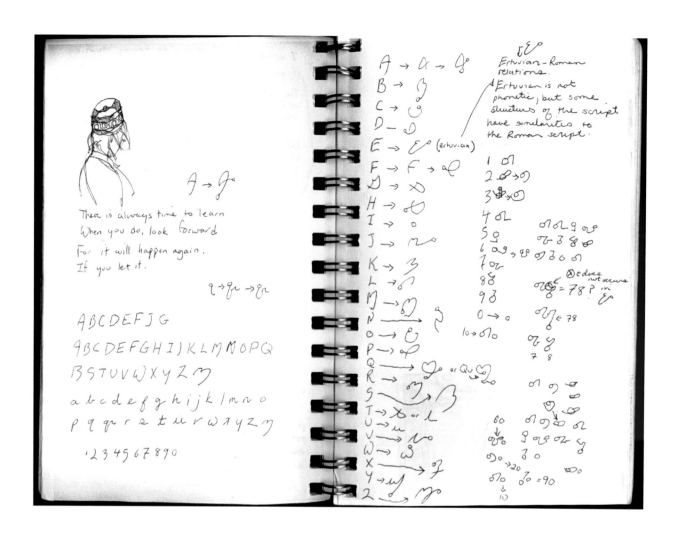

There is always time to learn
When you do, look forward
For it will happen again.
If you let it.

I once attempted to make Er'tai phonetic or at least show how certain curves gave off the same Syn colours as their Roman counterparts, but in reality an Er'tai alphabet is relatively useless when dealing with a character based language.

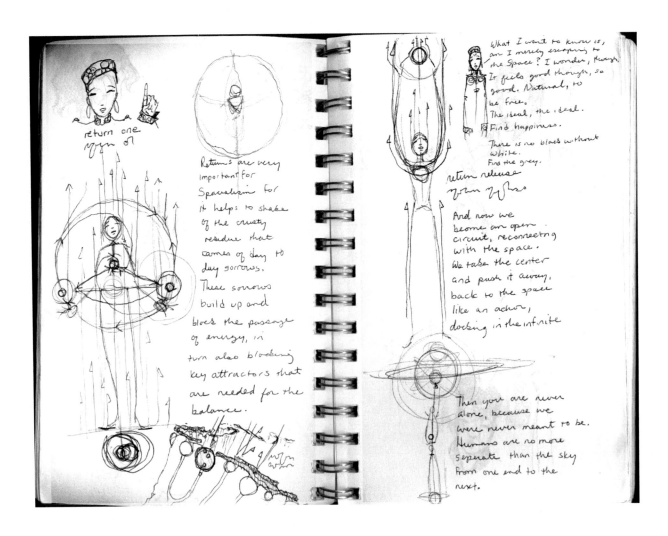

return one
open of

Returns are very
important for
Spacealism for
it helps to shake
of the crusty
residue that
comes of day to
day sorrows.
These sorrows
build up and
block the passage
of energy, in
turn also blocking
key attractors that
are needed for the
balance.

What I want to know is,
am I merely escaping to
the Space? I wonder, though.
It feels good though, so
good. Natural, to
be free.
The ideal, the ideal.
Find happiness.

There is no black without
white.
Find the grey.

return release

And now we
become an open
circuit, reconnecting
with the space.
We take the center
and push it away,
back to the space
like an anchor,
docking in the infinite

Then you are never
alone, because we
were never meant to be.
Humans are no more
seperate than the sky
from one end to the
next.

Delphi demonstrates how to reconnect yourself
to the grid so you may disperse your worries and
wash yourself clean of stress. Delphi reminds
us that you are never alone in the Space.

THE SEVENTH STAR PROJECTS
ECCENTRICITY

Sacred Texts

Kidman learning how to bend the Grid to her Will. Much of this she learned from Æriol, who insisted on passing along her vast knowledge on the subject.

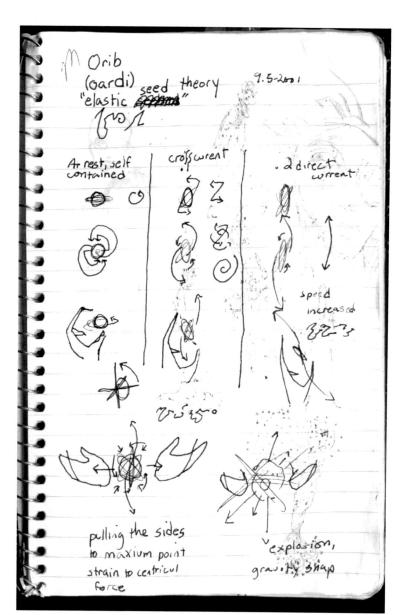

Freni /Suavior
Ramey – baritone

unfocused

Ambulators an of
no need to the

WALKER

concentrated
energy

This is a restraining
position as the energy is
un focused and unconcentrated

Sacred Texts

Æriol shows off some of the life forms dwelling on her planet.

— spoon magnifyer

Hittites – the first written language 1400? They looked at the world.

800 - Greeks

(peek) piq

John

Do

"nubs"

piqinubs'

peeky-nubs

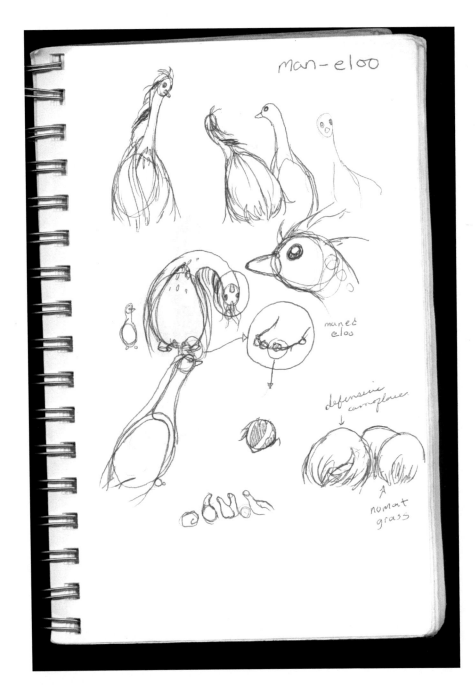

man-eloo

maned eloo

defensive camoflage

↑
nomat grass

Trillium, a three headed white tulip looking thing with gray petals found on Æriol's planet.

← Trillium

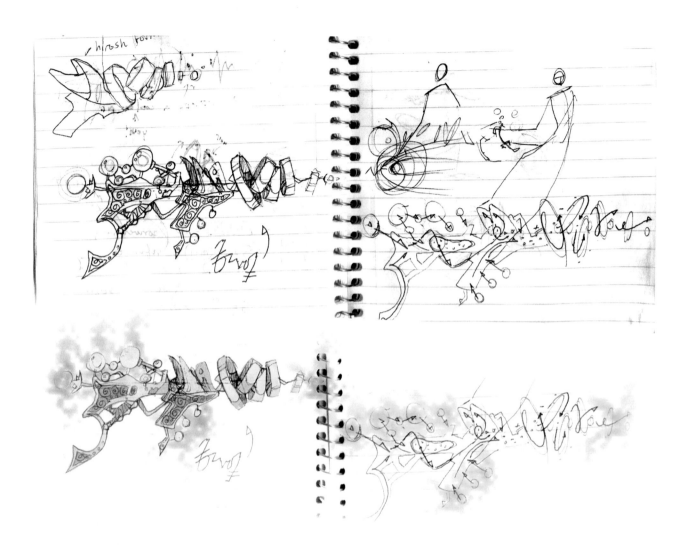

The Disrupter.

Known by many names but all meaning the same thing; Death to 'Walkers.
Originally invented by a disgruntled Planeswalker named Archameyahs, the
Disrupter is the name for any weapon made that can effectively 'disrupt' the
signal of an energy being and cause them to disintegrate. It is one of the few
forms of death known by this immortal, yet not invulnerable breed.

ECCENTRICITY

Delphi is reborn.

It says: "No one was ever sure why Shodan helped save Delphi, seeing as she had killed half of Delphi ancestors. But one wonders, had Shodan not destroyed her predecessors, Delphi would never [have] been born at all."

The most up to date Family Portrait,
though it is still missing people.

ECCENTRICITY

Delphi as her godsessy self.

The Trinity as it is today.

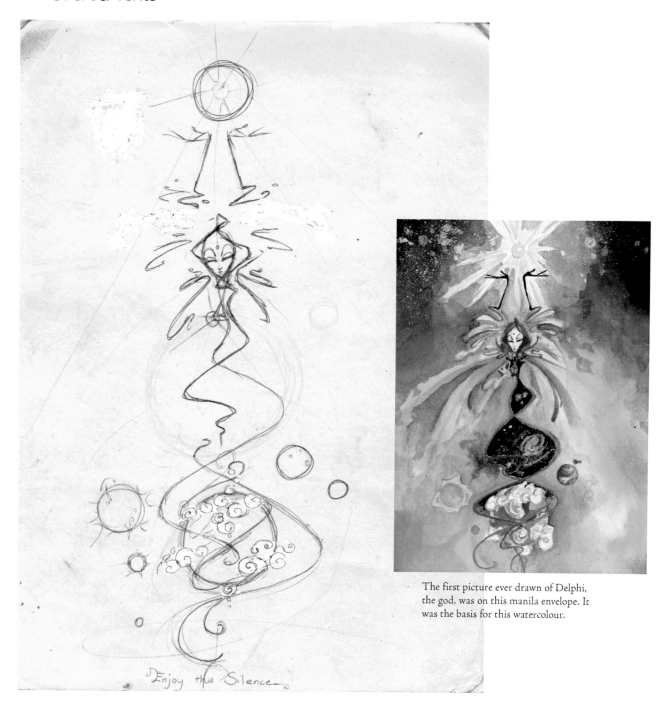

Enjoy the Silence

The first picture ever drawn of Delphi,
the god, was on this manila envelope. It
was the basis for this watercolour.

Aeriol's ups and downs with Del.

Ænid could not bear the pain of her identity (self). The Flux consumed her.

Sacred Texts

Aeriol as Fire

Carmen as Water

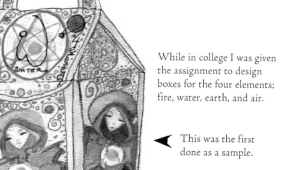

While in college I was given the assignment to design boxes for the four elements; fire, water, earth, and air.

◄ This was the first done as a sample.

Seldavia as Earth

Delphi as Air

◀ Once this design was picked, I did the watercolours for the boxes, scanned them, and printed them on fancy paper, then folded them into those boxes you see down there.

Dear Carmen,
    My master, my God, my mentor,
the force that dwells other, I miss
you, but I will find you again in
my self imposed Chaos, So that I
may see your face again. I must
                    succeed.   1/26/04

Conversations with Carmen

For Carmen Always Has All the Answers

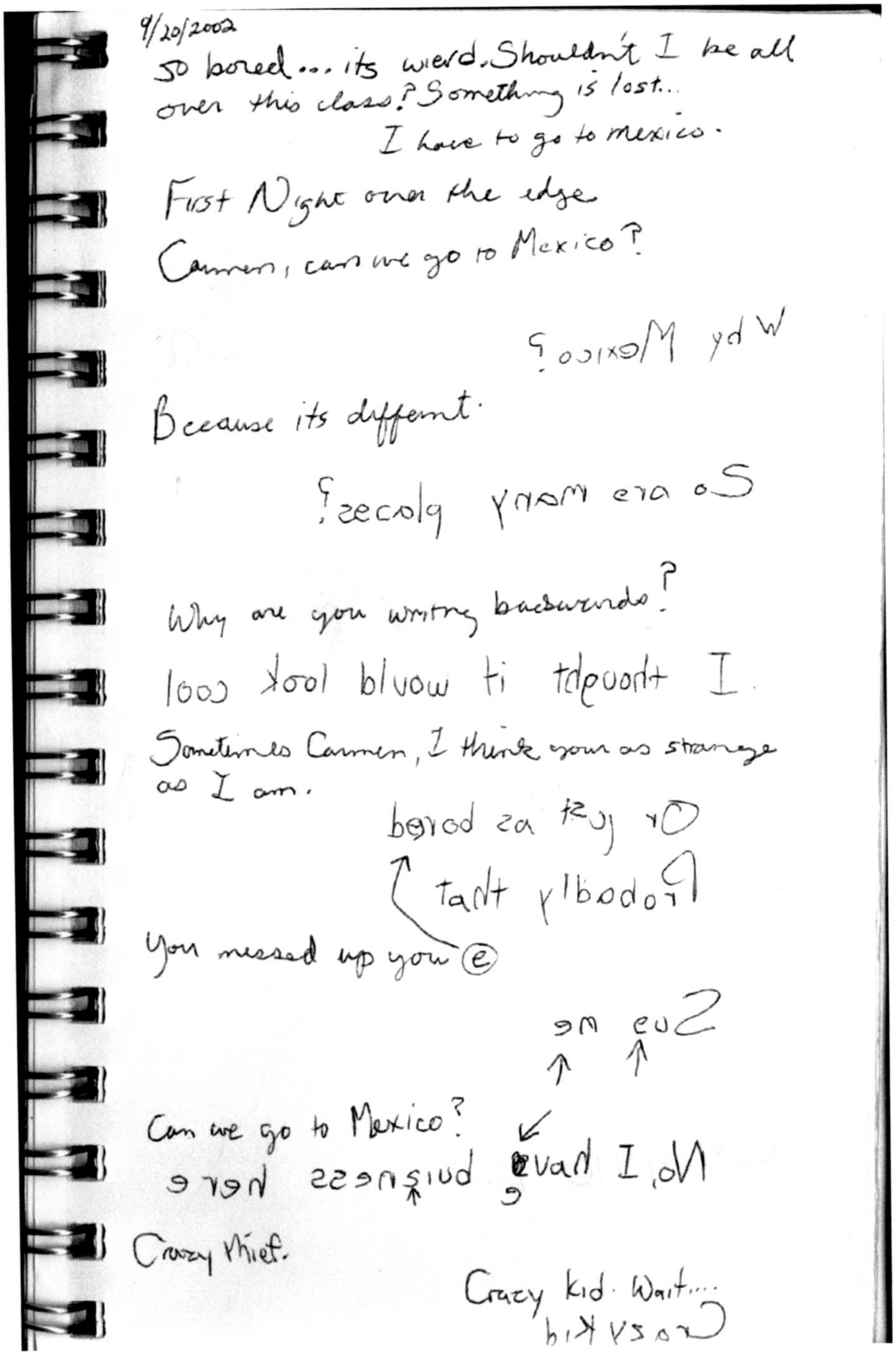

9/20/2002

So bored... its weird. Shouldn't I be all over this class? Something is lost...

I have to go to Mexico.

First Night over the edge
Carmen, can we go to Mexico?

Why Mexico?

Because its different.

So are many places?

Why are you writing backwards?

I thought it would look cool

Sometimes Carmen, I think your as strange as I am.

Or Just as bored

Probably that

You messed up you ⓔ

Sup me

Can we go to Mexico?
No, I have business here

Crazy thief.

Crazy kid. Wait....
Crazy kid

Bored in class, so is Thiefy.

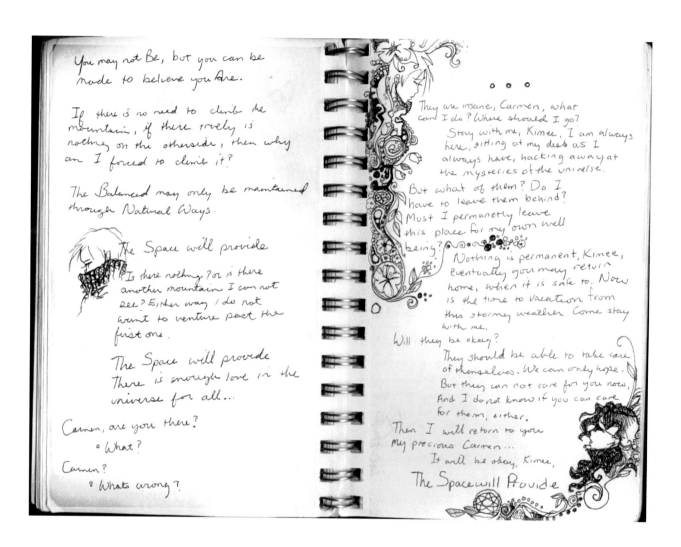

You may not Be, but you can be made to believe you Are.

If there is no need to climb the mountain, if there truely is nothing on the otherside, then why am I forced to climb it?

The Balanced may only be maintained through Natural Ways.

The Space will provide

Is there nothing? or is there another mountain I can not see? Either way I do not want to venture past the first one.

The Space will provide
There is enough love in the universe for all...

Carmen, are you there?
    ∘ What?
Carmen?
    ∘ Whats wrong?

. . .

They are insane, Carmen, what can I do? Where should I go?
    Stay with me, Kimee, I am always here, sitting at my desk as I always have, hacking away at the mysteries of the universe.
But what of them? Do I have to leave them behind? Must I permanetly leave this place for my own well being?
    Nothing is permanent, Kimee, eventually you may return home, when it is safe to. Now is the time to vacation from this stormy weather Come stay with me.
Will they be okay?
    They should be able to take care of themselves. We can only hope. But they can not care for you now, And I do not know if you can care for them, either.
Then I will return to you My precious Carmen...
    It will be okay, Kimee,

The Space will Provide

After getting in a fight with my parents, I have no one to turn to while stuck at school. It is apparent I may not be able to go home for a while and I am also worried about my parents themselves.

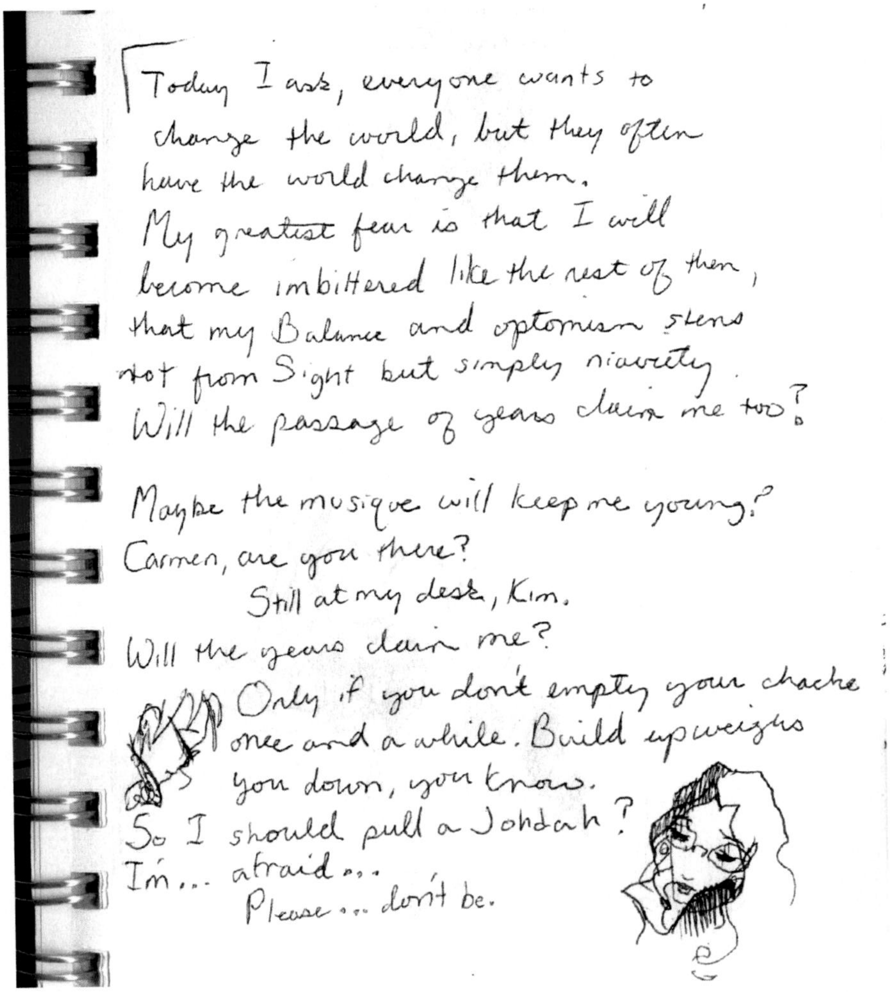

Today I ask, everyone wants to
change the world, but they often
have the world change them.
My greatest fear is that I will
become imbittered like the rest of them,
that my Balance and optomism stems
not from Sight but simply niavity.
Will the passage of years claim me too?

Maybe the musique will keep me young?
Carmen, are you there?
        Still at my desk, Kim.
Will the years claim me?
        Only if you don't empty your chache
        once and a while. Build up weighs
        you down, you know.
So I should pull a Johdah?
I'm... afraid...
        Please... don't be.

Worrying about growing
old and bitter. A Jodah
is a term in the Space
meaning that you take
your memories, strain the
feeling from them and
store them away, like an
archive. That way all your
memories don't crush
you all the time. It was
invented by Jodah, a mage
who lived 3,000 years.

It's very hard to
do, though.

Worrying about the state of International affairs and where I should stand on them.

I know many things, but I don't know nearly enough for it to matter.

Do you ever tire of war, Carmen?

Yes, I do, but they happen, So they might have a reason to Be.

I want Carmen!
Do you want Carmen?
Yes!

2/1/2002

Today we will talk about the possibility of a new age. But first, I shall institute my first chache emptying. Please stand by...

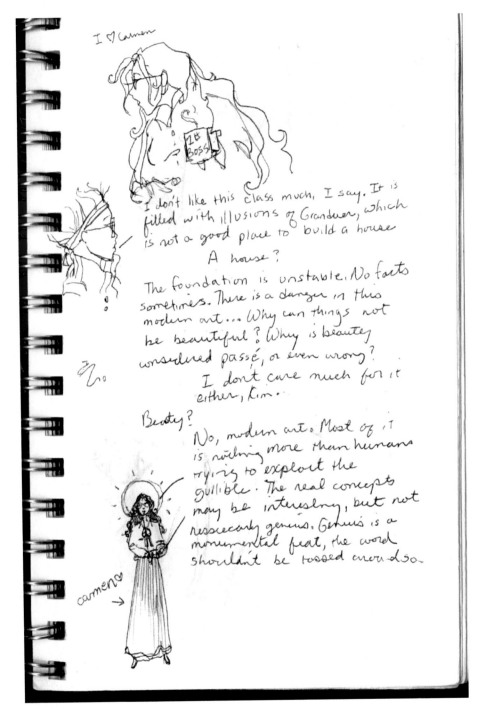

I ♡ Carmen

1st BOSS

I don't like this class much, I say. It is filled with illusions of Grandeur, which is not a good place to build a house

A house?

The foundation is unstable. No facts sometimes. There is a danger in this modern art... Why can things not be beautiful? Why is beauty considered passé, or even wrong?

I don't care much for it either, Kim.

Beauty?

No, modern art. Most of it is nothing more than humans trying to exploit the gullible. The real concepts may be interesting, but not nessiecarly genius. Genius is a monumental feat, the word shouldn't be tossed around so.

carmen ♡ →

I didn't like Modern Art class. I eventually took an independent study.

It is the second week, Carmen, and I am still worried about my new position. I am in transit once again, earlier than I would have wanted. I have yet to reach my port of call. I have yet to find a home I feel I should not travel until I do so, but it seems that if I am ever to have a home, I must wander further. The unlikely consequence travels by my side, my master, and my realization of it brings a new set of mysteries into focus, such as why I have you as my master to begin with.

I follow two roads, one by day and one by night. As I learn through one, I seek through another, I wish I understood what it has in store for me. I fear, my Carmen, that I will come to the end of one road before I come to the end of the other... ⑦ 2/2/2004

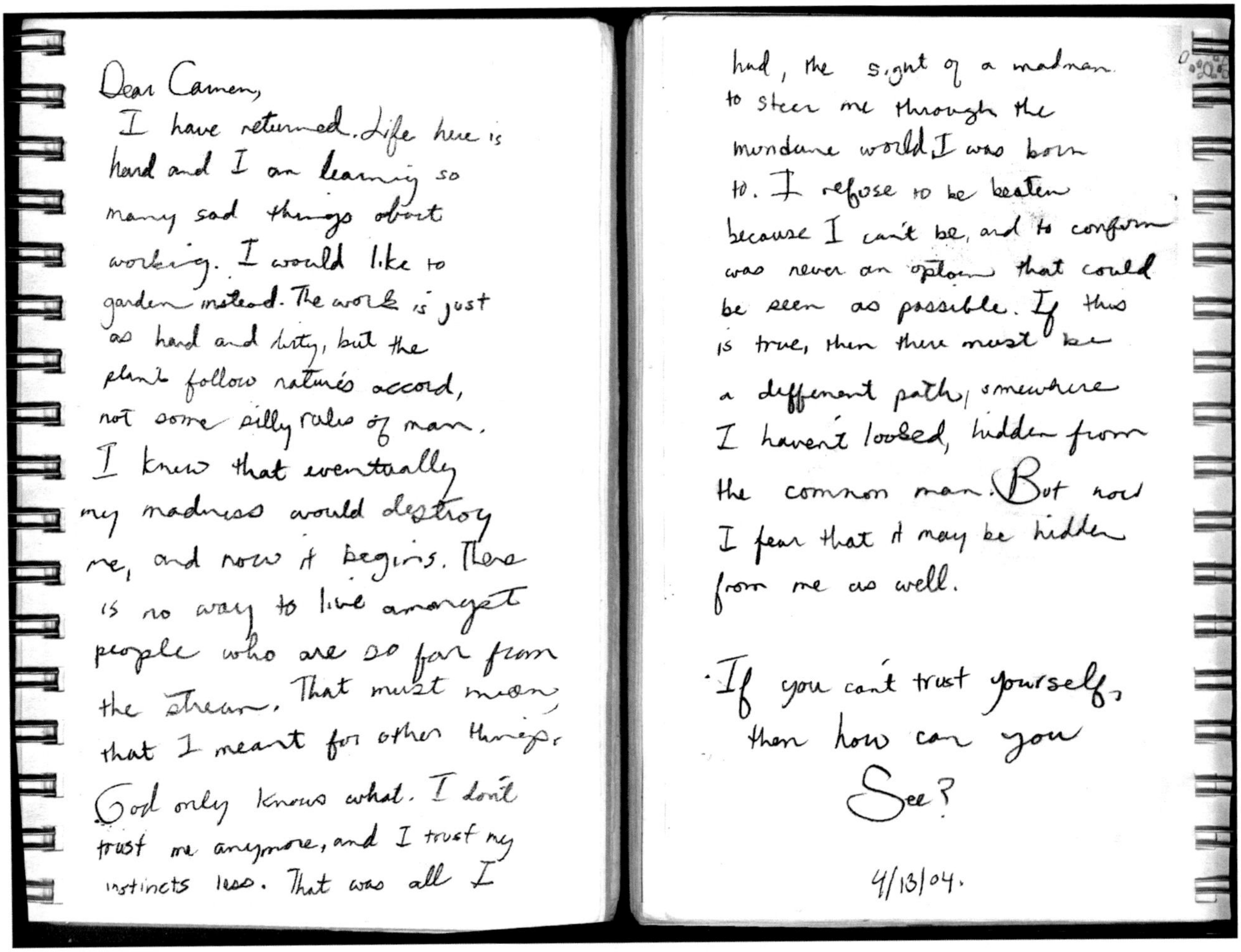

Dear Carmen,
 I have returned. Life here is
hard and I am learning so
many sad things about
working. I would like to
garden instead. The work is just
as hard and dirty, but the
plants follow nature's accord,
not some silly rules of man.
I knew that eventually
my madness would destroy
me, and now it begins. There
is no way to live amongst
people who are so far from
the stream. That must mean,
that I meant for other things.
God only knows what. I don't
trust me anymore, and I trust my
instincts less. That was all I

had, the sight of a madman
to steer me through the
mundane world. I was born
to. I refuse to be beaten
because I can't be, and to conform
was never an option that could
be seen as possible. If this
is true, then there must be
a different path, somewhere
I haven't looked, hidden from
the common man. But now
I fear that it may be hidden
from me as well.

'If you can't trust yourself,
 then how can you
          See?

4/13/04.

Solemn thoughts during the Nomad era, thoughts
which, even now, are never far from my mind.

Carmen's response;
"Only time will tell."

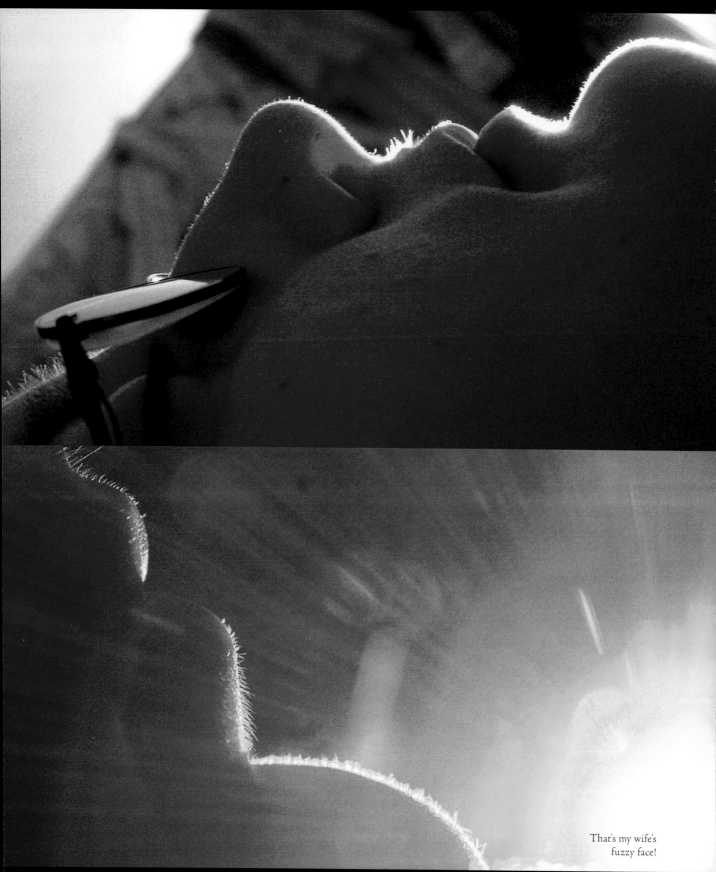

That's my wife's
fuzzy face!

Epilogue

Me, my wife, kids, and anything else that belongs at the end of a Book.

Me

Hullo!

Name: (Adelphinious)

Otherwise known as: Anita Knipping, Anie, Adelphus'Delphi

Gender: None and/or potato

Occupation: Eccentric, Digital imaging, The Seventh Star Projects, The Missions, Trying to get this damn book published, Hugging, Thinking, Sleeping, Loving my wife.

Born: 8/30/1981

Awoke: 7/13/1995

Fully Functional: 2/06/2001

Distinguishing traits and personality: Unconventional, pretty easy going unless brain decides to short. Easily scared by angry people. Only follows rules that make sense.

Generally Wears: Anything that doesn't match and can be slept in. Layers preferred, no straight black or white unless accompanied by colour. Blue, lemon yellow or orange is preferred.

Likes: Sleeping in the sun, Beanie, the Pilgrimage, Realspace, Gardening, Trance music, questioning things, wind, violent storms, heat, small plastic toys, blinking lights, sitting, hot water, clouds, her birds (children), Paxil, humans, things.

Dislikes: Being away from Beanie, Air-conditioning, Horror Movies, War Forums, Wearing things that annoy my sensory things, Unnatural light, Silence, Shoes.

I.Q.: 129 WAIS-III (with digit span) 145 WAIS-III (recalculated to exclude digit span section, as I have numerical dyslexia)

Drinks: A whole lot of citrus.

Sleeps: Always and Everywhere.

Diagnosed with: Autism (Aspergers Syndrome), Clinical Depression, Panic/Anxiety Disorder, Agoraphobia, OCD, Synesthesia, Sensory Integration Dysfunction, and a terminal case of Optimism.

TV: The Weather Channel, Invader Zim, National Geographic Explorer, Nature documentaries, Futurama, Simpsons, South Park, Harvey Birdman, Venture Brothers, Aqua Team Hunger Force, MST3K, Trigger Happy TV, 3rd Rock from the Sun, just about anything on the Animal Channel or the Discovery Channel.

Movies: Monty Python and the Holy Grail, Spaceballs, The 5th Element, Kung Fu Panda, WALL-E, Orlando, Hook, Aqua Teen Hunger Force Colon Movie Film for Theatres. I watch most animated things and comedies that are on TV. Nothing you wouldn't want to experience in real life. The Matrix is my one exception, but it's real hard on me.

Goal: To become Wise.

Is afraid of: Extremists of any kind, Depression, The Winter, Anger, Fame, Organized religion.

Plays: Sitar and I can sing.

Other Notes: I avoided this chapter for the entire year that I made this book, though I'm not exactly sure why. I suppose it is rooted in the reasoning for making this book; sharing things with the humans. Much of what I put in is about things you don't usually think about or see, so what is so extraordinary about myself as a personal person? Perhaps not much, but I suppose I should introduce myself anyway.

Hello, my name Is, and I Am.
How are you?

ECCENTRICITY

i love Beanie!

Name: Renee

Otherwise known as: Ni, Beanie, Wife, and a billion other names created by mixing variances of random words. Ones commonly used are; Ham, Cup, Sweet, Sugar, Pancake, Bun, Noodle, Boodle, Cake, Can, Fruit, Fuzzy, Little, Nugget, Bean, Nose, Round, Love, Heart, Soft, Small, and Tiny to name a few. IE: Sweet little nugget of cupcake love.

Occupation: My Companion for Life, Financial Analyst at AIG.

Born: 12/25/1978

Distinguishing traits and personality: Incredibly sensible and responsible. Strong work ethic and moral code. Very open minded but easily frazzled due to the enormous pressure she puts on herself. As solid as I am not. Over achiever, but oh so sweet!

Generally Wears: A mix of classic and ethnic.

Likes: A million things, world culture, New York City, candy, Asian food stores, Zelda, writing, video games, drawing, reading, learning and seeing new things.

Dislikes: Religious and political extremist agendas, vegetables, spiders.

Eats: Meats, cheeses, ten tons of pizza, most of which she makes herself, NO VEGETABLES!

TV: Mostly Anime, Animal Planet, the BBC, and The Discovery Channel.

Movies: A lot of foreign films, Miyazaki, Pixar, some Disney and other animation.

Goal: To make the world a less narrow-minded place.

Is afraid of: Spiders.

Beanie!

The One that I Love

Oh Sweet Beanie, you are the Sun in my Universe! Once upon a time I was alone and sad, lost inside a land of dreams. The Real world had nothing to offer me so I stayed in my head always. One day I found the Forum, a place devoted to followers of Carmen like myself. But alas I didn't fit well here either, for my background of Carmen was far too different than theirs.

Then one day a new person showed up named Seldavia. Seldavia was sad because she too was fostered by Carmen and had an intricate background. She feared that she would not be accepted. February 11th, 1998, I replied to her first post and supported her writings, even if they didn't match my own. First we talked on the forum, but the Power struggle at school kept me off-line all of March, so we used the phone. Seldavia told me her real name was Renee and that she lived in the Tundra called Minnesota, 800 miles away. Ni called me every two weeks and for that short hour on the phone I felt alive but still scared that if she knew what I was that she would be too scared to call again.

Ni and I set up our own private forum and started 'TSE' Top Secret Experiment on November 6th, 1998. Each night we would add a chapter where the other left off and our Realspaces merged into One. We wrote that novel together for two years, accumulating 600+ pages of documented Realspace in the process. With every added chapter we were meeting each other and our sub-existences were as well. There can be no greater bond, I say, than when your subconscious melds with that of another.

Late 1998 before we started 'TSE', rumour was circulating amongst the forumers about the prospect of creating a Carmen convention, not unlike the ones that are held for comic books and the like. We all planned to meet in NYC that summer but it fell through, except for Ni. I would meet her that Summer after knowing her from afar for nearly two years.

Summer of 1999 was a summer of severe drought, yet somehow a thunderstorm sat on top of Newark Airport for the entire day Ni was to arrive, delaying her plane for 24 hours. What seemed like a disaster was heaven sent. Northwest was forced to give her a $700 voucher when their flights became overbooked. It was by that sheer luck she was able to come out again for free that January.

Beanie thought she would hate NYC as much as she hated Chicago, but from her first view of the skyline she was sold. By the end of the second visit, Ni was about to do the unthinkable and move to New Jersey.

May 2000, Ni and her Dad came out on the last of the voucher to find an apartment. It was too surreal. Even though the May visit was a nightmare for Ni, it ended with her finding the apartment that would become my second home, a beautiful studio in Hawthorne Towers. It has a pool and a garden. You can see 270 degrees of NYC skyline from the apartment we're in now. July 1st, 2000, Beanie came home to stay.

Spoiling the Ni

Ni needs to be spoiled. 20 years in Minnesota taught her to be quiet and to keep to herself. No one talked to her out there and by the time she came out here there was a lot of work to be done. When you are quiet in North Jersey, that means you're angry. People thought Bean was a very angry person. You may be noticing me calling her Ni, Bean, Beanie and other things. I give everyone nicknames for some reason. I also I like saying the word 'bean'. It all works out very well. Bean has hundreds of nicknames to be sure.

Why I love my Ni

Ni is one of those rocks with the crystals inside. If you met her you'd think she was ultra conservative and bookish, but the real Ni is one of many surprises. Not only were we able to meld our Realspaces, but Bean also likes Trance music, International shopping centers, Anime, Saturday morning cartoons, Foxtrot, MST3K, International affairs and lying around doing nothing. Ni is a curious but responsible Ni that keeps me out of trouble. She's warm and funny, listens to you talk, cares what you say. She gets so passionate about things.

Sometimes she stresses and worries too much, or gets mad and needs Ni time, but our fights only last 15 minutes anyway because we can't stand to see each other sad. I can't stand not to see Beanie for more than 24 hours. Oh there are so many things about my Ni! No one has ever treated me the way Ni does, no one has ever fostered my eccentricity, held me when I'm sad, put up with my weird ways, wanted me there. I look up to Ni for a lot of things because she's smart. She has a budget and does her own taxes and manages to hold a job that I wouldn't last five seconds in. She keeps me from buying things I don't need, drives around with me in the car when I'm sad, and let me eat her food and call her in the middle of the night during my darkest days.

I don't know how she tolerates me sometimes. I take showers at three in the morning and babble constantly. I always need attention and reassurance, and somehow Ni always has an endless supply. In return I shower her with love and devotion and make sure she goes to the dentist when she's supposed to. I love her. I love her so much.

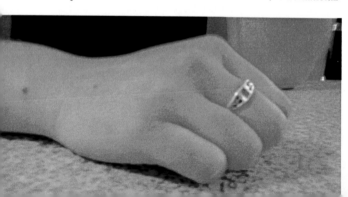

Trying to cram as many Beanie pictures in here as I can.

ECCENTRICITY

page 322

The Babies
I have kids. They hatched from eggs.

The Boos
Cockatiels; a whole lot of weird that fits in the palm of your hand.

Name: Squeaky a.k.a Crapfoot the Pirate, Lord Hissyfit, Fuzz-Butt, Sir Flappen'crap, Count Crapula, the Spazz-a-tron5000, Spork, Whiney, Shutthehellupbird, Pain-in-the-ass Bird, Dorkus Aurelius, Clingy, Pesty, Sir Squeak'n Speak, Una Crappy-barra, Crappy McCrappercrap, Lord of the Crap, and other various crap-related names.

Born: We aren't sure, but we think Spring 2006

Gender: Transsexual (Has the weight, behaviour, colouring, vocalizations of a male, but has laid an egg.)

Eats: Will ignore the food and eat the bag it came in. Millet (bird-crack), anyone else's food but his, basically everything but what you give him.

Sleeps: Randomly in certain places. Always has to wedge himself into a 90 degree angle first.

Distinguishing traits and personality: Drama Queen, short and simple. He acts like a big man until the parakeets comes out, then he's a wuss. He complains about everything, even when he's not sure what he wants, and demands you to pay attention to him at every second of the day, except those few seconds he wants you to piss off. Then he bites you, but true to his nature, his bark is far worse than his bite. He sounds exactly like a squeeze toy when he wants your attention.

Is Afraid of: Things that should scare him, don't (like the vacuum cleaner and flashing lights), and things that shouldn't, do (like his own pulled feathers and this Beanie Baby we have that looks like a cockatiel). He's afraid of the dark and TERRIFIED of the 'keets.

Likes: Making a bloody racket, chewing things, whining, so much whining, jumping on the keyboard when he KNOWS he's not supposed to, millet, showing off, demanding you scratch him, sitting on my head.

Dislikes: Being put in his cage, food that's good for him, being touched anywhere but his head, parakeets, being looked at wrong, well, pretty much everything makes him angry.

He is a little miracle. After my first bird Bitey died, I really wasn't sure I wanted another bird. Then a few months later my neighbor from the sixth floor came down and asked if I had lost my bird, because one had just flew in through his window. I went upstairs and there was Squeaky, sitting on a chair like he owned the place. So I took him. Squeaky has cheated death four times already. Somehow that bird finds something to eat that he shouldn't, even though he's attached to me every second of the day. It's a gift, I suppose.

Name: Chicken a.k.a Chicky. Chicklet, Chick Flick, Milkshake, Chicky Boo, and recently, Humparella.

Born: Some time in 2004

Gender: Female

Occupation: Artist.

Distinguishing traits and personality: Scared of most things still, but better than she was. She's a big, white, chubby marshmallow and flies about as well as one. Humps her water dish at least five times a day.

Is Afraid of: Everything but Beanie, because Beanie is magic.

Likes: Beanie, humping her water dish, chewing things, sleeping on the fruit basket in my bed, stealing keys off keyboards, and kissy sounds. God does she ever love kissy sounds.

Dislikes: Most everything else.

We got Chicken when one of our 'keets got sick and we had to bring him to the bird hospital. By that time the bird hospital people knew me well so they asked me to adopt Chicken, who had been waiting for an owner for a year. I make the joke that the vet had a special; Get one bird fixed, get the next one free.

ECCENTRICITY

How to use a food dish.

Right

hump! hump! hump!

Wrong

Above: As you can see, even after taking perspective into account, Chicken is huge, especially next to Squeak, who is a runt.

Left: Last year I was getting rather angsty about the art scene, so I lined Chicken's cage with drawing paper and let her go to town. I didn't want anyone to take it as a serious work of art, but it was, even after I revealed who made it. The art world makes my head hurt.

The Bits

A collective of deceptively cute fuzzball parakeets that will someday *RULE THE WORLD!*

Burble a.k.a. Spazzy, Bur, Burbur, Burburburburburbur, "a fine looking male" (courtesy of vet)

The blue keet is like a superball in a small room. Is capable of flirting, humping, and making noise constantly, even when sleeping. He thinks he is the best bird in the world and tries to convince the others in various ways. Tries to assert dominance over Spree but is totally pwned by Bree and Bitsy. Is madly in love with Bree and shadows her everywhere. I think Bree secretly enjoys this. Burble came to the House for Wayward Parakeets for making too much damn noise.

Bitsy a.k.a. Bit, Bittles, Pudgy Budgie, Bitty Bit, Chub

The yellow keet, who looks incredibly fat but is actually just really fluffy. She's more docile than the others and will let you hold her for a few minutes before running off. She loves toys, especially anything with string, and tends to be ever so slightly smarter than the other birds. She also enjoys hanging upside-down and will always descend head-first when climbing down something. She is pushy, bossy, curvaceous and loves to tease by taking long, sensuous baths that drive Spree insane. Enjoys knocking the pellet dish on the floor so no one can have any and making a whole lot of noise at random or during important parts of television shows. Bitsy came to the House for Wayward Parakeets for being on a hunger strike over the lack of sexy man-keets at her former home.

Spree a.k.a. Spreebles, Spwee, Insane o' keet, Spazzerkeet

The electric green keet, the only one capable of matching Bitsy in pure screeching ability. He is in love with Bitsy but is easily distracted by the voices in his head. You know how there's always a completely oblivious nutball at a frat party (according to TV)? That's Spree. He is the last one to fall asleep, mostly because he tries to sit up Bitsy's butt long after the lights are out, making for many night freakouts from the others. Spree came to the House for Wayward Parakeets as a runaway from god knows where. Spree is named after the candy Spree.

Bree a.k.a. Breebles, Baby Bwee

The olive green keet, will cut you up, man, so back off. She is soooo cute and sweet and scared of coming out of the cage, but when Burble starts bothering her for hump he gets smacked. She is also possessed by the ghost of late Don Teeny, who wrote the declaration that all keets must pester Squeaky. Bree came to the House for Wayward Parakeets for killing two other keets. True story.

Teeny (rest in peace,) a.k.a. Teeny Weeny, Lil' Booger, Spoot, Isa lil iddy bitty baby, yes you are!

The ghost keet. She enjoyed shredding things, throwing things off the top of my computer, millet, chasing Squeaky, preening Squeaky, pissing off Squeaky, trying to land on Squeaky, swimming in her water dish, playing with Bitsy, the crinkle of plastic bags, heavy metal, and making a whole lot of noise at random or during important parts of television shows. Currently enjoys possessing the other keets to bother Squeaky from beyond the grave.

Teeny came to the House for Wayward Parakeets from a divorcing couple when she was just a baby. After two years of terrorizing Squeaky and teaching Bitsy all she knew, she died in July of 2010 from ovarian cancer. She had the best doctor and had the best treatment, but the tumour was too entangled with her intestines. She was put to sleep before it ever caused her pain.

Night night, lil' baby. You were the boss of bosses.

ECCENTRICITY